THE ECONOMICS AND POLITICS OF NGOs IN LATIN AMERICA

THE ECONOMICS AND POLITICS OF NGOs IN LATIN AMERICA

Carrie A. Meyer

Westport, Connecticut
London

Library of Congress Cataloging-in-Publication Data

Meyer, Carrie A.
   The economics and politics of NGOs in Latin America / Carrie A.
Meyer.
      p.   cm.
   Includes bibliographical references and index.
   ISBN 0–275–96621–6 (alk. paper)—ISBN 0–275–97099–X (pbk.: alk. paper)
   1. Non-governmental organizations—Latin America.
HC125.M495   1999
068′.5—dc21   98–56629

British Library Cataloguing in Publication Data is available.

Library of Congress Catalog Card Number: 98–56629
ISBN: 0–275–97099–X (pbk.)

First published in 1999

Praeger Publishers, 88 Post Road West, Westport, CT 06881
An imprint of Greenwood Publishing Group, Inc.
www.praeger.com

Printed in the United States of America

The paper used in this book complies with the
Permanent Paper Standard issued by the National
Information Standards Organization (Z39.48–1984).

10 9 8 7 6 5 4 3 2

Copyright Acknowledgments

Contents

List of Tables

Preface

Many scholars have struggled to understand the burgeoning nongovernmental organization (NGO) sector in developing countries. Over the past ten years, as an economist I have tried to add my two cents to the conversations among social scientists, development professionals, and practitioners about the role of NGOs in Latin America. With this book, I took the opportunity to review the history and to gather my insights into a unified political-economic framework that views NGOs in Latin America as producers of international public goods and contributors to global community.

Many of the chapters in this book borrow pieces from papers I have previously published in scholarly journals, but the first two chapters are completely new. Chapter 1 is an overview of the growth of NGOs in the international community, and Chapter 2 reviews the history of NGOs in Latin America. Together they set the stage for the subsequent chapters, which analyze the political-economic role of NGOs in Latin America. Chapter 3 draws from Meyer (1992b) to examine how the economics of NGOs matched practical experience, as of the mid-1980s, when donors began moving much more money through NGOs. Chapter 4 draws from Meyer (1992a) and from other unpublished case research to contrast the history of institution building in the rural public and private sectors of the Dominican Republic. The discussion of opportunism, NGOs, and entrepreneurship found in Chapter 5 is a revision of Meyer (1995a).

Chapter 6 presents NGOs as appropriate partners for the provision of complex public goods, based on Meyer (1997a). The analysis of NGOs and the political economy of information in Chapter 7 is based on Meyer (1997a). Finally, Chapter 8 draws from three papers (Meyer 1993, 1995b, and 1997b) to show how the interaction of Southern NGOs and Northern donors contributes to global community.

Research support came from various sources. Financing for the field research in 1990 that underlies Chapters 3 and 4 was provided by Development Alternatives Inc. through the DESFIL project; this assistance is gratefully acknowledged. Thanks are due to William Visser and the World Resources Institute (WRI) for sharing background case materials on national environmental funds gathered by the New Partnerships Working Group, which reinforced the empirical basis for Chapter 8. Moreover, some of the ideas were inspired and certainly enriched during my two years at WRI, especially through work on *Biodiversity Prospecting* with Walter Reid and others (1993). A special debt of gratitude is due to those persons I interviewed in the Dominican Republic and Ecuador in January and June 1990. Their names and affiliations in 1990 are listed in the notes to Chapters 3, 4, and 8.

Many people supplied information, read papers and chapters, and — not least importantly — provided moral support. Thanks are due to Ana Sittenfeld and Annie Lovejoy for providing additional information on National Biodiversity Institute and responding to queries, and to Randy Curtis, Jamie Resor, and Barry Spergel for information on national environmental funds. Several research assistants at George Mason University have provided invaluable support to my research program: Julia Devlin, Adolfo Laurenti, Mark Lynner, Keith Norbutt, Yesim Yilmaz, and Ruth Wu. Sally Harman and Carol Hlavinka helped with administrative assistance. Former colleagues from WRI read, commented, and encouraged: Walter Arensberg, Janet Brown, Sarah Burns, Kathleen Courrier, Thomas H. Fox, Robert Livernash, Owen Lynch, Roberta Nichols, Walter V. Reid, Kirk Talbott, Lori Ann Thrupp, Peter Veit, and Aaron Zazueta. Colleagues and former colleagues from George Mason have also read papers and provided constructive criticism: Michael Alexeev, Dora Ampuero, Tyler Cowen, Jack High, Susanne Kernan, David Levy, Karen Vaughn, and Richard Wagner. Many anonymous referees and editors of journals, including Christopher Bliss, David Booth, Janet Craswell, Rudolf Richter, and Dennis Young, have provided helpful criticism. Others who merit thanks for reading, commenting, and providing information or support include: Joan Anderson, Tony Artuso, Werner Baer, Anthony Bebbington, Dan Biller, Patricia Bonnard, Deborah Brautigam, Lorig Charkoudian,

Thomas F. Carroll, John Clark, John F. Due, Bruce Ferguson, Julie Fisher, Beth Floyd, Alan Fowler, Michael Gollin, Ann Hudock, David Kaimowitz, Stanley Katz, Jack Kloppenberg, Mary Laschober, William Millan, Pablo Molina, Mancur Olson, Carol Pandak, Charles A. Reilly, Susan Rose-Ackerman, R. David Simpson, Denise Stanley, Anne Ternes, Theodore Tsoukalas, Roberta Warren, and Anne E. Winkler. The forbearance of the Breuer family also deserves special mention for extending new invitations as I repeatedly postponed my visit before finishing this book.

The participants of many professional conferences over the past ten years have also contributed insight and suggestions to precursors of the ideas and chapters presented here. These conferences include the Latin American Econometric Society, Santiago, 1989; the Business Association of Latin American Studies, Albuquerque, 1990; the Midwest Economic Society, St. Louis, 1991; the Latin American Studies Association, Washington, 1995, and Chicago, 1998; the Association for Research on Nonprofit Organizations and Voluntary Associations, New York, 1996; and the International Society for Third-Sector Research, Mexico City, 1996, and Geneva, 1998. George Mason University seminar and brown-bag participants have also provided comments.

Finally, I owe an enormous debt of gratitude to my parents, Norman and Anne Meyer, for always believing in me.

Acronyms and Abbreviations

ACIPA	American Consortium for International Public Administration
ACORDE	Costa Rica Association for Development Organizations
ACVFA	Advisory Committee on Voluntary Foreign Aid
AHC	Academy of Christian Humanism
BIMS	Biodiversity Information Management System
BINGO	big nongovernmental organization
BTG	British Technology Group
CARE	Cooperative for American Relief Everywhere
CEBRAP	Brazilian Center for Analysis and Planning
CEDOPEX	Dominican Center for the Promotion of Exports
CIPAF	Research Center for Feminist Action
CIPCA	Center for the Investigation and Promotion of the Farmer
CNA	National Council of Agriculture
CORDAVI	Corporation for the Defense of Life
CRS	Catholic Relief Services
DESCO	Center for the Study and Promotion of Development
DGF	General Directorate of Forests
DONGO	donor-organized nongovernmental organization
EAI	Enterprise for the Americas Initiative
ECOSOC	Economic and Social Council

EDUNAT	environmental education project
FAO	Food and Agriculture Organization
FDA	Agricultural Development Foundation
FDD	Dominican Development Foundation
FEDIA	Ecuadorian Foundation of Agricultural Investigation
FONAMA	National Fund for the Environment
FORO	National Forum for Columbia
FSE	Emergency Social Fund
FSI	Social Investment Fund
FSLN	Sandinista National Liberation Front
FUNDAGRO	Foundation for Agricultural Development
FUNDEJUR	Foundation for Rural Youth Development
FUSADES	Salvadorian Foundation for Economic and Social Development
GAO	General Accounting Office
GDP	gross domestic product
GEF	Global Environment Facility
GONGO	government-organized nongovernmental organization
HIV	human immunodeficiency virus
IAD	Dominican Agrarian Institute
IAF	Inter-American Foundation
IDB	Inter-American Development Bank
IDEA	Institute for Agricultural Strategies
IDECOOP	Institute for Cooperative Development and Credit
IDIA	Dominican Institute of Agricultural Investigation
IEP	Institute of Peruvian Studies
IER	Institute for Rural Education
IICA	Interamerican Institute of Cooperation in Agriculture
ILD	Institute for Liberty and Democracy
IMF	International Monetary Fund
INBio	National Biodiversity Institute
INDRHI	National Institute of Hydraulic Resources
INEDER	Institute of Education for Rural Development
INESPRE	National Institute of Price Stabilization
INPROA	Institute for Agricultural Promotion
IPG	Interagency Planning Group
IRD	integrated rural development
ISA	Superior Institute of Agriculture
IUCN	International Union for the Conservation of Nature
JACC	Agricultural Enterprise Board of Consulting and Co-investment

MIRENEM	Ministry of Natural Resources, Energy, and Mines
NEF	national environmental fund
NGO	nongovernmental organization
NPF	National Parks Foundation
ODA	official development assistance
ODC	Community Development Office
OECD	Organisation for Economic Co-operation and Development
ONAPLAN	National Planning Office
PIDAGRO	Integrated Program of Agricultural Development
PPA	Program for the Small Farmer
PRI	Institutional Revolutionary Party
PROFONANPE	National Fund for Protected Areas of the State
PVO	private voluntary organization
SEA	Secretary of Agriculture
T & V	traning and visits
TNC	The Nature Conservancy
UEPA	Agricultural Policy Studies Unit
UN	United Nations
UNCED	UN Conference on Environment and Development
UNEP	UN Environment Programme
USAID	U.S. Agency for International Development
USAID LAC	USAID Latin America and Caribbean
WRI	World Resources Institute
WWF	World Wildlife Fund

1

The Explosion of NGOs in the International Community

Around the globe society's institutions — states, markets, and civil society — are struggling to keep up with change. Throughout modern history improvements in transportation and communication technology have expanded markets, connected peoples, and changed the role of the state. Now as the millennium ends, dramatic advances in communications technologies have unleashed powerful forces of economic globalization (Carnoy, Castells, Cohen, & Cardoso 1993). Markets around the world have opened up to foreign investment; financial markets are increasingly interdependent; and multinational corporations shop the world to find the best labor market for each stage of production. The role of the state, after some retrenchment, is under scrutiny (World Bank 1997). The Cold War ended when economies controlled by authoritarian regimes collapsed in Central and Eastern Europe. Privatization of state enterprise began in the United Kingdom under Thatcher and subsequently spread throughout Europe, Latin America, and Central and Eastern Europe. At the same time democratic governance has made substantial progress across these and other regions (Carothers 1997).

Institutions of civil society — including nongovernmental organizations (NGOs) — have also undergone revolutionary growth and change. Scholars and policymakers have called attention to the rise of global civil society (Mathews 1997; Commission on Global Governance 1995) and the global associational revolution (Salamon 1995), referring primarily to

the tremendous growth in numbers and influence of NGOs. As participants in a changing balance among states, markets, and civil society,
NGOs have both responded to and catalyzed change in a newly globaliz-
ing world order.

NGOs IN A NEW WORLD ORDER

NGOs play a fascinating role in this changing balance among states,
markets, and civil society because NGOs are both political and economic
entities. Nongovernmental organizations, as implied by the name, are not
of government; they are also not for profit. For purposes of this book, they
are independent organizations that receive outside funding to support
either staff, programs, or both — in effect, they are not purely voluntary.
Further, the NGOs discussed here are based in either the North or the
South[1] and engaged in activities related to sustainable development,
including advocacy, research, and service provision; and they work in
such fields as relief, health, human rights, agriculture, and environment.
Thus, although NGOs are nongovernmental, they are frequently very
much engaged in political life and may work in partnership with government; and although they are nonprofit, they may compete with for-profit
consultancies and service providers.

Civil society, of course, is a much broader term — too broad,
perhaps, to define precisely. Here civil society is used loosely to mean the
space where people interact. It includes the realm of voice (Hirschman
1970) and that of collective action. Governments participate in civil society, as do private businesses, but neither encompasses civil society. In
addition to NGOs, other institutions of civil society include voluntary and
membership organizations, professional associations, and grass-roots
groups.

As the globe shrinks, the demands on global civil society are growing.
Advanced communication technology facilitates economic and political
collaborations across borders that call for international civic input and
institutions (Commission on Global Governance 1995). Globalization
means that the world's economies are increasingly interdependent. Thus,
the governance of international trade, labor, and finance falls in the lap of
global civil society. Increasing demands are placed on intergovernmental
institutions, such as the World Trade Organization and the International
Monetary Fund. However, a myriad of supporting professional and trade
associations are expanding across borders. Increases in the human population and its level of economic development call attention to the shrinking
natural environment and the increased need for international collective

action to protect the global commons and to ensure international security. Two world wars marred the first half of this century and encouraged national governments to establish the United Nations and its associated intergovernmental institutions. The second half of the century, however, saw the rise of a wide variety of international NGOs dedicated to specific issues of international concern, such as Amnesty International and the World Wildlife Fund (Spiro 1995). These international NGOs have united the voices, energies, and financial backing of people around the world to address international problems.

Both intergovernmental and nongovernmental organizations engaged in addressing international problems are attempting to provide international public goods. Public goods, as distinguished from private goods, can be enjoyed by many at the same time. The benefits of international public goods are shared internationally; they include world peace, basic research, popular education, world health, and a healthy global environment.

Clearly international NGOs like Amnesty International and the World Wildlife Fund belong to global civil society and produce international public goods; what is less clear to many, however, is the political-economic role of NGOs based in the South and funded by the North. This book aims to clarify the role of Southern NGOs funded by Northern donors, specifically focusing on Latin America's NGOs. Like international NGOs, Southern NGOs funded by Northern donors belong to global civil society and produce international public goods.

The role of Southern NGOs requires special clarification, in part because these NGOs have suddenly exploded on the international scene in the past 15 years, and in part because Southern NGOs are frequently depicted as pillars of local civil society and forces of grass-roots democracy (Clark 1995; Fisher 1998; de Janvry & Sadoulet 1993; Reilly 1995). Southern NGOs and the grass-roots organizations they support are likened to the dense networks of civic associations that Putnam (1993) defined to be "social capital" — a positive contributor to better governance in Northern Italy.

This vision of indigenous NGOs and local democracy is neither accidental nor entirely misleading. Foreign donors, such as the U.S. Agency for International Development (USAID) have explicitly worked through Southern NGOs with the intention of strengthening institutions for democratic governance (U.S. Agency for International Development [hereafter USAID] 1994b). Chapter 2 supports the contention that Northern donors of Southern NGOs in Latin America furthered democratization. Donor efforts in this direction have been at least as intense in recent years, if not so deeply rooted, in the countries of Central and Eastern Europe; and donors are also assisting new democracies through NGOs in Africa and Asia (Hudock 1997). Upon examination, therefore, the raging fires of grass-roots democracy in developing countries are not purely indigenous; they are fanned with external funds directed at Southern NGOs.

Indeed, researchers confirm that the vast majority of Southern NGOs are funded by Northern donors (Fowler 1997). Edwards and Hulme (1996: 962) cite increased numbers of NGOs in Nepal and Tunisia related to the sudden availability of external funding: in Nepal registered NGOs increased from 220 to 1,210, and in Tunisia from 1,886 to 5,186 — both in the span of only three years. As NGOs have grown in numbers and power in developing countries, so too has local criticism. *The Economist* (1998) calls NGOs, like the Grameen Bank and the Bangladesh Rural Advancement Committee, "The other government in Bangladesh"; and it reports that local politicians complain that NGOs are powerful beyond their accountability. *The Economist* sides with the NGOs, however, and says that corruption is rare among NGOs (whose books are audited), but rife among local politicians. The magazine states, "the 20,000 or so NGOs" in Bangladesh provide "education, health, small loans and agricultural development far more efficiently than the corrupt and inefficient government. Yet, while outsiders have lavished praise on the NGOs, Bangladeshis themselves are ambivalent."

The above examples illustrate the two principal political-economic roles of Southern NGOs proposed in this study: Southern NGOs should be viewed as providers of international public goods — goods that may be valued both inside the host country and abroad — and although Southern NGOs may energize local civil society, they belong more properly to global civil society.

The world is changing, and NGOs around the world are responding. The power of the international private sector has increased dramatically.[2] States, in contrast, have retreated as economic powers and have increased opportunities for democratic participation. States have also looked for private-sector alternatives to provide public services. International donors increasingly use NGOs to provide international public goods. All of this means that the political and economic spaces for NGOs internationally have grown enormously. As NGOs interact in an increasingly complex global community, new institutional fabrics governing their relationships are woven. This book sheds light on pieces of these fabrics, beginning with an overview of NGOs in the international community.

THE GROWTH OF NGOs IN THE INTERNATIONAL COMMUNITY

NGOs and the United Nations System

Nowhere has the sudden influence of NGOs in the international community been more visible than at the United Nations (UN) conferences of the 1990s. The UN Conference on Environment and Development in Rio de Janeiro in June of 1992 was a turning point. Some 9,000 NGOs from 167 countries sent some 25,000 delegates to attend a forum parallel to official intergovernmental meetings (Fisher 1993: Spiro 1995). Some 1,500 NGOs were accredited to the official conference proceedings (Otto 1996). NGOs at local, regional, and international levels were recognized as key participants in the agenda for sustainable development that resulted from the conference.

The first UN conference to begin opening wider doors to NGOs internationally was the Stockholm 1972 Conference on the Human Environment; since then the relationship has deepened.[3] Maurice Strong, secretary general of the 1972 conference, proposed broadening NGO participation beyond those NGOs on formal consultative status with the UN. Later in the 1980s national and even local NGOs were admitted to UN conferences. Nonetheless, the number of NGOs from all over the world — particularly from the developing world — that came to Rio surprised the governments. Developing countries had initially been skeptical of (Northern) environmental NGO presence; they later sought to ensure adequate NGO representation from developing countries (Willetts 1996a).

Subsequent UN conferences in the 1990s built on the Rio experience. Although the 1993 World Conference on Human Rights in Vienna excluded NGOs from official proceedings, NGOs were still present in large numbers at a parallel forum. The conferences on population and development in Cairo, 1994; social development in Copenhagen, 1995; and women in Beijing, 1995 had more liberal criteria for NGO participation. Their agendas for action identified critical roles for NGOs as partners in follow-up activities. Almost 2,500 NGOs were accredited to the Beijing conference, making it the largest UN gathering ever held (Otto 1996).

NGO inroads to the UN system as a whole have been less visible to the world at large but real nevertheless. In 1994 Boutros Boutros Ghali welcomed NGOs to a meeting at UN headquarters saying, "I want you to consider this your home. Until recently these words might have caused astonishment. The United Nations was considered to be a forum of sovereign states alone. Within the space of a few short years, this attitude has changed. Non-governmental organisations are now considered full participants in international life."[4] In the original 1945 UN charter, article 71 allowed the UN Economic and Social Council to "make suitable arrangements for consultation with nongovernmental organizations which are concerned with matters within its competence."[5] In 1949 90 NGOs had consultative status (Spiro 1995). In 1968 the legal framework for NGO consultation was redefined under Resolution 1296 of the UN Economic and Social Council. Despite politicized UN–NGO relationships during the Cold War, the number of NGOs with consultative status grew from something under 400 in 1968 to more than double that in the mid-1980s. By 1994, this number had reached almost 1,000 (Willetts 1996a).

Growing Funding for NGOs

The new louder voice for NGOs in the international community has been backed by widespread increases in funding. Unfortunately, adequate numbers on the funding levels of NGOs around the world are difficult to attain. The Organisation for Economic Co-operation and Development (OECD) is the best single source.

The primary sources of funding for NGOs in developing countries are bilateral: Northern government donors and Northern NGOs or Private Voluntary Agencies, as termed by the OECD. The OECD tracks the amount of bilateral official development assistance (ODA) that is funneled through NGOs — to Northern NGOs and then typically to Southern NGOs. The OECD also tracks grants that originate outside of ODA, from Northern NGOs and foundations; most of this money also eventually flows to Southern NGOs. The total contribution from or through Northern NGOs, as tracked by the OECD, is currently on the order of $8.5 billion, close to 15 percent of total ODA.[6]

Inconsistencies in definitions and in data reporting across countries, however, lead to many omissions in the OECD data including, significantly, the figure for the amount of ODA channeled through U.S. NGOs. Outside analyses, however, provide complementary information that verifies what is common knowledge at the field level: funding increases over the last several decades have been substantial. Table 1.1 shows the increase in bilateral ODA channeled through Northern NGOs from three sources, all reported in constant 1992 U.S. dollars. Smith (1990) undertook extensive studies of North Atlantic funding of development NGOs, which built on baseline OECD data. Smith found that Canadian and European public contributions to NGOs quadrupled in real terms from

$199 million in 1973 to $844 million in 1983 (Table 1.1). For the same period he found that U.S. bilateral contributions to U.S. NGOs (termed private voluntary organizations [PVOs] in USAID jargon) increased from $794 million to $931 million in real terms. The OECD reports a further doubling of Canadian and European bilateral contributions to NGOs from 1984/85 to 1995. The U.S. General Accounting Office (1995) conducted a study of bilateral aid through U.S. PVOs that showed U.S. contributions to PVOs increasing by about 50 percent during this decade.

TABLE 1.1
Bilateral Official Development Assistance through NGOs
(constant 1992 $ millions)[a]

	United States	Canada and Europe	Asia
1973 (Smith)	794	199	NA
1982 (GAO)[b]	1,070	NA	NA
1983 (Smith)	931	844	NA
1984/85 (OECD)[c]	NA	481	29
1992 (GAO)	1,500	NA	NA
1995 (OECD)	NA	958	257

Notes:
[a]Figures are converted to 1992 U.S. dollars using the gross domestic product deflator.
[b]The GAO figures include food commodities and freight as well as funds provided to PVOs by U.S. government agencies other than USAID.
[c]The OECD figures are underreported because some countries are omitted. Smith's analyses built on baseline OECD data.

Source: Organisation for Economic Co-operation and Development 1996, Tables 13–20; Smith 1990; General Accounting Office 1995.

Grants by private voluntary agencies, which generally flow to Southern NGOs, have also increased in real terms between 1973 and 1995, but the increases have been more modest. U.S. grants by these Northern NGOs and foundations have actually leveled off, but increases have come from Europe, Canada, and Asia (Table 1.2).

Bilateral donors also increasingly fund Southern NGOs directly, rather than funneling the money first through Northern NGOs (Edwards & Hulme 1996). Later case studies in this book, for example, show dramatic shifts at the level of USAID field offices, in program aid to Southern NGOs, and the trend to fund Southern NGOs directly is generally

TABLE 1.2
Grants by Private Voluntary Agencies
(constant 1992 $ millions)

	United States	Canada and Europe	Asia	Total
1973	2,629	1,229	99	3,957
1984/85	1,931	1,461	162	3,554
1995	2,321	2,946	273	5,539

Note: Figures are converted to 1992 U.S. dollars using the gross domestic product deflator.

Source: Organisation for Economic Co-operation and Development 1974, Table 15; Organisation for Economic Co-operation and Development 1996, Tables 13–20.

recognized to be worldwide. However, funding that does not flow through Northern NGOs, in the OECD data, is likely to be lumped with bilateral aid. Thus substantial increases in total bilateral ODA over the last two to three decades are also indicative of increased funding for Southern NGOs (Table 1.3). Bilateral aid from the United States has declined sharply in real terms since 1965, but until 1992 this decline was offset by increased ODA from Canada, Europe, and Asia. Total bilateral ODA from developed countries in 1995 was more than 80 percent greater in real terms than the 1973 level. It is difficult to determine how much of this ODA was channeled directly from field offices to Southern NGOs; nevertheless, it has represented a growing source of funds. Between 1992 and 1995, however, total ODA fell by about 14 percent as Northern governments pushed to shrink budget deficits (OECD 1997).

TABLE 1.3
Bilateral Official Development Assistance
(constant 1992 $ millions)

	United States	Canada and Europe	Asia	Total
1965	13,471	7,490	1,352	22,313
1973	6,790	10,956	3,042	20,787
1984/85	9,497	12,576	4,030	26,104
1995	5,207	21,833	10,613	37,653

Note: Figures are converted to 1992 U.S. dollars using the gross domestic product deflator.

Source: Organisation for Economic Co-operation and Development 1974, Tables 15, 16–32; Organisation for Economic Co-operation and Development 1996, Tables 13–20.

A Brief History of Aid through NGOs

The history of foreign assistance through NGOs by European and Canadian donors is quite different from that of the United States, and support from Asia came much later. The data reviewed above revealed particularly strong support for NGOs in the United States. Although the percentage has been declining, 40 percent of grants from private voluntary agencies in Table 1.2 are from U.S. private agencies. Moreover, Table 1.1 reveals the substantial and growing percentage of U.S. ODA channeled through Northern NGOs.

The partnership between the U.S. government and PVOs dates back to World War II when a War Relief Control Board was established to coordinate the relief activities of U.S. PVOs. When that governing body was dissolved in 1946, the Advisory Committee on Voluntary Foreign Aid was established, consisting of representatives of both PVOs and government. The PVOs that have ever since played major roles for U.S. relief and development cooperation — CARE,[7] Catholic Relief Services, and Church World Services — were also founded at about the same time. Public Law 480, passed in 1954, authorized government surplus commodities to be donated to these and other PVOs registered with the Advisory Committee on Voluntary Foreign Aid and distributed in developing countries (Ruttan 1996).

Thus, by the mid-1950s U.S. PVOs were shifting relief activities from Western Europe to developing countries, and U.S. PVOs were established as cornerstones in the history of U.S. development efforts. Initially, much of the PVO work focused on commodity distribution, but efforts to provide technical assistance in agriculture, health, and education grew. Congress amended Public Law 480 in 1961 to allow more flexibility in the use of the commodities — for example, to use funds generated from the developing country government sale of the commodities for development purposes. In 1973 Congress declared, in an amendment to the Foreign Assistance Act, that PVOs should be encouraged to expand overseas development efforts with USAID support (Ruttan 1996; Smith 1990).

European and Canadian NGOs arrived later to the scene, food aid played a much smaller role, and NGOs were less establishment oriented. Before the mid-1960s contributions by European governments to international charities were insignificant (Smith 1990). Thus early European NGOs were much more independent of government and much less preoccupied with communism than their U.S. counterparts. Indeed, European NGOs, according to Smith, were based in a broad movement that involved labor, professional, religious, and political groups, and their orientation was leftist relative to U.S. PVOs.

After the mid-1960s Canadian and European governments began to support NGOs, but they lacked the anti-communist agenda of the U.S. government. While U.S. PVOs were still focused on relief, European NGOs began to work in development. Smith (1990) notes, "Oxfam in Great Britain prior to the 1960s had concentrated on providing immediate relief to the hungry, sick, or homeless overseas. By the end of the decade, however, it was spending 90 percent of its budget to improve medical and social welfare facilities or to support agricultural development and training" (p. 80). In the mid-1970s, European and Canadian government contributions to NGOs began to increase more rapidly, at a time of center-left politics in Europe. Meanwhile, U.S. bilateral assistance levels fell dramatically, as shown in Table 1.3, because of increased military spending in Vietnam; thus, the Europeans and Canadians could build new influence as international donors. Smith argues that European governments also tried to distance themselves from the image of the United States — now tarnished by the Vietnam War.

During the 1980s U.S. assistance levels rose again, as shown in Table 1.3; and assistance to PVOs in particular expanded rapidly. In 1981 Congress required that at least 13.5 percent of government expenditures for assistance activities be channeled through PVOs. By this time Ruttan (1996: 227–29) reports that USAID funding of PVO activities had about doubled from levels of the mid-1960s. As reported earlier, funding to registered PVOs increased by 50 percent from 1982 to 1992. Total PVOs registered with USAID have almost tripled since 1982 — although not all of those registered are regularly funded (General Accounting Office 1995). USAID data have indicated that 33 percent of development assistance was channeled through NGOs and PVOs in 1994, up from 19 percent in 1985, and with further increases (to 50 percent) announced by Vice President Gore at the Social Summit in Copenhagen in March 1995 (*Connections* 1995).

NGOs and the World Bank

The evolving relationship of NGOs and the World Bank is also a striking example of the growing influence and new relationships of NGOs in the international community. NGOs have changed the way business is conducted at the World Bank.

International and U.S.-based NGOs — especially environmental NGOs — have traditionally criticized World Bank activities. A popular exposé by Bruce Rich, then international director of the Environmental Defense Fund, an NGO in Washington, D.C., highlighted many of the difficulties in the World Bank–NGO relationship. Rich (1994) characterized the "Bank's preferred way of doing business [as] top down, secretive, with a basic contempt for public participation, access to information, involvement of democratically elected legislatures, and informed discussion of alternatives" (pp. 176–77). Other criticisms attacked the bank's overriding concern with economic growth, supply-driven pressure to lend money irresponsibly, structural adjustment policies in response to the 1980s debt crisis that were insensitive to the needs of the poor, and the bank's "unparalleled capacity to catalyze ecological destruction" (p. 32).

By the mid-1980s the World Bank's poor record on environmental management had attracted international attention. NGOs like Rainforest Action International, Greenpeace, Earth First!, and the Sierra Club helped focus this negative attention (Rich 1994; Cleary 1996). Major grass-roots movements provided credibility. Chico Mendes organized fellow rubber tappers from the Amazon in 1985 to lobby the World Bank to halt the subsidized transformation of the rainforest to cattle pasture. Although international environmental NGOs facilitated his efforts, the murder of Mendes by ranchers in 1988 made him a martyr. Grass-roots activism was also impressive in India. Indian NGOs successfully fought to halt the damming of the Silent Valley in the late 1970s and early 1980s. Later, from 1989 to 1993, World Bank plans to finance dams that would displace hundreds of thousands of people in the Narmada Valley were fought by even stronger combined efforts of Indian NGOs, grass-roots groups, and international supporters.

The fiftieth anniversary of the Bretton Woods Conference that founded the World Bank was marked in 1994. The efforts and words of Bruce Rich, the Environmental Defense Fund, and additional leadership from the Friends of the Earth led to the launch of the "Fifty Years is Enough" campaign in May 1994. By the time the fiftieth anniversary was celebrated in Madrid at the end of 1994, 120 U.S. NGOs had endorsed the program and 135 NGOs from Europe and elsewhere also supported the program (Cleary 1996: 88).

Meanwhile, the World Bank struggled to handle the public relations problems. In 1981 a formal World Bank–NGO Committee was established to develop and review approaches for cooperation. In 1984 the World Bank began publishing an annual progress report on cooperation between the World Bank and NGOs. Many NGOs viewed these efforts as public relations cover; nevertheless, some significant steps were taken.

When the committee met in 1987, it issued the "Santo Domingo Consensus Conclusions," which called for cooperation with developing country NGOs and grass-roots organizations, the exchange of research and experience between NGOs and the bank on policy issues, and NGO participation in project implementation, design, and monitoring (Cleary 1996). At that time, operational collaboration was still small: World Bank data show that on average from 1973 to 1988, only 6 percent of bank-financed projects involved NGOs (NGO Group 1997: 2).

The structural adjustment policies of the World Bank in the middle and late 1980s were the target of much criticism by NGOs, but the World Bank and NGOs also began some successful cooperative innovations in response to the social hardships of the time. The first social fund was created in 1986 in Bolivia with cooperation from other major donors; by 1990 it was being replicated across Latin America. Bolivia's Emergency Social Fund was funded primarily by international donors, including the World Bank. Some 25 percent of funds were disbursed through NGOs. As of 1997, the bank had invested more than $4.3 billion in more than 30 such funds around the world (Malena 1997). (See Box 2.3, Chapter 2.)

The late 1980s were also a time when the World Bank sought private-sector solutions to development problems; and NGOs belong to the private sector. Research, such as Gabriel Roth's *The Private Provision of Public Services*, was undertaken to explore such private-sector alternatives (Roth 1987). The World Bank began to consider that NGOs might be something more than a political nuisance; they might also offer efficiencies in service delivery. World Bank studies, such as Michael Cernea's *Nongovernmental Organizations and Local Development* and Paul and Israel's *Nongovernmental Organizations and the World Bank: Cooperation for Development*, examine analytically the economic and political roles of NGOs in development assistance (Cernea 1988; Paul & Israel 1991).

With assistance from the Swedish International Development Authority, the World Bank also began to study the participatory development methods practiced by NGOs. The 1996 *World Bank Participation Sourcebook* admits that "Until recently, the Bank looked to NGOs primarily for capability in service delivery" (World Bank 1996: 243). The *Sourcebook* claims that times have changed, and the World Bank now looks to NGOs for their skills in eliciting beneficiary participation. The first chapter begins by stating, "Some readers who know the World Bank well will note that the examples presented in Chapter II differ from their notions of how the Bank normally goes about its work"; it then criticizes the bank's traditional "external expert stance" and recommends the "participatory stance" for development assistance (World Bank 1996: 3). Perhaps more than anything else, this admission by the World Bank illustrates the powerful rise of NGOs in the global community; it reads almost like an apology.

The 1997 progress report on *Cooperation between the World Bank and NGOs* points to the bank's new president James Wolfensohn's personal interest in successful interaction between the World Bank and NGOs and his support for civil society. Wolfensohn has met with numerous NGOs from both the North and the South and has personally attended NGO–World Bank Committee meetings. At the operations level, World Bank–NGO collaboration has also increased. For 1996, 48 percent of projects are reported to have some NGO involvement. The report also claims that 42 percent of these projects involved NGOs during the design phase, although admitting that NGO involvement is still most significant during project implementation and maintenance. Data reveal that collaboration is most intensive with national indigenous NGOs (NGO Group 1997).

The Republican sweep of the U.S. Congress in November 1994 and subsequent sharp cuts to the U.S. foreign assistance budget forced NGOs, the World Bank, and the entire development community — especially in Washington — to rethink their relationships. Although anti-bank rhetoric was climaxing in 1994 with the "Fifty Years is Enough" campaign, only one year later Wolfensohn, together with NGO representatives[8] held a press conference to support development assistance (NGO Group 1997). In May 1998 the World Wildlife Fund and the World Bank announced a new major alliance for the conservation and sustainable use of the world's forests (Wolfensohn & Fuller 1998).

CHAPTER OVERVIEW

This chapter has provided an overview of the growth of NGOs in the international community, but remaining chapters focus on NGOs in Latin America. Latin America has epitomized, in the last 15 years, the changes in terms of democratization, expanding markets, and shrinking states that NGOs in the developing world have faced.

Chapter 2 recounts that history in Latin America and explains how it relates to the NGO revolution. By way of a painful economic crisis, Latin America moved from state-led development to private-sector–led development. At the same time democracy took hold in the region; 15 of 20 countries in Latin America replaced authoritarian regimes with democratically elected heads of state between 1978 and 1994. As states and markets realigned, the indigenous NGO sector came into its own. In the 1960s indigenous NGOs were the domain of the Catholic Church, U.S. food aid, and private foundations like Ford and Rockefeller. With each passing decade, Latin America's NGOs attracted more donor attention and funding. By the mid-1980s they had become a forceful presence in both providing public services and eliciting citizen participation in democratic processes. In Chapter 2, the explosive growth of NGOs over the past 15 years is juxtaposed against the dramatic economic and political change of the same period. Historical case studies of the growth of NGOs in Chile, Peru, Mexico, Brazil, and Central America are provided.

Subsequent chapters use case studies of specific NGOs in Latin America to illuminate their emerging political and economic roles in Latin America's development.

Chapter 3 uses case studies conducted in early 1990 on agricultural sector institutions in Ecuador and the Dominican Republic to question the sudden major funding shift of USAID in the mid-1980s from the public to the private, NGO sector. In so doing, the chapter examines from a rational economic perspective the roles of the public, private, and nonprofit sectors. It concludes that NGOs cannot substitute for the public sector.

Although NGOs cannot replace the domestic public sector, they may still be a better instrument for international donor projects. Chapter 4 uses historical case evidence on the ebb and flow of donor funds over 30 years to contrast the superior flexibility of a Dominican NGO with that of the Dominican agricultural extension service.

Chapter 5 returns to the doubts about the newly funded, powerful NGOs that surfaced in Chapter 3 and focuses on the complex topics of opportunism, altruism, and entrepreneurship. Rapid growth in the NGO sector caused confusion, criticism, and disappointment. The chapter clarifies the economic role of NGOs as producers of international public goods and contributors to economic production, employment, institutional innovation, and technology transfer.

The economics of partnerships between NGOs and public and private sectors is the topic of Chapter 6. It argues that nonprofit NGOs, as partners in complex contracts with public and private sectors, are well suited to the production of complex public goods. This analysis is illuminated with a case study of an NGO in Costa Rica that has an active array of public- and private-sector partnerships, as it produces biodiversity goods, some private and some public.

Chapter 7 examines NGOs as information-intensive producers in an age of falling costs of information transmission. Both the goods they produce and the inputs they use are information based. This explains the political nature of NGOs. As NGOs educate, train, network, and raise awareness, they build human and social capital — an economic investment as well as a political transformation of the parties involved. The falling costs of sharing information can be expected to increase the economic and political impact of NGOs.

Chapter 8 examines funding relationships between international donors and NGOs indigenous to Latin America as contributions to compromise and the building of global community. Case research on environmental NGOs in Ecuador and on national environmental funds throughout Latin America provides the fodder. Donors are criticized for coopting NGOs in developing countries, but funding relationships also build greater understanding, encourage compromise, and establish the basis for global community.

General conclusions are summarized in Chapter 9.

NOTES

1.   North and South here do not refer to precise geographical regions of the globe but rather to developed and less-developed countries, respectively.

2.   Some of these changes cause concern. See Korten (1995).

3.   Charnovitz (1997) traces the early history of NGOs and international participation back to 1775, although much of the history relates to organizations that here would be described as voluntary, membership, or professional associations. Nevertheless, he found that the establishment of the League of Nations and later the United Nations diminished space for early international NGOs until about 1972.

4.   As cited in Willetts (1996a: 59).

5.   As cited in Otto (1996: 109).

6.   Total ODA in 1995 was $58.9 billion. This includes multilateral and bilateral ODA (Organisation for Economic Co-operation and Development 1997, Table 21). See also Participation and NGO Group (1996).

7.   CARE was established as the Cooperative for American Remittances to Europe in 1945; it was later renamed the Cooperative for American Relief Everywhere (Ruttan 1996: 225).

8.   Oxfam International and InterAction were represented. This last is a large coalition of U.S. development NGOs.

2

New Spaces and Fabrics in Latin America

The relationship between states and markets in Latin America has changed profoundly in the last two decades. The Latin American state moved from a position of strength to one of utter weakness during the debt crisis of the 1980s. In its aftermath the market — long in bondage to state controls — broke free and the private sector ascended as the expected savior. However, although the economies of Latin America began growing again in the 1990s, the private sector has yet to generate the anticipated increases in employment and improvements in living standards for the region's poor. Thus, Latin America's leaner states and liberalized markets still face growing pains.

The relationship between the state and civil society has likewise undergone dramatic change. Between 1978 and 1994, 15 of the 20 countries in Latin America turned from authoritarian to democratic regimes. Only Cuba remains under dictatorial control. Indigenous nongovernmental organizations (NGOs) have played active roles in this transformation process — both responding to change and catalyzing it: engaging citizen participation, providing services the state could not, and absorbing international funds that shunned repressive or weak states.

With a newly liberal private sector welcoming foreign investment, democratic governance taking hold, a burgeoning NGO sector fed by international donors, and revolutionized communication systems, Latin America faces the next millennium with many new political and economic spaces: for new relationships and forms of participation, for innovation in the provision of public services, and for a new global order. New institutional fabrics with strong ties to the global community are being assembled in response to these opportunities as various parties pursue their self-interest and as civil society, private business, and public sectors attempt to address modern problems. The chapters of this book provide case studies analyzing new roles of Southern NGOs in the emerging institutional fabrics.

This chapter briefly overviews the economic and political change in Latin America over the past two decades and then describes the growth of an indigenous NGO sector funded by foreign donors. From quiet beginnings in the 1950s and 1960s, NGOs exploded onto the scene in the mid-1980s in the midst of the economic and political transformation. Although similar growth patterns are apparent in many countries of the region, case studies of the growth of NGOs in Chile, Peru, Mexico, Brazil, and Central America illuminate institutional fabrics unique to particular countries.

STATES AND MARKETS REALIGN

The economic trauma in Latin America during the 1980s was enormous. The debt crisis began in August 1982 when Mexico declared its inability to meet foreign debt obligations. Latin America had grown rapidly from 1970 to 1980 — real per capita growth averaged 3.5 percent per year (Inter-American Development Bank [hereafter IDB] 1997a: Table B-2). This growth was financed by heavy borrowing from commercial banks: from 1975 to 1982 long-term foreign debt increased almost four times. In 1982 total external debt was $333 billion (Edwards 1995: 17). Oil profits, funneled through the international financial community in the 1970s, had expanded dollar reserves and encouraged liberal lending to developing countries. Although at the time the loans were made it was clear that further loans would be required to pay them off, Latin America's sudden inability to service debt meant that virtually no further loans were forthcoming after 1982 (Sachs 1989).

Latin America got caught by a sudden change in global financial conditions, and the poor response policies exacerbated the crisis. Beginning in 1980, both the United States and the United Kingdom tightened monetary policy to fight inflation under Reagan and Thatcher. Interest rates rose and a worldwide recession resulted. With the recession came lower commodity prices for Latin America's exports. Meanwhile, debt obligations on loans, made at variable interest rates, rose as interest rates rose. As high U.S. interest rates attracted international investment and strengthened the dollar, speculation eroded the value of Latin currencies. Soon, coming up with the dollars to service the loans, now at much higher interest rates, became impossible (Sachs 1989). Efforts to maintain exchange rates only resulted in currency speculation, capital flight, further exchange rate devaluation, and spiraling inflation.

Poverty and hardship characterized the decade. Economic growth in the region came to a halt as countries struggled to make payments. Between 1980 and 1983 real per capita gross domestic product (GDP) fell by almost 10 percent on average in Latin America (IDB 1997a: 52). Not until 1990 did the situation turn around for the region as a whole. Some countries suffered sooner and others later, but none escaped the ravages of the 1980s. The bitter medicine of the International Monetary Fund required shrinking public sector services to address the public deficit, eliminating price controls (on subsidized food and transportation, for example), and liberalizing exchange rates. The poor took the hardest hit. Real wages dropped by close to 50 percent, and in some countries (Brazil, Mexico, Peru, and Venezuela) the drop was even greater (IDB 1997a: 38). Poverty levels increased from less than 25 percent of the population in 1982 to 35 percent in 1990 (IDB 1997a: 41). Measures of inequality worsened.

Nevertheless, toward the end of the 1980s, it became clear that those who took the bitter medicine early (like Chile and Mexico) were stabilizing their economies and starting to recover; soon, free market reforms swept the region. Opening markets to trade was an early priority: average tariffs on imports were reduced from 42 percent in 1986 to less than 14 percent in 1995; maximum tariffs fell from 84 percent to 41 percent; exchange rates were allowed to float freely; and free-trade agreements were pursued throughout the hemisphere (IDB 1997a: 42–43). Credit and financial markets were likewise liberalized, and foreign investment was ushered in. Stock markets grew as portfolio investment swelled. Privatization of state enterprises also attracted foreign investors. Mexico privatized assets worth almost 12 percent of GDP (US$ 27 billion) between 1988 and 1998; Argentina privatized about 8 percent of GDP (US$ 18 billion) over the same period. Only a few countries have yet to initiate privatization programs.

The reforms have dramatically changed the relationship of the public and private sectors in Latin America. The private sector and market forces have been unleashed to pursue economic growth, while the public sector has downsized and pursued macroeconomic stability. Other government functions have been passed back to the market or in some cases to NGOs.

Governments in Latin America worked hard to achieve macroeconomic stability, but they have yet to report convincing progress for the poor. Inflation rates have come under control, and public sector deficits have been nearly erased. Market reforms have encouraged growth, but the growth rates are disappointing given the magnitude of the reforms. The recovery in real wages has been modest and the poverty rate still hovers around 35 percent (IDB 1997a). Thus, governments are still struggling to address social needs.

DEMOCRATIZATION OF THE LATIN AMERICAN STATE

With incredible force, over the same economically traumatic decade of the 1980s, democracy swept Latin America. In the 1960s and early 1970s, military dictatorships — some reformist but many repressive — had become the rule in Latin America. Of the 20 countries south of the Rio Grande generally considered Latin America, only 4 had democratic regimes in 1975. After 1994 Cuba alone remained under dictatorship. In country after country, democratically elected leaders came to power.

Those 4 that managed to avoid authoritarian regimes in the 1970s are Colombia, Venezuela, Mexico, and Costa Rica. Colombia has a century-old tradition of democracy with only two successful military coups. From 1958 to 1974, a bipartisan coalition government, the National Front, shared power, as the presidency alternated between the two traditional political parties. In 1974 the National Front ended and, since that time, despite the threats of guerrilla insurgents and drug dealers, Colombia has maintained democratic elections (Kline 1990). Venezuela, in contrast, began the twentieth century with the long and brutal dictatorship of General Juan Vicente Gómez (1908–35). Thereafter, experiments with democracy alternated with dictatorships, but in 1958 Venezuela made a successful and lasting transition to democratic rule (Myers 1990). Mexico's democracy is still quite limited, but its civilian one-party state has provided stability for more than 70 years (Levy & Bruhn 1995). Costa Rica has the most liberal democratic traditions of the 4. Political parties were organized in the early 1900s, and political conflicts between the left and the right brought the country to civil war in 1948. The new constitution of 1949 abolished the military and has provided the basis for democratic governments ever since (Seligson 1990).

The Dominican Republic is debatably a fifth democracy to survive the 1970s, beginning with the election of the United States–supported presidential candidate, Joaquín Balaguer, in 1966. However, Balaguer had served as one-time vice-president during the 30-year dictatorship of Rafael Trujillo, and twice the presidency was returned to Balaguer with elections generally considered fraudulent. Thus, most would date the advent of democracy to 1978 when power was peacefully transferred to the opposition candidate Antonio Guzmán (Betances & Spalding 1997; Sanchez & Jesuit 1996).

All 15 of the other countries in Latin America were under authoritarian regimes in 1978; but beginning in South America, in one country after another, military regimes withdrew and democracy took hold. Military rule ended in Ecuador in 1979 and in Peru in 1980. Somehow, these and other fragile democracies survived the desperate economic trials of the 1980s. The case of Bolivia is particularly poignant. Military regimes ruled Bolivia from 1964 until 1982. During the next three years the newly elected Hernán Siles presided over the worst hyperinflation ever to hit Latin America. Then, as described by Gamarra and Malloy (1990: 359), "At age seventy-eight, Víctor Paz Estenssoro returned to the presidency in 1985 for the fourth time since 1952. His return to the presidency was dramatic. . . . Paz stabilized the economy and established the basis for the short-term survival of political democracy in Bolivia."

The two largest economies in South America, Argentina and Brazil, also made the transition to democracy at the height of the debt crisis. Argentina experienced a particularly high level of political violence and repression in the 1970s and indeed had had constant political turmoil since 1930 — 13 presidents were forcibly removed from office. The Argentine military government collapsed in 1983 after defeat in the Falklands-Malvinas War and the democratically elected Alfonsín came to power (Snow & Wynia 1990). In Brazil 20 years of military rule ended with the election of Tancredo Neves by the Electoral College in 1985. Unfortunately, Neves died before he could assume power and the vice-presidential candidate Sarney became the new president (Lamounier 1995; Wiarda 1990).

Uruguay and Chile both had long experiences with democracy before their military regimes began; they returned to democracy in 1985 and 1990 respectively. Sigmund (1990: 201) says that "Until the 1973 coup [Chile] was one of the oldest constitutional democracies in the world. Since 1833, with only two interruptions . . . its political system had followed regular constitutional procedures, with civil liberties, the rule of law, and periodic contested elections for a bicameral legislature and a directly elected president." This democratic tradition was broken in 1973 by the repressive regime of General Augusto Pinochet, which lasted 16 years. The first large-scale privatization and free-market reforms also took place in Pinochet's Chile.

Paraguay has the shortest tradition of democracy in Latin America. Roett and Sacks (1990: 337) comment that, "Dictatorship is to Paraguay what democracy is to Sweden or Great Britain: normal, traditional, and — for many Paraguayans — comfortable." The 35-year dictatorship of Alfredo Stroessner ended in 1989 with a military coup. Subsequent elections in May 1989 "were the freest in Paraguay's history, but they were still run by the same team that used to run Stroessner's phony elections" (p. 352). Since then liberalization has continued; the presidency was transferred in 1994 and again in 1998.

Civil wars, funded by Cold War politics, plagued most of Central America throughout the 1980s, and the arrival of democracy was accompanied by heavy U.S. support if not troops. Nicaragua was the first to shake its repressive authoritarian regime in 1979. The Somoza family had ruled Nicaragua since 1936 as leaders of the national guard established by the United States in the early 1930s to maintain order and fight the revolutionary Augusto Sandino. By the 1970s rule under the Somozas had become increasingly violent. They were overthrown in 1979 by the Sandinista National Liberation Front (FSLN), which sought support from Cuba and the Soviet bloc. Rebel opponents known as contras waged a guerrilla war with U.S. support from 1981 to 1988, while the FSLN government "reacted by building a massive, Soviet-armed, counterinsurgency-oriented army" (Booth 1990: 493). U.S. pressure also won Honduran, Costa Rican, and Salvadoran cooperation against the Sandinistas. Eventually, the efforts of Central American nations led by Costa Rica and Guatemala resulted in a Central American peace accord in August 1987. Nicaraguan elections followed in 1990 with the victory of Violeta Chamorro (Booth 1990).

Honduras was a critical ally of the United States during Nicaragua's civil war. The Honduran military government of General Policarpo Paz García, under U.S. pressure for democratization, called for constitutional elections in 1980 and presidential elections in 1981. It subsequently became the "recipient of an unprecedented amount of foreign assistance," and has successfully transferred power democratically since 1981 (Rosenberg 1990: 519).

Honduras had an early history of political party politics, but El Salvador was traditionally ruled by a few powerful families. Family divisions brought the military to power in 1932 and from that time until 1979 existed what Baloyra (1990: 490) calls a "tacit alliance between officers and the oligarchy." In 1977 the Carter administration suspended military aid to the increasingly repressive Romero regime; and in 1979, in the wake of the Sandinista Revolution, the Salvadoran military deposed General Romero. Not until 1982 did U.S. pressure orchestrate elections. Baloyra (p. 492) says that "Despite some controversy about their nature and relevance to [Salvadoran] politics, the Salvadoran elections of 1982–1988 had a positive impact in the process of transition." Nevertheless, the civil war initiated under the Romero regime, between leftist guerrillas and right-wing death squads, persisted until early 1992.

Guatemala's presidency passed from military to civilian hands in 1986 after the first free elections in 20 years, but close ties to the military remained. Ebel (1990: 500) states that the military, "made it abundantly clear that they would not give up their control of the countryside, where they had successfully suppressed a guerrilla uprising, or accept an investigation into what the Kissinger Commission had termed 'the brutal behavior of the security forces.'" Peace accords ending the 36-year internal conflict between the government and the guerrillas were signed in December 1996.

In Panama two decades of military rule ended in December 1989 when U.S. troops were sent to capture General Noriega and destroy his corrupt Panamanian Defense Forces, which had become heavily involved in drug trafficking and money laundering. With continued U.S. support, democratic elections were held and efforts to rebuild institutions continue.

The final Latin American country to hold democratic elections after long years of authoritarian rule was Haiti. The Duvalier regime began in 1957 and ended in February 1986 when a series of riots turned into massive anti-government protest. Baby Doc, son and heir of Dr. François Duvalier, fled to France with his family. Elections were held in 1987, but the elected leader was overthrown. December 1990 brought the landslide electoral victory of Jean-Bertrand Aristide, a radical Roman Catholic priest. His presidency also fell, in September 1991, to a military coup. Aristide was not reinstated until 1994, with U.S. military intervention followed by a UN peacekeeping force (Economist Intelligence Unit 1995).

Certainly democracy remains fragile, particularly in Central America and Haiti, but also throughout Latin America. Rebel movement and economic conditions have severely challenged democratic rule. Peru struggled with the Shining Path insurgent movement and a sharply deteriorating economy throughout the 1980s and until 1992 when President Alberto Fujimori closed down congress and suspended political liberties in what became known as the "autogolpe" (Sanchez & Jesuit 1996: 7). The following year the Guatemalan president also staged an "autogolpe."

Paraguay still struggles to put authoritarian traditions behind, and in Colombia drug-related violence threatens democratic governance.

Despite its frailty in many countries, democratic progress has been significant and is deepening as donors, such as the IDB and the World Bank, encourage the decentralization of the state. The IDB (1997a: 99) reports that "only three countries in the region elected their mayors directly in 1980, 17 countries today use this form of local representation." As democratic political processes move into state and local governments, the power to tax and spend and the responsibility to provide public services (like education, health, roads, and water) has also increased at the local level. State and local governments in 1995 accounted for 20 percent of total government spending — up from 15.6 percent in 1985 (p. 99). With increasing decentralization, NGOs and the grass-roots organizations they work with have become larger partners in development (Fisher 1998).

THE EVOLUTION AND GROWTH OF NGOs IN LATIN AMERICA

By the time of the political and economic transitions of the 1980s, NGOs had already taken firm root in Latin America. Their early beginnings date back as far as the great depression in some countries with Catholic Church charities. U.S. private voluntary organizations (PVOs), established to coordinate relief for World War II, began working in Latin America together with the Catholic Church by the mid-1950s. The Rockefeller and Ford Foundations funded early research NGOs; and U.S. Agency for International Development (USAID) funded the Alliance for Progress of the 1960s, which, with its push for agrarian reform, helped to organize peasant groups. The repressive military regimes of the late 1960s and 1970s encouraged increased funding of NGOs that provided alternative visions of economic development. The U.S. Inter-American Foundation (IAF) also began supporting NGOs in the early 1970s, when increased funding began arriving from European and Canadian donors. In the 1980s USAID shifted development funding from public sectors to NGOs, and multilateral donors also began to take notice of NGOs as efficient alternatives for providing public goods. In the 1990s NGOs are playing a central role in a development strategy based on partnerships among members of civil society.

This section briefly traces the forces that propelled the growth of NGOs in Latin America over the past 50 years. NGOs did not evolve along precisely the same path in all countries, but they were subject to a number of common currents in the hemisphere. The next section focuses on several case studies that illustrate variations in the development of indigenous NGO sectors in Latin America.

The Catholic Church, U.S. Philanthropy, and Popular Education

The Catholic Church has been a pillar of civil society in Latin America since colonial times, and most early NGOs are rooted in this heritage. Before World War II Catholic involvement with labor, student, and welfare groups was promoted under the aegis of Catholic Action (Lehmann 1990: 91). After the war, in the 1950s charitable organizations — Cáritas — were established by the various Catholic dioceses to provide medicine, food, and clothes to those in need. U.S. PVOs, particularly the Cooperative for American Relief Everywhere (CARE), Catholic Relief Services (CRS), and Church World Services, originally established to administer war relief, began working together with Cáritas after the war. The PVOs provided funding and, with the passage of Public Law 480 in 1954, they also supplied surplus commodities. European and Canadian NGOs followed in the 1960s (Smith 1990).

Many countries in Latin America also felt the early impact of the Rockefeller and Ford Foundations, which became active donors to research NGOs (see Box 2.1). Rockefeller began working in agricultural research and training in the 1940s. Ford began funding social science research in Latin America in the late 1950s and helped initiate many of Latin America's top private research NGOs in the early 1960s.

Box 2.1: Early U.S. Philanthropy in Latin America

Today many foundations from the United States, Europe, and Canada provide grants to NGOs in Latin America; but the Ford and Rockefeller foundations made major early impacts in identifying and nurturing research-oriented NGOs. Before 1950 the Rockefeller Foundation was the dominant philanthropy in Latin America. Early work (beginning in 1917) was in health and in cooperation with governments; after 1940 Rockefeller began to work in agricultural research and training. The foundation was particularly instrumental in the establishment of national and international agricultural research centers but also provided support to private research NGOs.

Although Rockefeller was strong in agricultural research, Ford quickly became the heavyweight in overseas social science research. The Ford Foundation was not established until 1936 and worked primarily with Michigan philanthropies until 1950. In that year, Ford charted a new future with objectives focused on five priority areas including world peace, freedom and democracy, economic opportunity, educational opportunity, and the study of human behavior to enhance citizenship. Between 1950 and 1977 Ford spent more than $900 million in its less-developed countries program and an additional $335 million in international training and research. India was a major recipient as Ford began its work; work in Latin America came a bit later. In 1959 Ford created a Latin America office in New York and in 1961 opened a field office in Rio de Janeiro.

Ford made a unique and lasting imprint on social science research in Latin America. Although Ford started much later than Rockefeller, by 1968 the assets of the Ford Foundation were more than four times those of the Rockefeller Foundation. Daniel Levy (1996: 93), in an extensive study of private research centers (or NGOs) in Latin America notes that, "Among U.S. foundations, Ford is number one, easily. Its support has been important to almost all the important and some of the not-so-important [private research centers] in the region." At a time when Latin American social scientists were questioning the relevance of development theories that originated in the developed world, Ford took up the challenge to invest in indigenous social science research.

Some scholars have argued that U.S. foundations, including Ford and Rockefeller, have worked primarily to support U.S. foreign policy; but Levy (1996) found that Ford and Rockefeller encouraged autonomy in the research centers they funded and frequently deviated from U.S. policy. Ford in particular is credited with a broad research agenda designed to promote pluralism and including both Marxists and neoclassical economists among grant recipients. As military regimes overtook Latin America in the 1970s, Ford shifted funds from universities to private research centers and specifically worked to protect human rights and intellectual freedom in the Southern Cone. Ford even helped to relocate specific individuals who were trained by the foundation and exiled from their countries, in addition to providing protection and resources in the form of funding for private research centers for those who could remain at home.

Sources: Berman 1985, Cueto 1994, Levy 1996, Magat 1979, and Nielsen 1972.

However, although Northern PVOs and foundations provided funds, indigenous institutions and intellectuals provided the basic tenets of popular education, community action, and empowerment of the poor. The Catholic Church became increasingly committed to the poor in the 1960s and concerned with development as opposed to charity. In 1967 the pope denounced the increasing inequalities between nations, including the inequities in trade relationships. This echoed the doctrine of anticapitalist, dependency theory developed by Latin American economists in the 1950s. In 1968 Latin American bishops met at the Congress of Medellín and issued a document that marked the beginning of the Theology of Liberation. It pronounced the Church's "preferential option for the poor," urged the creation of base communities, and condemned the extreme inequality within Latin America (Lehmann 1990; Bebbington & Thiele 1993).

The ideas of Paulo Freire, a Brazilian professor of social work, also fed into the ideology that surrounded the formation of many early NGOs. Freire promoted consciousness raising — popular education for the purpose of freeing the spirit of man. Freire published his ideas in *Education: The Practice of Liberty* in 1967 and they became popular throughout Latin America and in development circles generally. Lehmann (1990: 101) says, "Freire's ideas gained their special appeal from the fact that they cut across the conventional ideological barriers of the time: They emerged from technocratic developmentalism . . .; they appealed to the lay Catholic movements . . . ; they appealed to Conservative politicians sponsored by USAID; and above all they carried a clear message for practical activity." Freire was a Catholic himself and his ideas were taken up by the Basic Education Movement of the Catholic Church. His methods of teaching focused on training local community leaders to be the teachers. The movement became known as *basismo*.

U.S. Bilateral Aid, the Alliance for Progress, and Rural Development

Another early force that contributed to the organization and activation of peasant groups in Latin America was bilateral aid from the United States. Development aid from the United States began with Truman's Point Four program of technical assistance, which was passed into law in 1950. The land-grant model of research, extension, and education, successful in the United States, was adopted as an appropriate method of technical assistance in rural areas. U.S. land-grant universities and foundations, such as the Rockefeller Foundation and later Ford, made important contributions to the effort. Farmers' groups and cooperatives, women's groups, and youth groups (modeled after 4-H clubs) were promoted in Latin America as points of contact for technical assistance personnel (Ruttan 1996).

Castro's 1959 victorious socialist revolution in Cuba gave new meaning to North-South relations in the hemisphere and a shot in the arm to U.S. foreign assistance. Shortly after the revolution, Congress finally approved U.S. participation in the new IDB. After Kennedy took office in 1961 U.S. development assistance was reorganized under the USAID and the Alliance for Progress was launched. At the Punta del Este Uruguay Charter in 1961, the United States agreed to a ten-year, $20 billion development effort in Latin America (Ruttan 1996). As shown in Table 2.1, U.S. funding to the region ballooned during the decade of the 1960s. In real terms funding to Latin America in 1964 was more than nine times the 1955 level, and never again has it returned to those levels, not even with the increased funding to Central America in the 1980s.

TABLE 2.1
U.S. Agency for International Development Loans and
Grants to Latin America and the Caribbean

Fiscal Year	$ millions	Fiscal Year	$ millions
1952	97.4	1975	870.5
1953	91.7	1976	843.3
1954	141.1	1977	638.4
1955	339.9	1978	653.8
1956	455.5	1979	711.8
1957	487.8	1980	730.5
1958	546.9	1981	843.5
1959	659.7	1982	1,127.3
1960	535.0	1983	1,517.8
1961	1,228.1	1984	1,531.7
1962	2,297.8	1985	2,321.9
1963	2,804.7	1986	1,754.3
1964	3,215.3	1987	1,912.4
1965	2,718.0	1988	1,415.5
1966	3,167.9	1989	1,471.6
1967	2,399.4	1990	1,917.7
1968	2,626.3	1991	1,463.1
1969	1,408.1	1992	1,185.5
1970	1,907.2	1993	1,149.0
1971	1,355.6	1994	785.3
1972	1,319.6	1995	562.0
1973	1,141.1	1996	525.8
1974	751.8		

Note: Figures are in 1992 constant dollars.

Source: U.S. Agency for International Development, U.S. Overseas Loans and Grants, 1947–95; U.S. Agency for International Development, Latin America and Caribbean, 1996 as shown at Web address: www.info.usaid.gov/regions/lac/sesd/assist.htm, October 7, 1998.

Agrarian reform was a centerpiece of Alliance for Progress efforts, and this meant continued focus on peasant organization and technical assistance for agriculture. Certainly, NGO development efforts in the 1960s were overwhelmed by USAID-funded government efforts — not only in agriculture, but also in health and education. The enormous attention devoted to peasant organization and education furthered the ideas of Freire and prepared the social infrastructure for the indigenous NGOs that later sprang up to work with these grass-roots groups. Although the Alliance for Progress began to run out of steam at the end of the 1960s, in many countries agrarian reform efforts continued. A new phase of integrated rural development was picked up in the 1970s by the IDB and the World Bank.

State Repression and NGO Alternatives in the 1970s

Dwindling USAID funds in the mid-1970s resulted in declines in government services for the poor and gaps for indigenous NGOs to fill. The heavy aid flows of the 1960s did not produce the desired results. Disillusion with top-down, government-led development increased attention on the potential of indigenous NGOs to work with grass-roots groups. The IAF began working with indigenous NGOs in Latin America in 1971, quite independently from USAID efforts (see Box 2.2). In 1973 Congress encouraged expansion of PVOs as conduits of U.S. foreign assistance.

Box 2.2: The Inter-American Foundation

By the mid-1960s the U.S. Congress was disappointed with the results of the Alliance for Progress under USAID in Latin America; the search for alternatives produced the creation of the IAF in 1969. The IAF was expected to support innovative approaches to development and bring back lessons learned to donors. It was also expected to elicit participation from community organizations among the poor. The IAF began work in 1971 with a board of directors with representatives from both the public and private sectors.

The size of IAF operations is modest. Staff size is limited by statute to 100 and has remained well below that level. The IAF is funded both by annual Congressional appropriations and by the Social Progress Trust Fund of the IDB. Funds from the latter are drawn from what Latin American countries owe in repayment on loans from the U.S. Government under the Alliance for Progress; 1973 legislation made these funds available in domestic currency for projects in the country of origin. Table 2.2 records appropriation levels since the beginning of operations. Although funding from the Trust Fund appears to exceed Congressional appropriations, it was available in local currency not in dollars. IAF annual reports state that Congressional appropriations made up more than 60 percent of the budget. Because administrative costs have been kept low — under 15 percent of total budget (Ruttan 1996: 243) — despite modest Congressional appropriations, field presence has been significant.

Vernon Ruttan notes that initially the IAF "was characterized by a mandate and a degree of operational autonomy that were highly unusual, if not unique, among U.S. government entities" (Ruttan 1996: 242). The IAF worked outside of normal government-to-government channels and was not controlled by State Department or USAID policy priorities. It sought social and institutional development, not merely economic growth. Perhaps most importantly, the IAF responded to the needs of community organizations rather than imposing initiatives from the outside.

Conservative elements in the United States were concerned about IAF activity. A 1978 Heritage Foundation investigation "grudgingly acknowledged the unique role of the foundation" (Ruttan 1996: 243–44). Although the research failed to establish evidence that the IAF supported groups with communist connections, it warned against unwittingly doing so. The Reagan administration moved to control the IAF board but, according to Ruttan, was unsuccessful in diverting the IAF from its original mandate.

The IAF has primarily funded local intermediary NGOs that work with grassroots organizations. About two-thirds of IAF grants have gone to such intermediary NGOs and one-fourth to the grass-roots organizations directly (Ruttan 1996: 243). Project grants range in size from less than $25,000 to more than $400,000, but typically more than half have been under $50,000. During the first 15 years, the average grant size was about $100,000. The IAF also sponsors research on Latin America for about 20 U.S. graduate students at the masters and doctoral levels each year (Inter-American Foundation [hereafter IAF] 1986).

In the first ten years of operation, more than 40 percent of grants focused on agriculture and rural development. Education and training followed with 16 percent of grants. Urban enterprises, community services (including health and housing), and research and learning also each received 10–13 percent each; just over 2 percent of grants were for legal assistance; and cultural expression received 4 percent (IAF 1981). By the late 1980s, less funds were allocated to agriculture and more to urban enterprise development as Latin America urbanized. Education and training remained an important component, at more than 20 percent of funds in the late 1980s. In 1996 agriculture grants made up 24 percent of the total, education and training absorbed 26 percent, and small enterprise development accounted for 38 percent. The remaining 12 percent covered research, housing, health, ecodevelopment, and other (IAF 1996).

Over the years the IAF has identified and promoted NGOs that have later been funded by donors with much larger resources, like the IDB and USAID. Currently, in keeping with the trend to decentralization and local level initiatives, the IAF is refocusing from funding NGOs to supporting broader local development initiatives involving local government, alliances of citizens, businesses, and NGOs (IAF 1998).

TABLE 2.2
Inter-American Foundation Funding
(million current $)

Period	Congressional Appropriations[a]	Social Progress Trust Fund
1970–73	10.0[b]	—
1974–76	20.0[b]	31.0
1977–79	30.0[b]	48.0
1980–82	40.4	48.0
1983–85	39.0	48.0
1986–88	36.3	48.6
1989–91	58.5	44.1
1992–94	86.8	24.6
1995–97	70.9	44.0[c]

Notes:
[a]Congressional appropriations are made annually for the fiscal year, Social Progress Trust Fund is renegotiated every three years.
[b]These are estimates based on grant levels in these years and the reported levels of $50 million for FY 1970–78 and $10 million for FY 1979.
[c]For 1995–2000.

Source: IAF Annual Reports: 1983, 1992, 1996.

The shrinking USAID presence in Latin America was filled in part by an increase in official development assistance from Europe and Canada, although most of Latin America's bilateral aid in the 1970s still came from the United States (Organisation for Economic Co-operation and Development [hereafter OECD] 1974: Table 74). Private aid from Europe and Canada also expanded, as indicated in Chapter 1, as governments from Europe and Canada channelled more resources to Northern NGOs. European foundations also increased activities as expanding European economies generated increased wealth (Smith 1990: 234).

The military governments that came to power in the late 1960s and early 1970s caused a flight of intellectuals and political leaders to NGOs. Brazil came under military control in 1964 and the Southern Cone countries of Chile, Uruguay, and Argentina followed. In countries where military command already existed, control was tightened. Many of the regimes were quite repressive and ousted their opposition from public agencies and universities. In reaction to the repressive regimes, foundations like Ford shifted resources away from public universities and toward private research NGOs, which grew staffed with social scientists purged from public universities. Smith (1990: 236) reports that "the Ford Foundation alone [donated] $3.5 million to support eleven private research centers in Argentina, Chile, and Uruguay between 1975 and 1978." The research centers provided asylum, useful work, and frequently connections to grass-roots organizations. International governments reluctant to support the regimes also shifted funding to NGOs.

The NGOs of the 1970s provided services the state was not providing and they were frequently at conflict with the state. According to Smith (1990), almost all of the funding for indigenous NGOs during this period came from abroad. However, Liberation Theology, volunteer efforts, and grass-roots groups provided the energy. NGOs were established throughout Latin America to provide legal services for human rights violations with funding from church-based NGOs in Europe and Canada. Some of the European funding came with leftist intents of fundamental social and political change. USAID funding was more reformist or in some cases counterrevolutionary, and the IAF attempted to respond to grass-roots demands rather than to impose a political agenda (see Box 2.2).

Political and Economic Transitions of the 1980s

By the 1980s the entire donor community was getting into the act with NGOs, particularly USAID. The Reagan administration came into power in 1981 and outlined four pillars of development assistance. Two of the four were policy dialogue and technology transfer. The other two were institutional development, which involved reducing the central power of the state and encouraging NGOs to step in, and private sector development, which meant enlarging the role of the private sector in solving development problems. Meanwhile, Congress required in 1981 that 13.5 percent of development assistance be channeled through U.S. PVOs (Ruttan 1996: 122, 228). This money is typically passed on to indigenous NGOs. As later case studies show, however, the shift of USAID emphasis from the public to private sector was most apparent in USAID in-country operations.

The Central American and Caribbean region was also a priority area for the Reagan administration. As shown in Table 2.1, USAID assistance to Latin America, after falling in the mid to late 1970s, rose dramatically in the 1980s and most of this aid was targeted on Central America and the Caribbean. In 1981–82 Latin America and the Caribbean absorbed 12 percent of the official development assistance portfolio from the United States; in 1985–87 this figure was 20 percent (OECD 1994: Table 38). During the mid-1980s, only a few countries in South America — namely Bolivia, Ecuador, and Peru — received significant amounts of U.S. assistance. In 1985, for example, 89 percent of USAID loans and grants to the Latin American region went to Central America and the Caribbean.

Thus conservative USAID-funded NGOs in Central America and the Caribbean exploded during the 1980s. Central America saw a strong new breed of NGOs allied with the right wing of the civil wars that infested the region. As later case studies in this book will show, in Ecuador, Peru, and the Dominican Republic, new NGOs supportive of the private sector arose that rivaled the clout of state agencies in policy circles. The NGO community became increasingly complex, and former NGO enthusiasts looked skeptically at these modern powerful NGOs that were frequently far more closely allied with the state than had been the NGOs of the 1970s.

Meanwhile, Latin America was engulfed in an economic crisis of dramatic proportions, and the World Bank and the IDB also preached the virtues of reduced public sectors and looked to NGOs for more efficient provision of public services. Top-down development had enlarged the public sectors of Latin America without accomplishing its goal; NGOs had the reputation of reaching the grass roots with innovative solutions. Social funds to mitigate the pain of economic adjustment became one of the first innovations involving both NGOs in Latin America and these major multilaterals. The Emergency Social Fund in Bolivia began operation in 1986 and soon there were attempts to replicate it in Peru, Ecuador, and Central America. The funds were typically set up as autonomous institutions providing funding to contractors and NGOs for the construction of social infrastructure and the delivery of emergency social programs. The social funds bought time for the structural adjustment programs to work and provided some employment and relief (see Box 2.3).

Box 2.3: Social Funds, Multilaterals, and NGOs

For the World Bank and the IDB, social funds provided the first real opportunity to work with NGOs in a concrete way; and the multilaterals were pleasantly surprised with the results.

The first social fund was innovated in Bolivia in 1986 as a means to soften the hardships of structural adjustment. Bolivia's Emergency Social Fund (FSE) operated as a semi-autonomous agency, skirting government bureaucracy and working directly with foreign donors on projects of economic and social infrastructure, microenterprise lending, and basic needs. The FSE funded 3,300 projects in four years. Private contractors built schools, health clinics, and water systems. Although employment generation was relatively low, the completed projects were a tangible sign of good faith during the economic crisis. NGOs worked alongside the public sector providing complementary services and accounted for 25 percent of funds spent and one-third of all projects funded (Sollis 1992). Donors credit the FSE with providing the impetus for dialogue between NGOs and government. By the time the FSE reorganized in 1991 as the Social Investment Fund, it had already become a model for nine other similar funds in Latin America.

The funds are now found in most countries in Latin America; and although few can boast the popular success of Bolivia's FSE, donors have certainly found them useful. Many of the funds have relied on foreign donors for up to 90 percent of total funding. The IDB is the single largest contributor to Latin America's social funds. With more than $1.3 billion invested in the funds, the IDB has provided about half of their total external financing. The World Bank has providing an additional 25 percent, and USAID and the UN Development Programme have also been major players (Goodman, Morley, Siri, & Zuckerman 1997; Siri 1996). World Bank and IDB documents promote social funds as indication of a new stronger working relationship with NGOs. A World Bank document calls social funds "one of the most accessible forms of World Bank financing for NGOs" (Malena 1997: 9).

In fact, most of the funding that flows through social funds in Latin America has gone to the private contractors that build the economic and social infrastructure — the schools, health clinics, sanitation systems, and roads. Fewer projects are devoted to microenterprise lending and rural development; NGOs are more active in these. On average, the World Bank estimates that 15 percent of total social fund disbursements flow through NGOs (Malena 1997).

Social funds have attracted a fair share of criticism as well as acclaim. Housed in modern buildings and staffed with professionals not subject to the salary caps in public-sector positions, the social funds, although generally efficient, can be flashy and elitist. Some have viewed social funds as a political shield, designed to lessen popular resistance to the structural adjustment reform (Arellano-López & Petras 1994). Others focus on the extent to which the funds have displaced public-sector social spending and allowed governments to abandon their responsibilities. "Funditis" is defined as a disease that afflicts weak governments interested in attracting international funding but unable to effectively coordinate the efforts of disorganized groups of social funds and NGOs.

The multilaterals have also used social funds to showcase a new, more participatory style, but the commitment of the funds to participation is also subject to question. As a result of the 1993 Popular Participation Law, Bolivia's municipalities have become the principal users of the Social Investment Fund and NGOs must coordinate with the municipality to obtain funding. Other countries have a less participatory style. Projects funded by El Salvador's social fund must also be solicited by communities, but the Center for Democratic Education found that in most cases the community participation amounted to no more than acquiescence to the suggestions of private contractors who developed the proposals for schools or health clinics.

Launched as temporary institutions (four to six years) to alleviate poverty, for better or for worse, most funds in Latin America seem likely to become permanent fixtures of social policy.

Sources: Arellano-López and Petras 1994, Goodman et al. 1997, Malena 1997, Siri 1996, Sollis 1992, and Wurgaft 1992.

Civil Society in the 1990s Latin America

The 1990s have ushered in a new era in Latin America on a variety of levels, and NGOs are finding their role in a new civil society. One of the biggest changes is the tremendous increase in private capital flowing into Latin America. From 1990 to 1993 private flows increased eight times. Over the same period development finance fell by about one-third (OECD 1995: Chart III-1, p. 60). Economies had begun to grow, and newly democratic states faced the challenges of the decade with a new array of relationships and potential partnerships for development. Without a doubt the relationship with the international private sector is far more important than it has been in the past.

The drop in international development finance has certainly affected NGOs, although many donors, including USAID, are still increasing the proportion of funding channeled through NGOs as shown in Chapter 1. Nevertheless, in real terms, from the 1980s peak in 1985 to 1996, Table 2.1 shows that USAID assistance to Latin America fell by more than three-quarters. Thus, NGOs reliant on USAID funds have been forced to diversify.

Although NGO resources may have shrunk since 1990, the entire aid community and many new democratic governments seem to have bought into the concept of the full participation of civil society in democratic governance and sustainable development. In practice this often means greater participation for NGOs. In 1995 the IDB established a new office, charged with modernization of the state and civil society, based on the conviction that a "strong civil society requires a strong and effective state, and vice versa" (Reilly 1996: 8). The unit is providing technical assistance for governments at national, regional, and local levels designed to encourage greater citizen participation, including the participation of entrepreneurs, NGOs, local governments, and community-based organizations. Building democracy is also currently one of USAID's major goals. USAID is working with NGOs to ensure that elections are conducted transparently, to strengthen civil society, and to implement judicial reform.

NGOs are included in an array of participatory policy processes. Bolivia, for example, in 1994 passed a popular participation law that decentralizes governance to the municipal level and links municipal governments to grass-roots organizations through a designated representative. Costa Rica, as part of an effort to modernize the judicial system, undertook in 1993 a major process of national consultation that attempted to give voice to employees of the judicial system and other stakeholders in the community. Regional workshops, fora, and grass-roots consultations were held throughout the country with the help of support committees. Colombia in 1990 undertook constitutional reform with massive popular participation. The reform strengthened the legal system, transferred increased power and responsibility to citizens, and sought to fight corruption by increased accountability to the people (IDB 1997b).

The information revolution has also strengthened NGOs. As argued later in Chapter 7, NGOs are information intensive, and as the costs of transmitting information fall, the productivity of NGOs can increase. The impact of the information revolution on NGOs in Latin America has only just begun. With economic reform and privatization, telecommunications in particular have attracted enormous interest. In 1997 Latin America was anticipating a growth potential of $10 billion annually in the telecommunications market over the next five years (IDB & Together Foundation 1997). Under an Informatics 2000 Initiative, the IDB has organized a civil society task force that seeks to further the use of information technology while strengthening civil society organizations in Latin America. The task force has found NGOs to be leaders in introducing information technologies and has documented numerous ways that NGOs have used information technology, including desktop publishing, fax, electronic mail, and Internet, to network, share information, and reach a large constituency in their development efforts (IDB & Together Foundation 1997).

From an infancy that began 50 years ago, Latin American NGOs have matured into sophisticated and cosmopolitan partners in the pursuit of sustainable development. A variety of forces, both indigenous and international, have fostered their growth. The role of the Catholic Church has been pervasive throughout Latin America and has linked indigenous civil society to international charity. The Ford and Rockefeller foundations and other Northern foundations have supported the development of Latin American scholars and have shielded them from repressive regimes. The efforts of the Alliance for Progress helped to organize the peasantry into active grass-roots organizations. Through NGOs, international donors have overtly influenced local politics. Yet as markets open, as democracy deepens, and as modes of communication multiply in Latin America, local and international processes have become increasingly intertwined in complex patterns.

Much of the rest of this book is devoted to more careful examination of the complex relationships among international donors, indigenous NGOs, and the public sector in a changing environment. The next section, however, moves from the general to the specific by examining country case studies of NGO development.

COUNTRY CASE STUDIES OF NGO DEVELOPMENT

The general historical development of NGOs in Latin America recounted in the previous section is significantly enhanced by a closer examination of the nuances of each country. Offered here are a selection of countries (Chile, Peru, Mexico, and Brazil) and one region (Central America) that represent some of the more distinct prototypes within the general experience in Latin America. Later chapters provide additional country experience.

NGOs Challenge Repression: Chile

Chile, more than any other country, illustrates how NGOs have challenged and survived repression and have gone on to become partners in development with a newly democratic government. Much of the history of NGOs in Chile parallels that in other Latin American countries: early roots tied to the Catholic Church and the grass-roots groups of agrarian reform programs, increasing growth supported by leftist funds in the 1970s under military repression, and even faster growth as repression lifted and international funding swelled.

Thomas Carroll (1992) traces the beginning of NGO networks in Chile to the peasant-based organizations that developed with state support under the agrarian reforms of Eduardo Frei (1964–70) and Salvador Allende (1970–73). The socialist Allende was overthrown by Augusto Pinochet in 1973, the reforms were reversed, and the peasant-based groups were harassed during the long and repressive regime of Pinochet; however,

Carroll notes that "the movement provided some of the conditions leading to the emergence of new kinds of civic institutions" (p. 236).

Loveman (1995) documents beginnings in the early twentieth century stemming from the role of the Catholic Church in education, charity, and health care. In response to Protestant inroads and fears of socialism, Catholic Action was founded during the depression of the 1930s. It created grass-roots support organizations to work with youth and labor organizations. In the early 1950s it was followed by Catholic Rural Action, which promoted community development among peasant organizations and established the Institute for Rural Education (IER) — an NGO that still exists today. The Institute for Rural Education has been funded by international donors, the Chilean government, U.S. government agencies, and the church. Cáritas/Chile also worked in rural areas in the 1960s. In addition, the Catholic Church sponsored the Institute for Agricultural Promotion, which began working during the Frei regime on agrarian reform, agricultural cooperatives, and technical assistance to farmers. The Institute for Agricultural Promotion (INPROA) also continued working through the Pinochet dictatorship to the present time, relying solely on private and international assistance.

However, of the universe of NGOs in Chile today (approximately 700),[1] those founded prior to the Pinochet regime are clearly the exception; the vast majority sprang up in response to the junta policies. Although the regime banned political parties and controlled unions and many community organizations, many grass-roots community organizations remained, and NGOs expanded to support them. The NGOs were staffed in large part by intellectuals, professionals, and former government officials who had been removed from their positions in public agencies and universities. Funding came from external sources, many of which preferred not to support the military government directly. NGOs provided alternative channels for charitable and development assistance. The Ford Foundation and the IAF provided critical support in early postcoup years. Although the local conservative press attacked IAF support for left-wing opposition, international diplomatic concerns convinced the Pinochet government to permit the questioned projects to continue (Loveman 1995: 132).

Loveman defines three generations of postcoup NGOs: those that emerged initially (1973–76), a second generation (1976–79) that "tested the limits of junta tolerance" (Loveman 1995: 124), and further rapid growth in the early 1980s as the new political constitution — emphasizing open markets and privatization of government production and services — was adopted and implemented. In all three generations, academic and research centers and human rights organizations formed the basis of the NGO movement. Many of the early NGOs required the intervention of the Catholic Church for protection. However, by the third generation, an increasing diversity of services was provided by increasingly secular organizations.

One of the most important NGOs that arose and grew in response to the Pinochet regime was the Academy of Christian Humanism (AHC). Cardinal Raúl Silva Henríquez established the AHC in 1975 after military intervention at the Catholic University. The academy provided refuge and work in the social sciences for academics who otherwise might have left the country. The AHC grew rapidly to become a large umbrella of research groups and centers, each responsible for its own funding and programs. The Ford Foundation provided most of the early funding; later donors included the IAF, the International Research Development Centre (Canada), the Swedish Agency for Research Cooperation with Developing Countries, and the Netherlands Organization for International Development Cooperation. Levy (1996: 49) notes that from 1977 to 1987, more than 40 Ford Foundation grants supported research projects.

When Pinochet turned over power in 1990 to the democratically elected Patrício Aylwin, NGOs played a major role in the transition and in the new government. The Concertación, the party to assume power, publicly recognized the role that NGOs had played in the transition to democracy and in development activities in a document issued just prior to the elections. The document praised NGOs for their role both domestically in furthering socioeconomic development and internationally in providing informal diplomatic linkages to the international community. It encouraged the maintenance and expansion of NGO programs. When the party took office in March 1990, prominent personnel from NGOs were among those appointed for government posts (Loveman 1995: 138–42).

Substituting for a Weak State: Peru

NGOs in Peru have been induced not so much by state repression as by state weakness (Levy 1996; Díaz-Albertini 1993). The economy of Chile since the late 1970s has become the strongest in Latin America; the economy of Peru, in contrast, has one of the poorest records since that same time. NGOs have stepped in to provide services that the state could not. In particular, the state has been unable effectively to provide services to the large ethnically and culturally distinct indigenous population. Many of Peru's NGOs have worked with the indigenous population, both in rural areas and more recently in urban squatter settlements. However, despite the differences in character and role between NGOs in Chile and Peru, they also have some common roots.

Most Peruvian NGOs were created after the mid-1970s; but, as in Chile, a few prominent independent research institutes were founded earlier. The Institute of Peruvian Studies (IEP) was founded in 1964 "by philosophers, historians, anthropologists, engineers, and others chagrined by the [public] university's incapacity" (Levy 1996: 69). Like the AHC in Chile, the Institute of Peruvian Studies has received strong support over decades from the Ford Foundation. The Center for the Study and Promotion of Development (DESCO), also a Ford recipient, was founded in 1965 and grew to be the largest of Peru's research NGOs. In contrast to Chile's heavily Catholic orientation, however, both of these major research centers have secular roots.

Agrarian reform in Peru, perhaps even more so than in Chile, organized the rural populace into grass-roots groups that NGOs later served (Carroll 1992). The major agrarian reform took place under the leftist military government of Juan Velasco Alvarado (1969–80). Large collective enterprises were created from expropriated estates in a dramatic transformation of existing rural institutions (Meyer 1989: 15–17).

It soon became clear that worker-owners were not prepared for the management challenges, and NGOs stepped in to provide support. One such NGO was the Center for the Investigation and Promotion of the Farmer (CIPCA), created in 1972 by a group of Jesuits and laypersons experienced in informal education. Carroll (1992: 196) reports that CIPCA performed multiple roles, "acting as social promoter, communicator, technical specialist, coordinator, articulator of beneficiary needs, researcher, documenter, and policy adviser," and became "the key development institution of the North." When the conservative Belaúnde returned to power in 1980, CIPCA also helped to preside over the breakup (demanded by the beneficiaries) of the collective enterprises. CIPCA's success, according to Carroll, has resulted from its flexibility and cooperative relationship with the public sector. CIPCA was recognized as an educational institution and the Ministry of Education paid the salaries of about 20 percent of its staff of about 100 full-time employees. Carroll calls CIPCA a link between the "formal" and the "real" Peru because of its legitimacy with both government and peasant groups.

Most NGOs in Peru arose after the mid-1970s, when the Velasco regime started to decline, and into the 1980s — a period of severe socioeconomic trauma and state weakness (Caravedo 1995; Díaz-Albertini 1993). Crises in Peru's important fishing industry in 1976 and 1983 exacerbated the kinds of economic problems that developed in most of Latin

America during the late 1970s and 1980s. The Maoist Shining Path movement was launched in 1980 with violence that continued throughout the 1980s, while debt crisis and rampant inflation also plagued the country. By the end of the 1980s urban infrastructure had become critically deficient and posed an environmental threat to burgeoning urban populations, especially in Lima. A cholera epidemic alerted the world to the severity of the crisis.

As the state weakened and salaries fell in government agencies and in the universities, professionals and academics fled to NGOs. Levy (1996: 295) reports salaries at DESCO at $500 per month compared to only $60 per month at public universities. Thus, while the state floundered, NGOs proliferated, both bidding away most competent personnel and providing the services the state could not. The Peruvian NGO sector by 1994 numbered close to 900 (IAF 1995: 19). Its total budget was estimated between $50 million and $60 million by the late 1980s (Levy 1996: 10).

European donors are particularly prominent in Peru, and most NGOs lean left; but Peru's NGO sector has strong representation on the right as well. Peru's Institute for Liberty and Democracy (ILD) — strongly identified with founder Hernando de Soto — provides a prominent right wing example. The ILD was created in 1980 at the end of the military regime; under the Reagan administration it began receiving support from USAID and soon grew to a staff size of 75 (Levy 1996). The ILD and De Soto's pathbreaking book, *The Other Path* (which linked the growth of Peru's informal sector to excess government regulation), became well known to Washington Republicans and conservative think tanks. After his election in 1990, Fujimori formed a close relationship with the ILD to gain access to ILD's Washington connections (Levy 1996).

State Supremacy Begins to Ebb: Mexico

Mexico, for the size of its population, has far fewer NGOs than either Chile or Peru. A directory of Mexican NGOs lists only about 600 (IAF 1995: 16), a somewhat smaller number than either Chile or Peru, which were noted earlier at 700 and 900, respectively. However, the population of Mexico is about 90 million compared to only 14 million in Chile and 23 million in Peru.

The primary reason for the more limited NGO presence in Mexico has been the ever-present state (Hernández & Fox 1995; Levy 1996). Mexico's Institutional Revolutionary Party (PRI) has maintained stable governance since 1929, with an electoral process controlled by the party. The state has played a strong role in providing basic services and in funding social science research. Whereas in both Chile and Peru the Ford Foundation played an early role in establishing private research centers that became prominent members of the NGO community, much of Ford's early research support in Mexico went to El Colégio de Mexico. El Colégio is only quasi-independent from the state — more than one-half of its income is directly subsidized by the state through a budget line. Combining social science research and graduate education, El Colégio has preempted other social science research NGOs. Moreover, although Mexico's democracy could be called a mirage, it has not had the brutal repression of Chile's military regimes. Social research was able to develop within the public universities as well; in Chile and Peru, research NGOs housed all the major social science scholars.

Mexico also had more limited access to international resources — in part by choice and in part because international donors considered it to be more democratic and less needy (Hernández & Fox 1995). Levy (1996: 58) says that openness to international assistance is considered anti-Mexican and frowned on by the PRI. Hernández and Fox (1995: 204) found that grass-roots social movements were also skeptical of international funding. Much of the early funding of Mexican NGOs came through the Catholic Church. In the 1950s and 1960s, NGOs distributed food and worked in health and popular education; with the spread of Liberation Theology in the 1970s, NGOs grew more rapidly. However, according to Hernández and Fox, in Mexico a rift developed with the Catholic Church and NGOs on one side with their access to international funding. The more skeptical left shunned international funding, but garnered the energy of the grass-roots social movements.

As they did throughout Latin America in the 1980s, NGOs continued to increase in number and became more "secular, technical, and politically oriented" (Hernández & Fox 1995: 193). Their interest in democratization increased. The 1985 earthquakes marked a turning point in NGO history, as they helped guide an enormous citizen response. Foreign relief and development funding flooded in and NGOs sprang up to receive it. These NGOs worked in such areas as housing and urban issues. The volunteer efforts in reaction to the earthquake also led to the expansion of women's development NGOs.

The hold of the PRI weakened during the debt crisis of the 1980s and NGOs assumed more prominence. In 1990, as the government considered a tax law to treat NGOs like corporations, 75 major NGOs came together in a Convergence of Civic Organizations for Democracy. In addition to the new tax laws, they discussed the growing problem of extreme poverty and opportunities to participate in debt swaps. With numbers increased to

120, the convergence joined with other human rights groups to monitor polls in the August 1991 governor's race in San Luis Potosí, in a precedent-setting move (Hernández & Fox 1995: 200). Still, Hernández and Fox (p. 203) conclude that "Mexican NGOs have far to go before achieving the institutional life, the political impact, or the social presence of their counterparts in Chile, Brazil, or Peru."

Active Social Change: Brazil

Brazil has many more NGOs than does Mexico[2] and Brazilian NGOs are more actively integrated in the process of social change and democratization. Hernández and Fox (1995: 204) report that this may be caused in no small part by the contrasting actions of the Catholic Church in the two countries: "most of Brazil's bishops sheltered movements for social change and democratization in the 1970s and 1980s," while the hierarchy of the Catholic Church in Mexico was often hostile or indifferent.

The political environment in Brazil has also been more repressive than that in Mexico since the 1960s. Brazil experienced a long authoritarian period from 1964 to 1985 with violent repression in the 1960s and early 1970s. As it did in Chile (but not to the same extent) the repression led to the founding of some major private research NGOs. The Brazilian Center for Analysis and Planning (CEBRAP) is an example, founded in 1969 as a result of repression at the University of Sao Paulo. Still, much social science research was undertaken in Brazil's universities, and research NGOs have received significant government support, both from the state and federal level. Levy (1996: 102) notes that government funding at the Brazilian Center for Analysis and Planning began before democratization and increased after it.

Most NGOs in Brazil, however, are action-oriented as opposed to research-oriented and have strong relationships with grass-roots movements. Cesar and Piquet (1995) report on the results of a 1991 survey of 102 leading Brazilian NGOs. The survey was conducted at the first national assembly of Brazilian NGOs held in Rio de Janeiro in August of that year. They describe NGOs as: "'microarticulators' that mediate relationships between their clients and beneficiaries and the major institutions of society. Like small craft, they navigate under the sway of larger ships such as the state, churches, political parties, universities, social movements, the private sector, the mass media, and so on." Further, "NGOs are rather like the Lilliputians besieging Gulliver on all sides. Where they differ from Swift's fantasy, however, is in the source of their power, which lies not only in their numbers but also in their flexibility and in their role as social catalyst" (Cesar & Piquet 1995: 78, 72). Many of the leaders of the NGOs reported that they had been affected directly by the authoritarian repression; some were imprisoned, fired from jobs, tortured, or exiled. Most NGO leaders are associated with the Workers' Party.

Funding for Brazilian NGOs, in keeping with their leftist orientation, has been primarily European. More German and Dutch donors had relationships with Brazilian NGOs than any other nationality — both are well ahead of the United States in relationships with Brazilian NGOs; Great Britain and Canada follow and then other European countries. Most NGO leaders surveyed reported that in the future they would continue to rely primarily on European funding (Cesar & Piquet 1995: 81–82).

Most NGOs in Brazil were founded during the long authoritarian period, but growth has exploded since democratization. Forty percent of the NGOs in the aforementioned survey were founded between 1985 and 1990; less than 10 percent were founded during the 1960s, 22 percent during the 1970s, and 21 percent from 1980 to 1984 (Cesar & Piquet 1995: 73).[3] Although human rights and popular education were the key words during the 1970s, civil society, democracy, and ecology appear the dominant issues of the 1990s.

Cold War Politics: Central America

The Sandinista revolution in Nicaragua and subsequent U.S. efforts to topple the communist-supported FSLN distinguish the history of NGOs in Central America. Leftist international NGOs worked alongside the Sandinista government, while USAID funded an explosion of conservative, production-oriented NGOs in Honduras, El Salvador, Guatemala, and Costa Rica.

In the 1960s charity-oriented NGOs began to emerge in Central America in response to the efforts of Catholic Action groups and Christian base communities. Most had ties to CARE, Cáritas, and Catholic Relief Services and access to U.S. Public Law 480 food aid (Kaimowitz 1993a; Sollis 1995). These early NGOs often worked in cooperation with the state. Private research centers were quite limited in Central America, except in Costa Rica. Although Costa Rica became the host for a number of international research centers, a healthy university environment supported by a democratic state also limited the proliferation of research NGOs there.

A series of natural disasters in the 1970s — earthquakes in Nicaragua in 1972 and in Guatemala in 1976 and a hurricane in Honduras in 1975 — brought in increased numbers of international NGOs. Many stayed and later moved into rural development activities with peasant groups. The indigenous NGOs during the 1970s became associated with peasant movements opposed to the repressive regimes; collaboration with those governments halted (Sollis 1995).

After the Sandinista revolution, NGOs became increasingly polarized in Central America. Donor agencies from Western Europe and Canada funded leftist NGOs. Meanwhile, the conservative regimes welcomed U.S. Pentecostal church agencies and USAID helped found business-related NGOs and NGOs to support microenterprise development (Sollis 1995). Kaimowitz (1993a: 182) reports that NGO local networks reflected the competing ideologies: "USAID sponsored coordinated bodies in Costa Rica, Guatemala and Honduras that brought together and funded NGOs sympathetic to its aims. Separate, alternative leftwing coordinating institutions were set up in Costa Rica, El Salvador, Guatemala and Nicaragua." For example, USAID created the Costa Rica Association for Development Organizations (ACORDE) in 1987 to oversee USAID funding to the NGO sector. The association's board of directors was initially chosen by USAID entirely from the private sector (Macdonald 1997: 63).

The growth of NGOs during the 1980s accelerated with peace efforts. Sollis (1995: 527) reports that, "by 1989 there were over 700 NGOs in Guatemala; in 1990 there were 300 Nicaraguan development NGOs; and by 1992 there were over 700 Salvadoran development institutions and associations, over half founded after 1985." Kaimowitz found that 64 percent of agricultural NGOs in Honduras were formed after 1980. By the late 1980s, donor support for indigenous NGOs in the region had increased to $200 million a year (Kaimowitz 1993a: 182; Sollis 1995: 527). As revealed earlier in Table 2.1, USAID support in the region began to grow sharply in 1983, peaked in 1985, and subsided gradually from 1988 to 1993, after which it fell markedly. With the Sandinista defeat in 1990, however, USAID funds began to enter Nicaragua.[4] The lack of USAID funding in Nicaragua prior to 1990 had limited the growth of NGOs in that country. Costa Rica also had more limited NGO growth during this period than Guatemala, El Salvador, and Honduras because of a relatively strong public sector, a higher living standard, and more limited military involvement in regional conflicts (Kaimowitz 1993a).

Kaimowitz (1993a) reports that ideological polarization has diminished along with USAID funding in the 1990s, and cooperation between governments and NGOs has grown. The new Nicaraguan government has successfully worked with Sandinista-inspired NGOs. Moreover, the social funds, established with the support of the IDB and the World Bank in the late 1980s to relieve the economic crisis, have directly encouraged cooperation between public sectors and NGOs. According to Kaimowitz (p.

183), "ideological polarization has not vanished, . . . [but] it has become less confrontational."

CONCLUSIONS

Although NGOs began to take hold 50 years ago in Latin America, their rapid emergence in the past 20 has coincided with a political and economic environment also characterized by swift and radical change. In the process, NGOs have developed an enormous diversity of objectives and political viewpoints. Many NGOs are still closely connected to the Catholic Church, but others are secular. Some are powerful advocates for the right, the left, the poor, or the environment; others are efficiently providing public services; others both advocate and efficiently provide public services. Some NGOs are close to grass-roots groups, and others are close to powerful elites. Some NGOs are accused of opportunism, illegitimacy, and commercialism; others are attributed greater indigenous authenticity. Still, almost all NGOs in Latin America receive substantial funding and other support from international donors.

As their role in civil society expands, so does the importance of coming to grips with what that role is and can be. The remaining chapters in this book apply some rational economic analysis to the evolving puzzle of the political economy of NGOs in Latin America, their role in providing international public goods, and their place in the global community.

NOTES

1. Loveman (1995: 132).

2. Environmental NGOs alone number more than 1,500 in Brazil according to a 1992 directory (IAF 1995: 3). Fisher (1998: 164) estimates that total NGOs may number around 4,000. The population of Brazil is about 160 million compared to Mexico's 90 million.

3. Some NGOs did not answer the question and this accounts for an additional 7 percent.

4. Had it not been for the almost $400 million destined to Panama in 1990 and the $223 million to Nicaragua, the 1990 figure in Table 2.1 would have been much lower (USAID 1996).

3

From the Public to the Private Sector

Reducing the public sector and expanding the private sector were arguably the primary goals of much of the aid community during the 1980s. Reagan was in the White House cutting taxes, Thatcher was privatizing public enterprises in the United Kingdom, and the debt crisis in Latin America was drumming home the dangers of enlarged public sectors. The Washington consensus turned decidedly free-market, as the World Bank, the International Monetary Fund, U.S. Agency for International Development (USAID), and the Inter-American Development Bank all pushed for reduced public sectors and private-sector initiatives in Latin America.

Nongovernmental organizations (NGOs) benefitted financially from this turn to the private sector. As shown in Chapters 1 and 2, the 1980s saw large increases in resources going to NGOs. Bilateral donors around the world expanded their contributions through NGOs at the same time that private aid flows were increasing. Multilateral donors, like the World Bank and the Inter-American Development Bank, also became significantly involved with NGOs for the first time with the establishment of social funds to provide services to the poor during the economic crisis that engulfed the decade. The case studies in Chapter 2 demonstrate the resultant explosion in the numbers of NGOs in Latin America.

The NGO presence attracted worldwide attention, as spaces opened up when the public sector shrank and increasing democracy created opportunities for new voices not only domestically but internationally as well. NGOs became part of the fabric of new institutions and relationships in a world that was rapidly changing.

The 1980s, however, were also a time of considerable confusion for the image of NGOs in Latin America — a time of identity crisis. With increased resources and opportunities to participate, NGO success stories began to proliferate. However, the sudden empowerment of NGOs created jealousies and doubts as well. Latin American countries were not as enamored with NGOs as was much of the aid community. Reagan policies in the 1980s promoted the establishment of powerful right-wing NGOs throughout Central America, the Caribbean, and a few countries in South America. Long-time NGO advocates developed second thoughts on the advantages of NGOs and reexamined in what those advantages were rooted.

For better or for worse, NGOs were also caught up in confusion surrounding the newly popular private sector. What did it mean to be part of the private sector? What did NGOs share with the competitive profit-seeking enterprises of the modern global economy? What did they share with public-sector service providers?

This chapter addresses some of the questions raised during this tumultuous time on the role of the public, private, and NGO sectors. After describing many of the growing pains encountered and reflections on them at the time, the chapter appeals to economic theory to lay out fundamental characteristics of the public, private, and NGO sectors in the context of a closed economy. Case experience from the Dominican Republic and Ecuador illustrates the theoretical points made in the economic literature, while documenting a dramatic shift on the part of USAID from working with the public sector to working with NGOs. Implications of the international context of the donor–NGO relationship for NGOs indigenous to Latin America are brought to bear in the concluding section.

GROWING PAINS AND REFLECTION

NGOs began to attract the attention of scholars and development professionals in the late 1960s when it became clear that the top-down blueprint approach generally administered in the public sector had serious flaws (Korten 1980). By the mid-1980s the superior flexibility and sustainability of local-level efforts was well known (Uphoff 1986; Honadle & VanSant 1985; U.S. Agency for International Development [hereafter USAID] 1988). Top-down approaches had left beneficiary groups out of the planning process; they had failed to reach the poor; and when donor resources were removed, aid projects proved unsustainable because of insufficient local commitment to project goals (Montgomery 1979; Israel 1987). Local organizations, however, had produced some successful development initiatives. NGOs became associated with the advantages of a community-oriented "people-to-people" approach (USAID 1989). They acquired the reputation of reaching the poor and of promoting local participation because of their small size and political independence; and they were considered to be low cost and innovative (Tendler 1982; Annis 1987; Cernea 1988).

At the same time that NGOs had begun to demonstrate their effectiveness the development community was championing the private sector and calling for smaller government. Certainly in Latin America past aid programs had contributed to unsustainably large public sectors. The debt crisis of the 1980s made painfully clear the folly of such action. World Bank and International Monetary Fund structural adjustment and stabilization mandates required slashing public-sector expenditures. Development professionals at the World Bank, for example, explored ways to use the efficiency and vitality of the private sector toward public-sector goals (Roth 1987). USAID turned increasingly to NGOs — both Northern and Southern — as flexible and inexpensive instruments for their development activities (USAID 1989). The World Bank also recognized opportunities for increased work with NGOs (Paul & Israel 1991).

The time had also come to separate the mystique of NGOs from the reality. Judith Tendler was among the first to attempt this. NGO mythology typically identified NGOs with grass-roots organizations, but even in the mid-1970s many NGOs were large intermediaries. Tendler gave evidence to show that NGO development projects, like public-sector projects, were often "topdown, non-participatory, reliant on known techniques, or dependent on government" (Tendler 1982: iv). Even so, despite the fact that NGOs did not always live up to their reputation in these respects, she found them to be working successfully.

A 1987 conference convened in London by the *World Development* journal brought together many of the questions and growing pains surrounding the NGO sector in the 1980s (Drabek 1987). Academics joined with development professionals to begin to come to terms with the enormous changes and new responsibilities in the NGO sector for both Northern and Southern NGOs.

Annis (1987) addressed the question of whether Latin American NGOs could successfully "scale up" to receive heavier doses of donor funds without losing the virtues of smallness, and he answered it in the affirmative.

Annis recognized that in part the dynamism of the NGO sector in Latin America was caused by external funding. Joining with Tendler in debunking the NGO mythology, he stated,

In the face of pervasive poverty, for example, "small-scale" can merely mean "insignificant."

"Politically independent" can mean "powerless" or "disconnected."

"Low-cost" can mean "underfinanced" or "poor quality."

And "innovative" can mean simply "temporary" or "unsustainable." (p. 129)

Part of scaling up for Annis meant working in closer proximity with a state that may previously have been an adversary: rather he envisioned a complementary relationship. He found NGOs to be "providing services that states cannot provide, will not provide, or provide in a manner that local groups do not like" (p. 131).

Korten (1987) also expressed optimism about the potential of a new generation of NGOs to improve their management potential, scale up, and take a larger role in "people-centered development." He commented however, that some NGOs were historically "pre-bureaucratic," lacking in "adequate development of basic management systems and procedures" (p. 155). He reported that these NGOs may fear, with justification, that the professionalization required with increased funding could make them "more like the conventional bureaucracies of government that they commonly believe to be ineffective."

Many others expressed concern that large donor funds could jeopardize the autonomy and integrity of NGOs and could tempt them away from their basic priorities. Thomas Fox (1987: 13), referring to U.S. NGOs, questioned "how private and independent an NGO [could] be if it would go out of existence were government funding to dry up." He also pointed to controversial NGOs in Nicaragua providing support to families of contras and to other Latin American NGOs that steer clear of USAID funding. Garilao (1987) warned of the danger that Southern NGOs might be reduced to mere conduits of development assistance and encouraged the development of local resources and constituencies.

Van der Heijden (1987) found that the increasing dependency of U.S. NGOs on government was not unique, that this was also true of NGOs from other countries in the Organisation for Economic Co-operation and Development. He also noted more generally the financial dependence of both Northern and Southern NGOs on Northern funds, recognizing that most NGO funding "revolves around some 200 . . . international NGOs"

(p. 106). "These international NGOs are rooted in the donor societies from which they derive their support and income. . . . It is, thus reasonable to expect that the agenda and operations of these NGOs reflect their origins." Similarly he noted that the Southern NGO community was extremely dependent on external support and, thus, their work reflected the international agenda. He claimed that reliance on a single donor (often government) was the most problematic aspect of NGO dependency and that such government dependency limited the ability to criticize government actions. He also commented that large donors posed administrative burdens with complicated accounting procedures and recognized the inevitable trade-off between accountability for donors and independence for NGOs.

The heterogeneity of NGOs was another major theme at the *World Development* conference (Elliot 1987; Fox 1987; Garilao 1987). Participants agreed that heterogeneity was a source of strength for the NGO sector in both Northern and Southern countries, and that because of NGO heterogeneity generalizations about the sector were difficult if not impossible.

Studies by donors were by this time also pointing out areas where NGOs were weak relative to the public sector for carrying out development programs (Cernea 1988; USAID 1989). One major weakness highlighted was limited replicability of NGO services, because project success may depend on the highly motivated staff of a particular project. Low capacity to generate funding was another problem found to result in limited self-sustainability when external donor funds are absent. Limited technical and managerial capacity comprised a third area for concern; and finally, NGOs' focus on the micro rather than the macro level and lack of a global strategy was also seen as a disadvantage.

The next section helps to sort out some of these questions and concerns about the private, public, and NGO sectors, with the help of some economic analysis. Later chapters also return to address further the complex issues confronted as NGOs came into their own in the 1980s.

THE PROFIT, PUBLIC, AND NONPROFIT SECTORS

Although nonprofit NGOs are private and nongovernmental, they share many characteristics with government public service providers. Economists have begun to refer to nonprofits as the third sector, the other two sectors being the for-profit sector and the public sector.[1]

Nonprofit NGOs play important roles in the production and provision of public goods.[2] Public goods are jointly consumable — they can be consumed by more than one individual at the same time. A single agricultural research project, for example, can benefit a large number of farmers and even the country as a whole if a healthier rural sector stimulates the wider economy. Pure public goods are both nonrival and nonexclusive — nonrival in that one person's consumption does not interfere with another's consumption of the same goods and nonexclusive in that it would be impossible to keep another from enjoying the goods once they are produced.[3] Because of these qualities, the private for-profit sector fails to provide public goods in sufficient quantities, and traditional welfare economics has assigned public goods to the public sector (Samuelson 1954).

This section distinguishes between these three sectors from an economic viewpoint and helps to clarify some of the confusion that surfaced in the 1980s about the role of NGOs in developing countries. Few economists have paid attention to the international dimension of nonprofit activity; thus, this section begins with the insights to be gained from the perspective of a closed economy.

The Profit Sector

Profit-maximizing firms have clear incentives to minimize cost and use resources efficiently, particularly in competitive markets. Unfortunately, neither the public sector nor the nonprofit sector enjoys this advantage of for-profit production. Managers from the nonprofit, NGO sector do not maximize profits and thus lack the incentive to minimize costs; they may enhance their career, their salary, or the comfort of their workplace at donors' expense (Hansmann 1980; Easley & O'Hara 1983). Governments also do not maximize profits; political agents may maximize votes and seek rents rather than the social good. Centralized government decision making and bureaucratic provision and production of goods curtail flexibility to respond to opportunities for increased efficiency or changes in consumer demands. The private for-profit sector is relatively free from these kinds of political entanglements.

However, for some goods and services, the private sector may be considered insufficiently trustworthy. When monitoring — of either the quality of the goods or how much the quality is affected by the consumer's contribution — is difficult, as it often is for public goods, for-profit firms have incentives to lower quality and increase profits (Hansmann 1980). Because nonprofits do not distribute profits, they lack this incentive to cut quality and are often considered more trustworthy.

The Public Sector

The public sector is traditionally considered the primary provider of public goods. Because the benefits of public goods — like roads, a healthy environment, and an educated populace — cannot be withheld from those who fail to contribute, the private sector will typically underprovide them (Samuelson 1954). This is commonly known as the free rider problem. The political process may uncover demands for public goods even though in the private marketplace individuals are not willing to purchase public goods. The public sector has the power to tax to ensure the production of public goods, as well as the power to regulate to restrict the production of public bads.

The principal limitation of government as well as its basic source of strength is its reliance on the political process (Weisbrod 1988: 20–21). Public choice theory has done much to uncover the government failures associated with the government provision of goods and services. As mentioned earlier, bureaucrats may seek to maximize their budgets, and politicians may be more concerned with their reelection than with the social good.[4] The public sector also lacks the efficiency incentives and flexibility that the for-profit, private sector enjoys. Nonetheless, central government legitimately represents the political desires of the country as a whole.

However, government is a compromise made by voters; and, as pointed out by Weisbrod (1977), the politically determined level of public services is likely to leave some consumers oversatisfied and others undersatisfied. The undersatisfied consumers, then, may turn to the nonprofit sector.

The Nonprofit Sector

According to Weisbrod (1988), the public sector is the institution of choice when consumer demands are homogeneous. When consumer demands are heterogeneous, the nonprofit sector can meet the demands of those who are willing to pay for additional public services. A related advantage of the nonprofit sector over the public sector is better flexibility. Outside the centralized bureaucracy and political entanglements of government, it can respond quickly and directly to changes in consumer demand.

Others see nonprofits as the natural providers of public goods; but there are some disadvantages that, according to Salamon (1987), require the government to step in. Nonprofits cannot enforce contributions from free riders, but the government can tax. The nonprofit sector may provide public services in an uneven fashion because it has the further disadvantage of being responsible only to its donors, but the government is responsible to the general public. Thus, government contributions to NGOs can help to broaden the scope of nonprofit activities.

Because neither the nonprofit nor the public sector distributes profit, both can be seen as trustworthy, in the sense described above; donors need not fear that their contributions will go directly to profit rather than to the production of the public good. The nonprofit sector, however, allows the donor to direct funds more specifically to the desired public good.

However, like the public sector, the nonprofit sector is subject to inefficiencies and poor incentives. The same monitoring problems that encourage consumers to choose the nonprofit sector over the private profit sector because it may be more trustworthy ensure that opportunities exist for abuse of this trust.

Partners in Public Goods

Increasingly the public and nonprofit sectors work in partnership.[5] Salamon (1995) has proposed that the strengths and weaknesses of the government and nonprofit sectors are complementary. The nonprofit sector is particularly subject to the free rider problem, but the government can tax and ensure provision. The nonprofit sector may leave gaps in social services or let these services be determined by the wealthy; the government can help fill gaps and broaden the decision-making base. Furthermore, he notes that nonprofits can "personalize the provision of services, operate on a smaller scale than government bureaucracies, reduce the scale of public institutions needed, adjust care to the needs of clients rather than to the structure of government agencies, and permit a degree of competition among service providers" (Salamon 1987: 113). Thus, the public sector can use the flexibility of the nonprofit sector to its advantage and also benefit from the competition among nonprofit service providers for government contracts.

Others, including participants at the aforementioned conference on NGOs saw disadvantages to the partnership. Heavy dependence on government funding can compromise "some of the inherent advantages of being an NGO — their independence, their credibility, and their objectivity," (Fox 1987: 13). The nonprofits also risk increased bureaucracy, and the public sector may face potentially inflated costs (Kramer 1985; Salamon 1987).

Clarifying the roles of the public, private, and nonprofit sectors provides an important backdrop to the sudden shift in donor policies from the public to the private sector in the 1980s. The next section examines that shift in both the Dominican Republic and Ecuador and the reactions of local professionals intimately involved in it.

U.S. AGENCY FOR INTERNATIONAL DEVELOPMENT FIELD OPERATIONS IN THE 1980s

The increased concern of USAID with promoting the private sector, including NGOs, in the 1980s has already been established. In 1981 Congress specified that 13.5 percent of development assistance be funded through U.S. private voluntary organizations (PVOs) (Ruttan 1996: 228). The effects in the field, however, were much larger than this overall percentage might suggest. In fact, USAID increased appropriations to PVOs in programs of agriculture, rural development, and nutrition by sevenfold during 1979–86.[6] Because U.S. PVOs have typically worked through indigenous NGOs, such changes in appropriations surely resulted in increased funding to Latin American NGOs. However, the most striking evidence of USAID's shift to the private sector is seen at the level of country USAID offices and the programs they funded directly. Case research conducted in early 1990 in the agricultural and natural resources sectors of Ecuador and the Dominican Republic revealed an almost exclusive focus on indigenous NGOs.

Although the Dominican Republic and Ecuador did not receive such intensive levels of U.S. assistance as did Central American countries during the 1980s, both received substantial program funds. For example, over the 1984–89 period, development assistance to El Salvador averaged more than $80 million per year, the figures in the Dominican Republic and Ecuador respectively were $25 million and $22 million.[7] El Salvador's population was also the smallest of the three countries at this time, about 5 million compared to populations of 6 and 8 million in the Dominican Republic and Ecuador respectively. Thus, the experience presented next in these two young democracies was more moderate than what was experienced in countries like El Salvador, Honduras, and Guatemala.[8]

The Dominican Republic

USAID has had a heavy hand in the Dominican Republic ever since the assassination of the long-time dictator, Rafael Trujillo, in 1961. The Alliance for Progress was launched the same year, and during the next few years — which included the U.S. occupation of the Dominican Republic in 1965 — this country received more U.S. aid per capita than any other country in the world (Wiarda & Kryzanek 1982: 85). Exceeded only by Honduras and Haiti in 1986, 23.2 percent of Dominican government expenditures were financed by official development assistance (USAID 1989: 148).

NGOs began to grow in the Dominican Republic following Trujillo's death, but the bulk of the foreign aid at this time was directed toward the public sector. The major public agricultural institution, the Secretary of Agriculture (SEA) relied on foreign aid for approximately 20 percent of its budget until the early 1980s. However, because most of SEA's budget went to maintaining the bureaucracy, estimates suggest that 80 percent of the operations budget came from external sources.[9]

Beginning in the early 1980s, donors — particularly USAID — refused to work in the rural public sector and instead directed new programs to NGOs. Luis Crouch states that this attitude on the part of donors, combined with the financial crisis that hit the Dominican Republic in 1981, left SEA "paralyzed, practically non-operational" (Crouch 1986: 6). For the preceding 150 years, SEA was the most politically powerful agricultural institution in the country.[10] Other rural public institutions were similarly afflicted.

Meanwhile, two new influential NGOs were established under the guidance and with the financial support of USAID: the Agricultural Enterprise Board of Consulting and Co-investment (JACC) and the Agricultural Development Foundation (FDA), established in 1984 and 1987 respectively.[11] Planners intended that JACC eventually be self-supporting, but its major project in 1990 — the project for agricultural enterprise promotion — received about 40 percent of its financing from USAID and 12 percent from the Dominican government.[12] The mission of the FDA is agricultural research and technology development; however, professionals in agriculture, interviewed in January 1990, commented widely that output thus far was small, given the considerable funding received.[13]

Prior to the establishment of the FDA, efforts were underway to establish the Dominican Institute of Agricultural Investigation (IDIA). The IDIA was to take over the research, extension, and capacitation responsibilities that belonged to SEA in an institution semi-independent of the state. The IDIA was created by law in July 1985 and approved for financing by USAID; local consultants were hired to make preliminary studies and some $20,000 were disbursed to begin work (Chanlatte 1986: 1, 4–5). The institute was to be governed by a board of directors with representatives from both the public and private sectors. The program was reportedly dropped by USAID when it became clear that the public sector would have a majority.[14] Without USAID support, the program dissolved. USAID then redirected its efforts to establishing the FDA.

Ecuador

The USAID made a similar shift in Ecuador from working with the public sector to working with the NGO sector. Major recipients of USAID funding in the area of agriculture and natural resources in the 1980s include these three NGOs: Fundación Natura, an environmental NGO; Institute for Agricultural Strategies (IDEA), a think tank on agricultural policy; and the Foundation for Agricultural Development (FUNDAGRO).

Fundación Natura was established in 1978, prior to the Reagan era, by a group of Ecuadorian businessmen and public-sector officials. Natura is a successful and well-respected NGO, with an identity quite independent from that of its donors. However, Natura began receiving funding from USAID in 1980, and USAID quickly became the major supporter of Natura: 85 percent of international grants in its first four years of operation were from USAID. From 1978 to 1988 this figure remained over 60 percent (Fundación Natura 1989a). Natura also received substantial support from the domestic private sector and maintained an active working relationship with the domestic public sector.

IDEA was founded in 1985 with considerable help from USAID. Like Natura, IDEA was working with the public and private sectors. IDEA is a policy think tank; its purpose is to provide a forum for dialogue regarding macroeconomic, agricultural, and natural resource management policy issues (Institute for Agricultural Strategies 1989).

FUNDAGRO was founded in late 1987, again with substantial USAID support. Like the FDA in the Dominican Republic, FUNDAGRO is devoted to agricultural research, training, and extension. Bolivar Navas, coordinator for extension and education for FUNDAGRO, explained that FUNDAGRO works mainly as a catalytic organization, funding projects through universities and the public sector. He commented that one of the principal reasons for the founding of the institution was that international organizations were more willing to donate funds to an NGO than to the public sector.[15] As in the Dominican Republic, the new private-sector organization was justified on the basis of the failure of public-sector research and extension and the politicization of the public institutions. FUNDAGRO was expected to improve efficiency, and the wages and working conditions attracted highly trained professionals away from the public sector (Bebbington & Thiele 1993: 137). USAID had contributed an endowment to FUNDAGRO to fund core costs. Navas reported that the NGO was working to diversify its funding beyond USAID, its primary support in 1990.

Finally, at about the same time that IDIA was being planned for the Dominican Republic, a similar agricultural research institute — the Ecuadorian Foundation of Agricultural Investigation (FEDIA), semipublic, semiprivate — was being planned for Ecuador with the backing of USAID. Coincidentally perhaps, the organization also lost USAID support midway through the planning phase, whereafter USAID shifted its support to FUNDAGRO. Navas explained "FEDIA didn't get going because of legal matters, because of political matters, because of a series of misunderstandings."[16]

Local Perspectives

Domestic resistance at the time to the policy shift by USAID from the public to the private sector was particularly apparent in the Dominican Republic. The career-long Dominican professionals in agriculture policy, interviewed in January 1990, agreed that donors had good reasons for not wanting to work with the public sector. Inefficiency, irresponsibility, lack of continuity, and diversion of funds were some of the problems that had discredited the public sector according to interviewees. Although they commented on the flight of personnel to better working conditions and salaries of the NGOs, they insisted that the public sector should not be abandoned. Some warned that the sharp turn from the public sector and toward the private sector was quite negative and was polarizing political forces. Dominicans expressed skepticism that improvement on public-sector experience would be substantial: Frank Rodríguez said the personnel working in the new institutions were the same people who had worked in the public institutions, "they aren't extra-terrestrials." He implies that donor-financed NGOs could be subject to the problems of inefficiency and corruption that plagued the public-sector institutions. Francisco Pérez Luna agreed, commenting, "there are devils everywhere."

Professionals in Ecuador also expressed feelings that USAID had swung too far from the public sector and that state action should supplement the work of the NGO sector. José Perreira, among others, said that although some nonprofit NGOs may be administered more efficiently than state institutions, this depended on the capacity of the personnel involved. Bebbington and Thiele (1993) also document initial criticism of the private-sector FUNDAGRO and the donor shift from the public to the NGO sector.

Professionals in both countries unanimously agreed that a principal advantage of the NGO sector over the public sector was its position outside the political process. The Dominicans explained that not only was the public sector subject to major turnover in personnel every four years but also that public resources (including personnel) were often used for political purposes. Further, it had become almost accepted to arrive at a political position poor and leave rich. Some also pointed out that although in the NGO sector incentives might exist for individuals to make themselves rich at donors' expense, supervision was politically easier. A donor like USAID would encounter severe political complications trying to supervise the Dominican government, but NGOs could be more easily supervised by the donor and by the Dominican government.

The primary disadvantage of the public sector emphasized in Ecuador was the enormously cumbersome bureaucracy. Arturo Ponce claimed that the main advantage of the NGO sector is that "the NGO sector . . . isn't involved in the huge administrative apparatus . . . it's an administrative monster." Others agreed that NGOs had more flexibility to act quickly, independently, and creatively.

The ability of NGOs to contract professionals for a particular project adds to their flexibility; when the project is over, they have no further obligations to employ those individuals. The same is not true when the public sector increases its staff. Both management and contracted professionals who occasionally worked on projects at Fundación Natura were happy with the way projects were managed.

Others recognized, however, that NGOs lacked responsibility to the general public. Fausto Maldonado, an Ecuadorian national at USAID/Ecuador, said this was his principal worry about the NGO sector. He went on to explain that as opposed to the public sector, the private sector had limited objectives and self-established responsibilities (protecting mammals, for example) and limited time frames as well. Because they were voluntary agencies the public could not demand any wider responsibility of them. Others stressed the importance of defining roles for each sector.

Despite a lack of direct responsibility to the general public, management in Fundación Natura expressed concern for their domestic reputation and their international reputation, because they depend on both for funding. Similarly, those at the JACC in the Dominican Republic were cognizant of the importance of their relationship with the domestic private sector as well as their international relationships.

Finally, there was general agreement that the public and private sectors should work together. Fundación Natura, for example, collaborated with the public sector on a number of projects. The director, Yolanda Kakabadse, explained that NGOs, capable of capturing international grants, supplied the financing and the public sector supplied the law. Agapito Pérez Luna and many other Dominicans were sorry to see public-sector resources in agriculture being abandoned and duplicated in the private sector. They suggested that NGOs could contract out projects to the public sector.

Thus, the experience of rural sector institutions in both the Dominican Republic and Ecuador illustrates USAID's sharp policy shift in the 1980s toward working through NGOs rather than through the public sector. The experience in institutional reform encouraged by USAID is strikingly similar, including the stillborn joint private-public agriculture research efforts in both countries. Although donors showed a bias for working with the nonprofit sector, domestic professionals in agriculture and natural resources were more resistant to the changes.

THE NGO – PUBLIC SECTOR
CHOICE FOR LATIN AMERICA

Southern NGOs funded by Northern donors demonstrate many of the same advantages over the public sector as do domestically funded NGOs: ability to cater to heterogeneous consumers and provide services that the state does not provide; flexibility to respond quickly to changes in consumer demand, unencumbered by the bureaucracy of government; freedom from the political entanglements of government; and finally, donors prefer NGOs because NGOs offer donors more control over their donations than does the public sector.

Similarly, Southern NGOs funded by Northern donors possess many of the same disadvantages relative to the public sector as do domestically funded NGOs: NGOs are subject to free rider problems and thus lack fund-raising capacity and NGOs are outside the political process and thus bear no responsibility to the general public. Moreover, like the public sector, the nonprofit, NGO sector is subject to administrative failings and has poor incentives for efficient use of resources, although committed management may compensate for poor economic incentives.

In many respects, however, NGOs funded by official foreign sources play a fundamentally different role than do domestically funded nonprof-its. NGOs satisfy their organizational goals by seeking grants and contracts consistent with their objectives. Donors provide funds so that public goods are provided. To stay in business, NGOs need to satisfy the clients — the donors who pay the bills and demand the services. Thus, the

essential role of NGOs funded by foreign donors is to serve the international community — they provide international public goods. Some
NGOs, such as Salvadorian Foundation for Economic and Social
Development (FUSADES) in El Salvador, have relied almost entirely on a
single donor.[17] Others, such as Fundación Natura in Ecuador, have
avoided cooptation by a single foreign donor and have gained independence by maintaining a diversified donor base. However, as long as
foreign donors are paying the bills, the primary client is the international
community.

In view of the advantages of the nonprofit sector — both theoretical
and as evidenced in practice — the enthusiasm of donors for NGOs is not
surprising; but the preference of external donors for working with
Southern NGOs in no way attests to evidence that public goods for the
domestic economy will be better provided by the NGO sector. The public
sector is responsible to the domestic populace and can tax to provide
necessary services. The scope, duration, and variety of services offered by
externally funded NGOs depend on the goals of donors.

Certainly the goods and services demanded by the international
community may overlap with those demanded locally — international
public goods may be valued both at home and abroad. NGOs may be
adept at handling donor funds. The inefficiency of the domestic political
process ensures that the public sector cannot perfectly represent the
demands of the populace (Mueller 1989). Indeed, it is those consumers
underrepresented in the political process whom foreign donors presume to
reach through NGOs. Further, the improvements in service provision
gained by freedom from the political entanglements and cumbersome
bureaucracy of government may be large. If the services demanded by
external donors are valued as public goods by the domestic clientele and
the NGO sector is a more efficient channel for service delivery, then the
domestic clientele will benefit. However, to the extent that there is a role
for the public sector in any country — the sector responsible to its citizenship, able to provide public services in a consistent manner through tax
revenue — externally funded NGOs cannot replace the public sector.

NOTES

1.   Economists began to pay increasing attention to nonprofit organizations
during the past 20 years. See Powell (1987) and Rose-Ackerman (1986) for
collected works.

2.   See Ostrom, Schroeder, and Wynne (1993: 74–75) on the distinction
between provision and production. Production refers to the technical operation of

transforming inputs into outputs, whereas provision refers to ensuring the finances and arranging for the production. Many NGOs are active in both functions. NGOs heavily dependent on a single donor may be only producers.

3.   This follows the recommendation of Blumel, Pethig, and von dem Hagen (1986) to use "joint consumability" as the sole defining characteristic of a public good, while recognizing a wide spectrum of public goods — some much closer to private goods than others.

4.   See Mueller (1989) for a review of the public choice literature, which deals with these topics.

5.   Kramer (1985: 378) dates this strengthening relationship in the United States to the Economic Opportunity Act of 1964.

6.   See Meyer (1992b).

7.   (USAID 1996). Total USAID assistance was considerably more, particularly in the case of El Salvador. Development assistance is complemented by Public Law 480 food aid and by the Economic Support Fund.

8.   See Macdonald (1997) and Sollis (1995) on the politics of NGOs in Central America.

9.   Interamerican Institute of Cooperation in Agriculture (1989: 9). The next chapter pursues in more detail the role that donors played in the creation and evolution of rural public institutions in the Dominican Republic.

10.   SEA was originally founded as the Ministry of Agriculture on February 27, 1854. National Planning Office (1983: 189).

11.   According to the "USAID Program and Project Semester Report as of September 30, 1989," the largest flow of funds was going through JACC, FDA, and the Superior Institute of Agriculture (ISA), a private agricultural university that USAID helped found in 1962 and has subsequently supported.

12.   The three and one half year project was to cost a total of $10.4 million (JACC 1989: 7).

13.   Those who made such comments include Angel Castillo, director of Center for Administration of Rural Development of ISA; Agapito Pérez Luna, Interamerican Institute of Cooperation in Agricultural Sciences since 1980, previous positions in SEA, Banco Agrícola in institutional support; Francisco Pérez Luna, executive director of the Agricultural Policy Studies Unit (UEPA), former Secretary of Agriculture; and Frank Rodríguez, private consultant at Consenso Agrario, previous director of the Dominican Agrarian Institute (IAD), previous positions at the National Institute of Hydraulic Resources (INDRHI), and the Institute for Cooperative Development and Credit (IDECOOP). Other Dominican agriculture professionals interviewed include: Carlos Aquino González, JACC vice president, former SEA director, Foundation for Rural Youth Development (FUNDEJUR) vice president; Fernando Durán, director of extension under Training & Visits system; Benito Ferreiras, rector of ISA; Virgilio Mayol, JACC agribusiness specialist, director of extension under the Integrated Program of Agricultural Development; Wilfredo Moscoso, researcher at ISA; Bélgica Núñez, IDB Dominican Republic Agriculture project officer, formerly researcher at

UEPA; Alberto Rodríguez, Peace Corps project officer, formerly teacher at ISA; Pablo Rodríguez, researcher at UEPA. Interviews were conducted in January 1990. The viewpoints of the interviewees should be considered as their personal perspectives and not as statements from their organizations. These interviews are further recounted in Meyer (1992b).

14.   This was reported by Francisco Pérez Luna, Angel Castillo, and Ken Wiegand of USAID in interviews with the author in January 1990.

15.   Interview with author, June 1990. This and subsequent chapters also draw on interviews with the following Ecuadorian professionals: Neptali Bonifasc, executive director, IDEA, Board of Directors, Fundación Natura; Yolanda Kakabadse, executive directive, Fundación Natura; Fausto Maldonado, Office of Agriculture and Natural Resources, USAID, former liaison with Fundación Natura; Gonzalo Oviedo, administrator of the debt swap project, Fundación Natura; Angel Paucar, Department of Administration of Natural Areas and Wildlife Resources, Ministry of Agriculture; José Perreira, executive director of Consejo Nacional de Ciencia y Tecnología, (a public sector conservation data center), employed on contracts for Fundación Natura, 1990; Arturo Ponce, formerly with Department of National Parks and Wildlife, Ministry of Agriculture, founder of Fundación Natura. Interviews were conducted in May and June 1990 and they are further recounted in Meyer (1993). The viewpoints of the interviewees should be considered as their personal perspectives and not as statements from their organizations.

16.   This and subsequent quotations from interviews are translated from the Spanish by the author.

17.   The Salvadoran Foundation for Economic and Social Development is a very large and powerful NGO serving in the 1980s and early 1990s as the principal arm of USAID in El Salvador. In 1991 USAID was providing more than 90 percent of their funding (Personal communication James Stevenson, USAID/El Salvador, September 1991).

4

Responding to Donor Demands

To critical observers in the mid-1980s, the new enthusiasm of major donors for nongovernmental organizations (NGOs) often seemed like the latest fad in a trail of failed efforts in institution building in developing countries (Sarles 1987; Brodhead 1987). However, NGOs have yet to fade into the litany of past mistakes. Rather, they have evolved with changing times, and although many NGOs have come and gone, others have withstood the pressures of changing donor fads. Constantly forging new relationships with domestic and international donors, some of Latin America's NGOs have provided international public goods — public goods valued both at home and abroad — since the 1960s or even earlier.

NGOs are not an alternative to the domestic public sector, but in many cases they have proved a good conduit for international funding — and more than that, as later chapters will show. International donors have many years of experience supporting national public sectors in the South. Thorough assessments of international aid have found that overriding political motives are often to blame when international aid is ineffective in furthering development goals (Cassen et al. 1994; Ruttan 1996). Other problems stem from the lack of coordination between donors and the short-term nature of most donor programs (Cassen et al. 1994). Donor governments have found that working through NGOs can moderate such traditional problems with international aid. NGOs are less political than governments and perhaps more able to coordinate other development activities (Ruttan 1996). NGOs may also elicit substantial participation from local beneficiaries, which improves the prospects for project sustainability by helping to align the incentives of donors and local stakeholders (Government Accounting Office 1995; Fairman & Ross 1996).

This chapter argues further that international funds have often been damaging to public-sector institutions. Public-sector institutions are intended to respond to domestic political processes and serve domestic interests, not international interests. NGOs, in contrast, respond to needs felt by the individuals who found them and give of their time and energy. They are also designed to serve the donors whose interests coincide with management goals. Thus, it may often be more appropriate to channel international funds through NGOs than through the public sectors of developing countries.

To demonstrate this point, this chapter provides two examples from the Dominican Republic: the public rural extension service and a rural development-oriented NGO. The chapter begins by reviewing some of the most frequent problems donors have encountered while building institutions in the public sectors of developing countries and by recounting the passing of development fads to hit rural sector institutions in Latin America. An overview of the rural institutional framework in the Dominican Republic follows before each case study is presented.

DECADES OF RURAL INSTITUTION BUILDING IN LATIN AMERICA

Rural development efforts have provided a rich graveyard of public-sector institution-building efforts. In spite of long experience trying to improve public institutions for rural development, Israel (1987) reported institutional weakness to be a major roadblock to development and rural development institutions to be particularly problematic. Sarles (1987: 29) reported that missions of the U.S. Agency for International Development (USAID) in Latin America and the Caribbean were enthusiastically creating new private-sector institutions in the 1980s, and she recommended caution, given the record of "failed new institutions" constructed by international donors.

The Pressures of Donor Demands

The discouraging experience with institution building created much literature during the 1980s, attempting to explain how donors might improve their institution-building skills.[1] The literature revealed that weaknesses in rural public institutions were donor related to a significant extent. In fact, it showed that institutions were responding not to the demands of the rural clientele they would be expected to serve but rather to the demands placed upon them by the donor agencies.

The Project Approach

A frequent criticism of donor efforts in institution building has been the short-term project-oriented approach. Lacroix (1985: 12–13) stated: "The emphasis on short term results, on meeting deadlines, on disbursement of funds, leads to a strategic approach of institution building that is equally short term and is often meant to serve mainly the direct interests of a specific project. . . . Special project units are established, using special incentives to lure personnel away from the more permanent institutions of the public sector, undermining the latter's potential for sustained long term action." These points are echoed in studies that stress longer time horizons for donor projects and greater continuity in donor personnel (Uphoff 1986; American Consortium for International Public Adminstration [hereafter ACIPA] 1986). Further emphasis was made on the harm inflicted on institutions by donor targets and their need for quantifiable indicators (Uphoff 1986; Sarles 1987).

New projects frequently meant new institutions. Lacroix (1985: 20), commenting on the poor experience with this tendency, said, "The idea to create a new unit for project implementation was the logical consequence of the frustration of the early project designers and supervisors. Their experience led them to regard existing institutions as inefficient, technically incompetent, understaffed and philosophically conservative. . . . Thus, they saw clear administrative advantages in establishing a brand new unit." Sarles (1987: 29), while reflecting on the movement of USAID to new private sector institutions, warned: "The history of failed new institutions supported by donors should serve as a stern warning to planners who think that 'beginning over again' will somehow in the long run solve organizational problems that are endemic throughout a country. Continuity is such an important aspect of long-term success in developing research capacity that it is preferable under most circumstances to reform existing institutions rather than to start from scratch." Many others stressed that for long-term institution building it was best to work within existing institutions (Uphoff 1986; ACIPA 1986; Honadle & VanSant 1985; World Bank 1988).

The Money Problem

Much of this literature hinted that donor funding was part of the problem. Uphoff (1986: 259) complained of donor "preoccupation with 'moving money'" and emphasized that the amount of money spent did not equal the amount of development achieved. Further, he recommended that the traditional role of donor agencies as sources of capital and expertise be replaced by a participatory role in identifying problems. A World Bank study (1988: xviii) supported Uphoff's points concluding that "In too many cases . . . rural development lending was supply-driven by funds and project slots and the need to meet arbitrary target criteria."

Donors, in many cases, have commanded a controlling share of the budgets of rural institutions in developing countries. Sarles (1987: 18) emphasized that national agricultural research goals have been distorted by their dependence on donor funds, "In an effort to keep money flowing from donors, the research organizations agree to take on projects that are not national priorities, thereby distorting a rational research agenda for the country or region."

Donor Coordination

The call for cooperation among donors is another suggested improvement in institution building efforts that has revealed the difficulties donors help to create. A report on a series of seminars on institutional development concluded that:

Achieving effective donor cooperation is considered extremely difficult primarily because of different goals of the several donors. Also emphasized was the frequent lack of cooperation within donor organizations as well as between donors. Improvement in coordination was considered to be an extremely important goal from the standpoint of more effective use of donor resources, enhanced opportunity to achieve goals, and lessened stress on host countries too frequently encountering bewildering and frustrating different donor requirements and direction. (ACIPA 1986: v–vi)

Lele and Goldsmith (1989) suggested that the lack of alternative sources of assistance (other than the Rockefeller Foundation) for the development of the national research system in India may have been a blessing in disguise. They found that in Africa countries have been hampered by the diversity of aid sources.[2]

These chronic problems of international donor funding have negatively affected institutions in developing countries; so, too, have the constantly changing fads among donors in approaches to institution building.

Fads and Fashions in Latin America

The international aid community has been involved with institution building for rural development in Latin America since shortly after World War II and a variety of approaches have come and gone. Some of these approaches were alluded to in Chapter 2 as the history of NGOs in Latin America was recounted; but, until the 1980s, most experience with institution building was in the public sector. Disillusionment with the early community development approach soon brought efforts to increase agricultural production. The Cuban revolution inspired the Alliance for Progress to push for agrarian reform programs in the early 1960s. In the 1970s integrated rural development came into fashion with an emphasis on providing basic needs. Donors built new public institutions with each new approach, but results disappointed.

Community Development

The 1950s began the era of community development, a politically motivated effort that responded to fears of totalitarianism taking over the underdeveloped world. The following remarks by Lacroix (1985: 8) hinted at linkages between the community development approach and the ideas of Paulo Freire: "The long term objective of community development was to build stable, democratic nations. With this background and origin, community development was described as organization, education and social action in, for and by the community. . . . The development of infrastructure and social services and even the increase in production, i.e. economic development, were seen as somewhat incidental to the basic political motive of community development."

U.S. developmental assistance attempted to model the successful agricultural extension service in the United States based on the land-grant universities. In the community development era, this meant organizing groups of farmers, housewives, and youth clubs.[3] Large new bureaucracies were established to administer programs and to coordinate their components.

However, the community development era came to an end. Lacroix (1985) reported that the community development efforts, partly because of their political goals, were viewed suspiciously by the rural poor. Additionally, as noted by Ruttan (1984), the global food crisis prompted by crop failures in South Asia in the mid-1960s emphasized the need for reorientation toward increasing production.

Land Reform and Production

In the mid-1960s the development community changed course and made production the priority in agriculture. In Latin America, however, the situation was complicated by the Cuban revolution. Land reform became a political priority with the launch of the Alliance for Progress under the Kennedy administration. In the same period USAID and other international lending agencies sponsored research to demonstrate that land reform would also improve productivity (Dorner & Kanel 1971; Dovring 1970).

Almost every country in Latin America, because of the political pressures that originated from the Punta del Este Charter of the Organization of American States in 1961, enacted an agrarian reform law and set up public institutions to administer the agrarian reform program (Grindle 1986). Usually more than one bureaucracy was established to serve the needs of the newly landed farmers. Some have argued that in fact there was no real land reform, only the new bureaucracies to carry out the will of the foreign superpower (Dore y Cabral 1982).

Integrated Rural Development

The 1970s saw another change of heart regarding the appropriate role of foreign aid in rural development efforts. Land reform ran out of political steam and disillusionment existed with the bureaucratic and technologically oriented green revolution. A renewed emphasis was placed on local participation and, with the advent of the basic needs approach and discouragement with the trickle down myth, goals were set to reach the rural poor.

The new buzz words became integrated rural development (IRD), although it was not entirely clear what the approach was all about. Ruttan (1984: 394) commented that it "drew on a complex of often mutually contradicting intellectual and ideological perspectives." For example, although IRD condemned the centralized bureaucratic approach, systems thinking about institutional design and program implementation grew. Efforts were also made to integrate local participation into the bureaucratic planning process (Montgomery 1979). Programs attempted to integrate agricultural production (including credit, extension, input supply, and marketing), social services (such as health and education), and infrastructure (largely roads and irrigation).[4]

In theory existing institutions would coordinate projects, but in practice this meant adding departments or perhaps new institutions to the already existing entourage of rural institutions. Lacroix (1985: 43) reported severe problems with the IRD approach, the most widely commented being that of: "the difficulty of coordinating the various agencies which usually participate in multi-component projects. The causes for this problem range from simple administrative chaos to political rivalry and power fights between the agencies which, unfortunately, more often than not affects the regular and timely provision of finance."

Ruttan also noted the problem of project complexity, which he blamed in large part on the basic needs targets adopted by the lending institutions. He found that it was difficult to reconcile, "(a) a commitment to the objectives of mass participation in local decision-making and building institutions capable of mobilizing local resource for development with (b) the objective of achieving measurable improvements in basic need indicators within the relatively limited time span between programme initiation and evaluation. A frequent result is that the participation and mobilization goals have been supplanted by bureaucratic approaches to programme delivery" (Ruttan 1984: 398).

A Move to the Private Sector

By the mid-1980s donors were trying to distance themselves from the IRD approach. A 1988 World Bank evaluation of rural development experience made the following comments that although IRD had not been explicitly identified, "as part of the Bank's program, there are sufficient references to the concept, in one form or another, to allow readers to assume that it was part of the strategy. . . . Senior Bank managers have commented, however, that IRD was never formally 'taken on board' by the Bank. Perhaps this was because early warnings of problems with the concept, including some staff opposition, indicated that it was not likely to become a useful rallying cry or slogan" (World Bank 1988: 6).

As explained in Chapter 2, under the pressures of the debt crisis, the development-aid community turned to the private sector during the 1980s. Structural adjustment programs were designed to encourage private sector development and export-led growth. As shown in Chapter 3, donors turned away from the public sector and toward NGOs to administer development projects. Although the sharp turn elicited merited criticism, NGOs had already begun to demonstrate significant advantages over the public sectors of developing countries for channeling donor funds.

The remainder of this chapter examines donor experience with rural institution building in the Dominican Republic, both in the public sector and in the case of an NGO founded in the early 1960s. The following section provides a brief overview of the rural institutional framework and the role of donors in building it.

RURAL INSTITUTION BUILDING IN THE DOMINICAN REPUBLIC

The last chapter pointed out the heavy role that international aid agencies — particularly USAID — have played in building institutions in the Dominican Republic since the end of Trujillo's dictatorship in the early 1960s. Indeed, Dominican professionals with experience in rural public-sector institutions said that almost every institution that sprang up did so because of international funding or politics.[5]

Much of the rural public institutional framework in the Dominican Republic was laid down after Trujillo's dictatorship ended in 1961 and with heavy support from USAID under the Alliance for Progress. The earliest rural public institutions included the ministry of agriculture, later called the Secretary of Agriculture (SEA), first created in February 1854; and the Agricultural Bank, established under Trujillo in 1945.[6] In the 1960s, however, many new rural public institutions were established. Among these is the Dominican Agrarian Institute (IAD), established in April 1962 due both to domestic pressure to redistribute Trujillo lands consolidated and to hemispheric pressure for agrarian reform. The IAD was given the responsibility to redistribute state and privately owned lands to the rural poor, and to establish irrigation projects, credit programs, and other services such as agricultural extension, marketing, and cooperatives. The Institute for Cooperative Development and Credit, whose purpose is to promote and establish credit cooperatives, was created in 1963; and in 1965 the National Institute of Hydraulic Resources (INDRHI), responsible for constructing and maintaining irrigation systems, was created.

Also in 1965 a new law was passed to reorganize and establish the legal basis of SEA as the head of the national agricultural policy and coordinator for all other institutions in agriculture. The same law established the legal jurisdiction of the Agricultural Bank, which became the primary source of credit for the agricultural sector. The legal jurisdiction of IAD, the Institute for Cooperative Development and Credit, and INDRHI were also established at this time. The 1965 law also created the The National Council of Agriculture (CNA) as the responsible organ to SEA for the formulation of national agricultural policy. It was reported, however, that the CNA functioned only during 1983–85 (Agricultural Policy Studies Unit [hereafter UEPA] 1987: 828). In 1984, under a grant agreement between the Dominican government and USAID (AID-517-0156) the Agricultural Policies Studies Unit was set up to serve as the research organism responsible to the CNA (UEPA 1989b).

The National Institute of Price Stabilization was created in December 1969 with the participation of USAID and is responsible for the commercialization and stabilization of the prices of primary commodities. Joaquín Nolasco said that when the National Institute of Price Stabilization was created, similar institutions were created in many countries in Latin America and the Caribbean; he noted that most were plagued with inefficiency and changes of policy (Nolasco 1982: 53–54).

Also within the realm of rural development is the Community Development Office, involved in community infrastructure and technical assistance in a variety of areas since the 1960s. The Dominican Center for the Promotion of Exports, created in 1971, is an institution established to promote mainly agricultural exports. Finally, the General Directorate of Forests, created in 1962 (law 5856) (National Planning Office [hereafter ONAPLAN] 1983: 219), subordinate to SEA, is responsible for protecting and managing the national forests.

These represent the principal public institutions for rural development active in the 1980s. Many other minor public-sector institutions and a number of private-sector institutions were also working in the rural sector. The major agricultural university in the Dominican Republic — the Superior Institute of Agriculture in Santiago — was also created in 1961 with substantial help from USAID. The Superior Institute of Agriculture also became a regular recipient of USAID support over the years.

In the Reagan years, as explained in Chapter 3, two new powerful private institutions were established with the help once again of USAID; the Agricultural Enterprise Board of Consulting and Co-investment in 1984 and the Agricultural Development Foundation in 1987. The Agricultural Enterprise Board of Consulting and Co-investment supports medium to large agricultural enterprise and Agricultural Development Foundation works in research and technology development.

This section has provided only the broad outlines of the major agricultural institutions in the Dominican Republic. Most of the major public institutions arose during the heavy U.S. presence in the 1960s. Some were added later, but still with the help of an international agency. The following section traces in more detail the experience of the agricultural extension service through 30 years of donor aid.

THE CASE OF THE DOMINICAN
EXTENSION SERVICE

The history of the Dominican agricultural extension service from the early 1960s mirrors the changing goals of the aid community in Latin

America. As donor goals changed, programs of extension rose and fell. Unfortunately, the credibility of this domestic public institution suffered as a result of fluctuations in international funding and program goals.

U.S. Influence in the 1960s

The agricultural extension service was established in the Dominican Republic in 1962 under the authority of SEA and was supported during 1962–67 by USAID through the Dominican government (ONAPLAN 1983: 194). The first 4 regional extension offices were established in 1963. By 1967 there were 21 agency offices, 70 extensionists, and additional resources for national programs as well (Naut 1984: 441–42).

The Dominican extension service was modeled after the U.S. extension service based on land-grant universities. Durán commented that if the Dominican extension service did not have all of the characteristics of that of its northern neighbor, at least it was built according to the land-grant dream.[7] In addition to substantial funding, in 1965 approximately 65 technical assistance personnel — enough to fill a whole floor of the SEA — were sent in by USAID. Established at the end of the community development era, the extension service was based on informal education for the rural family. In keeping with other rural development programs in Latin America at this time, the orientation of the effort was more social and political than economic. Rural organizations were encouraged according to the following types: producer groups for the heads of households, domestic oriented groups for housewives, and *clubes 5D* (modeled after 4-H clubs in the United States) for the rural youth. Carvajal (1982) describes the extensionists of the time as missionaries of rural development.

Substantial efforts and resources were devoted to the agricultural extension service in this period but it was not well accepted by the rural clientele. Some claim that the U.S. model seemed foreign and out of place in the rural Dominican environment. Carlos Aquino González, who headed SEA during the 1960s, was more positive on this early extension model. He reports that the extension service was accepted initially but began to fall out of favor in 1965, the year of the U.S. invasion, even though the support of USAID continued. By 1967, however, both the USAID project period and the funding ended.

As future reference for Dominican participants, the experience under the U.S. model made lasting impressions. Aquino González, for example, has put his public-sector experience to work founding NGOs. The Foundation for Rural Youth Development (FUNDEJUR) is one such

NGO that he helped found. This private organization resembles 4-H in the United States and its beginnings are rooted in the early experience of the extension service and the *clubes 5D*.

A Period of Decline

Between 1967 and 1973, as community development fell out of favor and USAID funds to Latin America shrank, the extension service was left to function on domestic resources. By 1972 it had practically disappeared. Several extension agencies were closed, services were reduced, and training of the agents was deficient (Pérez Luna 1989: 22). The end result was a destruction of the credibility of the extension service and to a great extent that of SEA. The SEA is cited as "one of the most dramatic examples of the erosion of institutional power, passing from the ruling organism of national agriculture policy, to a deficient instrument of technical assistance to the farmer" (ONAPLAN 1983: 200).[8] This report attributes the erosion of power of SEA, in part, to the personal role that then President Joaquín Balaguer took in the politics of the rural institutions. However, the inconsistency in resources offered the rural clientele through the extension service, occasioned by the fluctuations in international funding, certainly played its role.

Revitalization in the Mid-1970s

The extension service was revitalized in 1973–78 and reoriented according to the objectives of integrated rural development. The Integrated Program of Agricultural Development (PIDAGRO) I was initiated in 1973 with the financial support of the Inter-American Development Bank (IDB) and technical assistance from the Interamerican Institute of Cooperation in Agriculture. According to Rodolfo de León (1982: 49) a golden age then began for the extension service. Funded with $39 million from the IDB, 170 new agents were added, offices and housing for extension agents were built, and approximately 40 employees of SEA were granted scholarships for study overseas.[9] Conceived with the idea of integrating the areas of investigation, extension, and financing, PIDAGRO I also had a large budget for loans to small farmers. Durán (1982) reports that the mechanics of administering the credit absorbed all of the extension agents' time and was the downfall of PIDAGRO I. Although agents were considered to be technical assistance personnel with the objective of increasing production, they became converted into credit agents.

PIDAGRO was complemented by a USAID funded project, Program for the Small Farmer (PPA), which began in 1974. Like PIDAGRO although much smaller, PPA was involved in a variety of areas, but in extension it worked to support the youth groups and women's groups begun in the earlier period and added 29 additional personal (Naut 1984: 66).

The Training and Visits Period

While PIDAGRO II supplanted PIDAGRO I, an international consulting company (TAHAL from Israel) proposed a reorganization of the extension service according to a plan called Training and Visits (T & V) (Mazara & Nova M. 1982: 36). The method was gaining popularity at the time with projects financed by the World Bank around the world (Israel 1987). The plan was adopted under PIDAGRO III and financial support was provided by the IDB. The program began in 1978 with a pilot project and was later extended to the entire country beginning in 1981. Durán, the regional director where T & V was tried as a pilot project and national director of extension in 1981, reported that the program had good results as a pilot project but was accompanied by enormous resources for economic and technical assistance. These resources were not available in quantity adequate for the entire country; neither could they be supplied by domestic effort alone.

Under the new method the extension agent now directed his attention exclusively to technical assistance for a carefully specified set of farmers — a major switch from the credit agent of the previous period and the missionary of rural development of earlier days. The method was extremely disciplined, requiring the agent to program and account explicitly for all of his working time, and was resisted by the agents. Furthermore, when the IDB funds ran out in 1982, counterpart funds from the Dominican government were also discontinued.

The 1980s Crisis

After PIDAGRO III ended in 1982, SEA's extension service, like most other rural public institutions, languished throughout the 1980s, as donors began funding private-sector initiatives (Pérez Luna 1989). Angel Castillo commented that at the field level the extension service did not even exist; when the extensionists went on strike, the farmers did not even feel it. Doorman (1986: 58) reports on survey results of rice farmers, only 14 percent of whom sought technical assistance from SEA. A leader of an association of rice farmers is quoted as saying, "all the agencies have technical assistance personnel and not one is worth anything" (Meyer 1989: 64).

Attempts were made, however, to redesign the role of the extension service, and proposals have been written to secure international funding. An example is a 1989 proposal to direct the efforts of the extension service to those farmers of irrigated land, on the basis that they could take greatest advantage of the technical assistance (UEPA 1989a). At this time USAID had begun financing a program with INDRHI to privatize management of the irrigation canals by turning it over to groups of water users (USAID/DR 1989). It was hoped that complementary financing could be obtained for the extension program. Agapito Pérez Luna explained that despite considerable efforts, SEA lacked credibility with international agencies and financing was not found. The experience illustrates, however, the degree to which donor goals were accommodated in efforts to fund public institutions.

Implications

Dominican career professionals in agricultural institutions plainly stated that donors have been the decisive force in shaping their extension service. The close parallel between the evolution in donor goals and the historical changes in the extension service in the Dominican Republic emphasizes their point. The fads and fashions that overtook the aid community — the community development era and the disenchantment that followed, the integrated rural development era, the popularity of the T & V method with the World Bank, and the shift to the private sector — each found a counterpart in the major institutional changes in the Dominican Republic.

Not surprisingly, the institutional changes financed by donors in developing countries frequently reflect donors' interests. Because public institutions in developing countries should respond to domestic politics, NGOs may be a more appropriate vehicle for donor programs. The following case of the Dominican Development Foundation (FDD) illustrates how an NGO can more flexibly accommodate changes in donor demands.

THE CASE OF THE DOMINICAN DEVELOPMENT FOUNDATION

The FDD is an NGO that has seen the same tides of development aid come and go in the Dominican Republic, and arguably it has survived them much more successfully than did the agricultural extension service.

Like the extension service, the FDD was originally founded in 1962, after the death of Trujillo, as the Association for Social Welfare.[10] In 1966 it was reconstituted as the FDD — a private, nonprofit organization dedicated to promoting development in the poorest sectors of Dominican society — and it was associated with the Panamerican Development Foundation. Founding members of the FDD included 23 national and multinational corporations.

U.S. Funding in the 1960s, Diversification in the 1970s

The FDD was active in agricultural extension in the mid to late 1960s. It received funding from the IDB in FY 1966–67, and in FY 1967–68 it collaborated with six public agencies dedicated to the rural sector that were at the time receiving funding from USAID. Unlike SEA's extension service, the FDD was also involved in other programs, such as health, funded by corporate donors and international NGOs. The international NGOs that the FDD worked with in the late 1960s and early 1970s were primarily U.S.–based; they included Volunteers for International Technical Assistance, Junior Achievement, Heifer Project International, Partners of the Americas, and Youth for Understanding. The FDD also had unique fund-raising opportunities not available to public sector agencies; for example, the Pittsburgh Pirates baseball team came to the Dominican Republic in 1968 to play a series of games and raise funds for the FDD.

When the U.S. Inter-American Foundation (IAF) began working with NGOs in FY 1971–72, the FDD was among the first grant recipients. A large grant of $450,000 — about one-third of its previous operating budget — was designated for the extension of credit to small farmers. In the early 1970s grants also began arriving from donors, both public and private, in Canada, Germany, and the Netherlands. FDD's corporate founding members also provided program support during this period as did international organizations such as the UN Food and Agriculture Organization.

The Crisis of Integrated Rural Development

PIDAGRO and integrated rural development greatly expanded the small-farmer credit programs of the FDD in FY 1974–75. Following the lead of the IAF, USAID granted $2 million for the small farmer credit programs to FDD in a financial arrangement through SEA. The IDB also channeled PIDAGRO funding through the FDD at this time. In FY 1976–77 SEA expanded funding by an additional $3 million.

The PIDAGRO prompted one of the first major crises within the FDD, which resulted from fluctuations in international funding, according to Esmeling Genao. Genao was director of Public Relations and Project Elaboration at the FDD in 1990 and an employee of the FDD since 1973.[11] Genao explained that the FDD "expanded their institutional capacity to reach a much larger number of beneficiaries, than they had previously. This growth meant that the institution began to be managed at a level of complication greater than had been their experience . . . and it also happened that the resources of PIDAGRO didn't arrive with the agility or opportunity with which they should have, and thus the institution passed through a stage of crisis."

Genao considered, however, that a private institution, such as the FDD, had certain advantages relative to a public institution, such as the extension service, in terms of avoiding the crises brought on by donors. He pointed out that as an NGO, the FDD could much more flexibly respond to a variety of available international funding programs, because, according to its statutes, the FDD owed no specific service to any specific clientele. Further, as a private institution, the FDD was not subject to the political obligations of the public sector, and that permitted it greater flexibility. When funding ending abruptly the FDD could move on to other programs.

New Initiatives in the Late 1970s

One such program that became a new emphasis in the mid-1970s was the program of support to Dominican artisans that focused on small loans, training, and marketing assistance in ceramics, leather, and dolls. The program received initial support in 1976 from a variety of donors including international agencies, such as the World Craft Council, private corporations, and the government of Austria. In 1977 the FDD acquired space in the old colonial houses in Santo Domingo to house an Artisan Center for both training and merchandizing.

Hurricane David hit the Dominican Republic in 1979, and the FDD was active in arranging emergency care (food, medicine, clothing, and shelter) for those affected by the crisis. The FDD served as an important channel for domestic and international donations, both public and private.

Microenterprise in the 1980s

Genao explained that the FDD experienced a number of shifts in focus, depending upon fads in the international environment. He noted that the needs of beneficiaries of existing programs were sometimes sacrificed to begin new development models in style in the development community in order to gain access to new resources. "Obviously," he said, "this has been a factor that has caused some distortions in the institutional development."

One such shift occurred in FY 1980–81 when the FDD began a large new program in microenterprise development and finance. Until that time, the rural credit programs that had begun in the 1960s and expanded under PIDAGRO in the 1970s had occupied the major portion of the FDD's portfolio. After the USAID and the IAF began funding microenterprise development in the Reagan administration rural credit programs continued, but at reduced levels, with help from Canadian and European agencies. Throughout the 1980s microenterprise development was the major focus of the FDD. In FY 1988–89 loans to microenterprises exceeded loans to small farmers by 66 percent (Dominican Development Foundation 1989).

CONCLUSIONS

The vagaries of international funding can be inconsistent with building strong institutions in developing countries. Researchers such as Levy (1996) have compared the growth of NGOs in the Dominican Republic to their growth in Peru, that is, filling in for a weak state. Evidence from the extension service in the Dominican Republic, however, suggests that the weakness of state institutions was linked, at least in part, to their heavy dependence on donor funds.

The literature on institution building in the mid-1980s recognized many problems in institutions that were related to the pressures of donor demands: the short-term project approach that can sacrifice long-term success for results in the short run, a tendency on the part of receiving institutions to let their priorities be supply driven by donor funds, and the problem of coordinating the disparate projects of various donors.

Fads and fashions in the development community are clearly visible in the history of both the extension service and the FDD in the Dominican Republic; so are the difficult pressures of donor demands. Agapito Pérez Luna explained that the cycles of high and low in the extension service were almost always related to international funding. De León referred to "days of glory and crisis" of the extension service associated with (and without) donor projects. Aquino González agreed that, "Basically the extension service has been strong when it had international funding. When this [funding] ends a weakening process begins." This discontinuity of services undermined the credibility of the extension service as a public-sector institution. State institutions must be responsible to the public.

The FDD, in contrast, although subject to very similar tides of donor funds, had the flexibility to invest its energies in alternative programs without losing credibility in the eyes of the public. Genao remarked that NGOs were specifically designed to gather funds from a variety of donors and work with a project approach. They had no specific mandate to offer any particular kind of service. NGOs are free to respond to donors, providing services the state is not providing.

The FDD, unlike some of the newly powerful NGOs that sprang up in the 1980s, had slowly expanded a diversified portfolio of projects over a long period of time. By doing so it avoided the impression of being coopted by a single donor, a problem that plagued many NGOs of that time.

The following chapter directly addresses these doubts about the newly funded, powerful NGOs that surfaced in Chapter 3 and focuses on the complex topics of opportunism, altruism, and entrepreneurship.

NOTES

1. Blase (1986) surveys this literature in an annotated bibliography. Uphoff (1986) is also an excellent guide to the literature on institution building.

2. Lele and Goldsmith (1989) also point to the importance of firm country commitment, a long-term program, and a coherent, consistent message from the donor agency. These were present in India with Rockefeller Foundation programs, but were absent in aid programs in Africa.

3. Throughout its history, USAID has relied on the land-grant universities for technical assistance in research and extension (USAID 1989: 72).

4. See Lacroix (1985: 15).

5. This chapter draws on the same interviews of January 1990 that were used in Chapter 3. See Chapter 3, note 13 for a list of the professionals interviewed and their affiliations. Pablo Rodríguez made this particular comment and Frank Rodríguez made substantially similar comments.

6. A domestic study financed by the United Nations and Organization of American States documents the state of the rural institutions in the Dominican Republic and the history of their formation: ONAPLAN (1983: 202–221). See also Aquino González (1978).

7. This and subsequent references to statements made by Dominican professionals are taken from the aforementioned January 1990 interviews. Any

quotations are translated from the Spanish by the author.

8.   Translated from the Spanish by the author.

9.   This was reported as RD$39 mllion, however, the peso and the dollar were officially on par at this time (Pérez Luna 1989: 23).

10.   The history of the FDD told in this section is taken primarily from an FDD document celebrating the twentieth anniversary of the FDD in the Dominican Republic (FDD 1986) and from various annual reports.

11.   Esmeling Genao was interviewed by the author in January 1990.

5

Opportunism, Entrepreneurship, and North-South Transfers

The spirit of the 1980s led to growth of all kinds of nongovernmental organizations (NGOs); but, particularly in the years leading up to the 1992 Earth Summit in Rio, environmental NGOs in Latin America grew explosively. Heightened donor interest in NGOs coincided with increased interest in the environment; environmental NGOs blossomed and other Latin American NGOs embraced environmental concerns (Kaimowitz 1993b). A study of biodiversity investments from all U.S. sources found an increase of 180 percent between 1987 and 1991, with over half of all funding invested in Latin America and the Caribbean (Abramovitz 1993). Most of these funds were channeled through NGOs, both international and local.[1]

The example of Northern contributions to protect the global environment helps to clarify the notion of international public goods introduced in Chapter 3 and to analyze the larger role that NGOs are taking in providing and producing international public goods. This chapter analyzes two case studies of environmental NGOs in Latin America from the perspective of economic entrepreneurship. Southern NGOs reliant on Northern donors are viewed as producers of international public goods. They take their place alongside for-profit firms as contributors to economic production, employment, institutional innovation, and technology transfer.

However, looking beyond the purely self-interested economic agent, behavioral assumptions allow for loyalty, commitment, and altruism as well as opportunism. This helps to clarify confusion regarding the modernizing NGO sector.

The following section explores the attempts of some to classify NGOs into the legitimate and the illegitimate, the committed and the commercial. The subsequent section uses concepts of opportunism and entrepreneurship to build a behavioral framework that redefines the popular vision of NGOs. Case experience from Ecuador and Costa Rica is presented in the following three sections, and the final section summarizes conclusions.

THE RAP ON YUPPIE NGOs

The dramatic changes in the Southern NGO community described in Chapters 2 and 3 — including the rise of powerful elitist or right-wing NGOs that identified closely with the state or functioned as service providers for large international donors — created a need, among researchers and development professionals, to categorize developing-country NGOs. Terms such as "BINGOs" (big NGOs), "GONGOs" (government-organized NGOs), and "DONGOs" (donor-organized NGOs), came into usage to refer disparagingly to the new yuppie NGOs that were closer to the money, less politicized in orientation, and more technocratic.[2]

By the early 1990s experts began to question the legitimacy of such NGOs. Clark (1991) notes an increasing number of GONGOs organized because of the possibility of funds but acting merely as arms of governments. Brown and Korten (1991: 73–75) comment on the illegitimacy of GONGOs and DONGOs as "captive organizations" in bondage to either the local government or to the donor. Farrington and Bebbington (1993: 194) lament the proliferation of such illegitimate, opportunistic NGOs. Nevertheless, Korten (1990) notes that some GONGOs are formed with good intentions and good results.

The tendency to glorify the grass roots endured. Many researchers have focused on grass-roots organizations and define other NGOs in terms of their relationship to the grass roots (Carroll 1992; Fisher 1993; Uphoff 1993). However, not all indigenous NGOs work with grass-roots groups. Others have classified them according to their motivation — commercial or commitment — but then allow for hybrids (Korten 1990). Uphoff (1993) groups professional service NGOs together with profit-seeking enterprises to distinguish them from the voluntary organizations "of the people."

Even when they are not organized by the government, NGOs that work with the government have been viewed negatively. Farrington and Bebbington (1993) examine opportunities for productive NGO–state interaction — reluctantly because of the loss of independence it means for NGOs. Nevertheless, they and others recognize surfacing complementarities (Carroll 1992; Clark 1991; Kaimowitz 1993b; Díaz-Albertini 1993).

Clearly, scaling up to handle increased funds has challenged the NGO community in developing countries and required compromises (Uvin & Miller 1996; Hulme & Edwards 1997). The skepticism of yuppie NGOs has important roots. Many of the NGOs that in the 1980s received large funding from major donors had begun life on the voluntary energy of grass-roots groups. Their criticism of the state or of imperialist capitalism may have been silenced by the donor grants. NGOs may use the grass-roots mythology opportunistically to attract funding when they no longer serve a grass-roots clientele.

However, the establishment of new working relationships between the NGO community, a democratizing state, and the international community is not all bad. Grass-roots NGOs can also be filled with charlatans only after the money (Fisher 1994; Reilly 1993). Popular sentiment aside, economists would assume that all NGO managers are self-interested, irrespective of their proximity to the grass roots.

Thomas Carroll (1992) defends professional intermediary NGOs based on the history of the Inter-American Foundation (IAF) work in grass-roots development. Seventy-five percent of IAF grants between 1972 and 1986 went to intermediary organizations, not to the grass roots. Carroll notes that despite the importance of professional intermediaries for IAF operation, "they are viewed with skepticism and have been generally downplayed in IAF rhetoric," (p. 2). He challenges notions that NGOs with large-scale collaborations with donors or governments "lose their soul" or "abandon their mission" (p. 17), and he encourages NGO interaction with governments and in the marketplace.

Given the increased political and economic involvement of NGOs, a broader understanding of them is essential. This chapter challenges popular notions by developing a political-economic framework of nonprofit NGO behavior and applying it to two case studies of large professional environmental NGOs in Latin America. The NGOs chosen, although closely connected to government and founded expressly to capture Northern funds, are committed and play useful roles producing international public goods.

OPPORTUNISM AND ENTREPRENEURSHIP

To further understanding of the expanding role of Southern NGOs in the international development arena, this section establishes a political-economic framework of NGO behavior. Nonprofit NGOs are recognized to be the result of entrepreneurial activity and are viewed as producers of international public goods. Self-interested economic behavior is shown to be consistent both with opportunism and with altruism, and fundamental confusions between opportunism and entrepreneurship are clarified. NGO entrepreneurs respond to changing opportunities and contribute to a new fabric of relationships with innovations in public goods and institutions.

Green Opportunities for Entrepreneurs

In the midst of changing opportunities, entrepreneurs flourish (Schumpeter 1942). Although the vocabulary of entrepreneurship, with its profit-seeking capitalists, is often avoided in the NGO literature, explicit recognition of the entrepreneurial nature of NGO activity is essential to understanding.

Schumpeter (1942) characterizes entrepreneurs as individuals with a sense of adventure and the vision to act confidently when surrounded by uncertainty and get things done. The entrepreneur takes personal responsibility for his (or her)[3] success by exploiting an invention, producing a new good, producing the same good in a new way, or by reorganizing an industry. Entrepreneurial input can range from the humble to the spectacular and is motivated by more than material gain alone. That success plays a motivating role in no way diminishes the creative contribution of the entrepreneur for Schumpeter; on the contrary, it is viewed as an appropriate stimulant.

Increasing Northern funds for environmental protection in the South provides a similar stimulant for those with creative ideas for producing international environmental public goods that can be marketed abroad and at home as well.

Producers of International Public Goods

Entrepreneurs who recognize complementarities between local needs and international objectives can design ways to produce international public goods of value to both the North and the South.

As explained in Chapter 3, nonprofit NGOs play an important role in providing public goods. Governments may leave some consumers undersatisfied with the level of public good provision; thus, nonprofit NGOs arise to address the concerns of those undersatisfied consumers. Governments have also found advantages (of efficiency and effectiveness) in contracting NGOs to provide public services.

Naturally, the preferences of foreign donors differ from those of local public sectors; but foreign donor preferences may correspond with those of undersatisfied local consumers. The developed world places different priorities on investments in conservation and environmental activities than does the South (Porter & Brown 1996), but many in the South may prefer the higher level of environmental service demanded in the North. Because the nonprofit NGO sector is more flexible and responsive to the needs of donors than are local public sectors and yet is still in the business of producing public goods, NGOs are a natural vehicle for the transfer of funds to support this international public good, demanded by the North and produced by the South.

As exporters of international public goods, nonprofit NGOs in the South increase economic production and employment outside the public sector, provide opportunities for technology transfer and international networking,[4] and foster improvements in local human capital. Such benefits explain local government willingness to allow Northern funding of NGOs, despite its often political nature (Smith 1990; Bratton 1989). Yet, as with for-profit production, these benefits may not be provided in an egalitarian fashion.

Local support — by the people, the private sector, and the local government — can enhance the effectiveness of Southern NGOs producing international public goods. Local approval and support provide domestic funding for a diversified portfolio and respect, stature, and political influence at home. Successful local NGO entrepreneurs will seek out relationships with other members of civil society, government, and the for-profit sector to find the mix appropriate to their objectives.[5]

Opportunism, Loyalty, and Altruism

Entrepreneurship should not be confused with opportunism. Although much of the NGO literature has defined opportunism as activity motivated by financial gain, opportunities for financial gain can stimulate beneficial entrepreneurial activity. Oliver Williamson (1985) defines opportunism as "self-interest seeking with guile" (p. 30). This definition is consistent with some NGO behavior. Economists typically assume that humans behave rationally: that they assess facts and make an optimal decision according to their self-interest. Williamson makes the additional point that when information is cloudy or unevenly distributed, some people may conceal the truth or default on promises in the pursuit of self-interest.

Williamson (1985) advocates appropriate incentives and governance structures so that the self-interest of various parties is consistent; and credible, enforceable commitments can be made (pp. 48–49). This can be extended to NGOs as well, from the grass roots up. Adequate monitoring is often difficult and opportunistic behavior should be anticipated. Donors might devise mechanisms to provide for improved accountability if they are concerned that their money be spent in accordance with objectives.

Experts on NGOs, however, may object to a presumption of opportunistic behavior. Fisher (1993: 98) claims that most observers believe that committed NGOs vastly outnumber the corrupt and that most are characterized by a strong sense of mission.

Herbert Simon, who has written widely on economic behavior, provides a theoretical basis for committed NGOs. Simon argues that humans are unable continually to optimize their behavior because of uncertainty and limited cognitive capacities and must adapt their behavior to rules and norms. He claims that humans are docile and respond to suggestion, persuasion, and teaching as a basis for the behavioral choices they make. Simon explains traits like altruism, pride in work, and loyalty to one's country, employer, or mission with the notion of docility. He argues that these traits are widespread, provide long-run benefits, and from an evolutionary standpoint may be enlightened self-interest (Simon 1991, 1993).

George Akerlof (1983) also argues that loyalty, honesty, and cooperative behavior may pay off in the long run despite short-run costs. He notes that the appearance of honesty (for example) is a valuable trait and "the cheapest way to acquire such traits . . . is, in fact, to be honest!" (p. 56). Thus, concerns for long-run reputation may dominate Williamson's short-run provisions to ensure contract compliance.

Jane Mansbridge (1990) argues that although self-interest plays an important role in human interaction most of the time, humans also have benevolent and malevolent motivations. She concludes that establishing institutions to run purely on selfish motivations may be misguided and recommends judicious reliance on motivations like empathy and principle.[6]

Northern donors must expect complex motivations behind the behavior of the Southern NGOs they fund. Although individuals (and organizations) differ considerably, all have complex motivations. The idea that some NGOs are benevolent, others malevolent, and others interested only in financial aspects is unrealistic. The difficulty of supervising the production of public goods ensures openings for opportunism, but properly directed self-interest alone is unlikely to achieve the returns that commitment does.

Natural checks on opportunism exist in human societies, but they vary across cultures (Ensminger 1992; Granovetter 1985). Cultural norms that encourage loyalty to one's own people or country may not apply to international donors. Donors should be sensitive to social norms that might encourage or discourage cooperative behavior. Simon (1991) argues that promoting a strong sense of identification with goals and objectives can effectively reduce opportunism. Greater consistency between international and local objectives and values is an obvious beginning when working with Southern NGOs.

Self-selected Entrepreneurs and Altruists?

Another factor potentially responsible for a preponderance of committed personnel in NGOs is the phenomena of self-selection (Young 1986). NGOs offers entrepreneurs with ideas and commitment an avenue for their energy often more satisfying than public-sector work. Smith (1990: 231) finds that executives and staff of nonprofit NGOs in Latin America are filled with "intellectuals, professionals, clerics, political activists, and socially concerned business leaders who are often dissatisfied with prevailing public policies." Fisher (1994: 132) agrees by attributing the recent growth of Southern NGOs to "demands by unemployed intellectuals for both political shelter and meaningful work."

To what extent are nonprofits filled with self-selected altruists and otherwise committed personnel? Some researchers have claimed that NGOs are always the result of committed individuals responding to a felt need for additional public services.[7] Although this may often be the case, sufficient evidence suggests that financial incentives have encouraged the formation of Southern nonprofit NGOs. Earlier chapters have shown that salaries and working conditions are often superior to those in the public sector, and the prestige attached to NGO leadership may be substantial. Particularly because professional opportunities are limited in developing countries, these incentives are important; but they need not be corrupting. The fact that many who work for NGOs are self-selected, committed individuals can counteract opportunities for opportunism.

Two large, nonprofit, environmental NGOs in Latin America are analyzed in the following sections in light of the behavioral framework developed here. The entrepreneurs in both cases respond to an opportunity to put Northern demand for international environmental public goods to work in the South. Financial incentives and economic goals are taken into account by committed personnel, jobs are created, and human capital is increased. Strong relationships with the for-profit sector, local government, and international donors, although they may alter incentives, coexist with commitment and result in increased production by the nonprofit NGOs.

FUNDACIÓN NATURA AND ENVIRONMENTAL EDUCATION

The history of Fundación Natura (or Natura), founded in 1978, precedes the recent wave of environmental NGOs in Latin America. Environmental NGOs arrived early to Ecuador with the Charles Darwin Foundation for the Galápagos, an international NGO created there in 1959. Thus, the World Wildlife Fund (WWF) and the International Union for the Conservation of Nature were already active in Ecuador when they became founding supporters of Natura.[8]

Although not a grass-roots organization, Natura is an indigenous, nonprofit membership organization. Natura was formed by a group of 43 Ecuadorian citizens who both demanded environmental public services and acted as entrepreneurs. Membership increased to approximately 1,200 by 1983 and to around 6,000 by 1989. Natura is governed by a rotating 30-member general assembly that elects a board of directors. The board elects the executive director.

An Establishment NGO Seeking Northern Funds

The idea for Natura was born two years before its founding in the Department of National Parks and Wildlife. The principal impetus, according to one of the founding fathers, was based on the recognition that an NGO could attract and administrate international funds more easily than could the public sector.

Natura's membership includes public-sector officials and distinguished Ecuadorian businessmen. Their close connections in government and the private sector encouraged an elitist reputation (Lieberman & Wood 1982). With private-sector financial support, Natura has broken with other local environmental NGOs occasionally and taken the industry side on contentious environmental issues. Natura's leadership in 1990 said their good working relationship with the government enhanced effectiveness. Also, with the independence that a sound and diversified financial base provided, they could pressure the government when necessary.

Natura's Work

Natura's objective when founded was to promote environmental education and protection in Ecuador, conduct or facilitate scientific conservation studies and international scholarships and scientific exchanges, and promote the creation of parks and conservation areas (Lieberman & Wood 1982).

The U.S. Agency for International Development (USAID) found these interests compatible and soon became Natura's principal foreign donor by sponsoring the first major education program aimed at the Ecuadorian government. In Natura's first four years, USAID accounted for 85 percent of their international portfolio with grants totaling close to $500,000. USAID and Natura agreed on subsequent education programs in 1983 and 1988, each five years in duration, budgeted at $659,000 and $1 million respectively. The focus of these programs was to institutionalize environmental education in the schools and to extend it into the communities along less formal channels.

Although USAID encouraged grass-roots action, Natura was never inclined in this direction. Early evaluations commented on successful "'hands-on' projects with local communities" but noted that this was not Natura's strength and would not be expanded (Lieberman & Wood 1982: 115). The coordinator of Acción Ecológica (a grass roots-oriented NGO) commented that Natura preferred more elitist media, such as television, newspapers, and other publications.

Natura has consciously maintained independence from USAID and other major donors with a diversified portfolio. It covered all administrative costs during the first seven years with membership fees and income earned through the sale of advertising time during the television broadcast of a program purchased from the National Geographic Society. Natura later began to charge overhead on projects and to supplement further the administrative budget with income-earning activities. Between 1978 and 1988 USAID support dropped to 60 percent of international grants. Domestic private-sector corporations also financed small projects.

With the debt swaps negotiated in 1987 and 1989, Natura's financial independence increased. Under the agreement, WWF and The Nature Conservancy purchased at a discount $10 million face value of Ecuador's external debt. The debt was converted into local bonds, and Natura was encharged with investing the interest in the management and expansion of national parks, in research, and in park personnel training. The principal becomes an endowment for Natura when the bonds mature (World Wildlife Fund 1988).

Flexible, Accountable, and Committed

Despite an elitist reputation and strong support from USAID, Natura has improved environmental education in Ecuador enormously and has also furthered its other goals. It has maintained a high profile and a positive image both domestically and internationally. For example, Yolanda Kakabadse, executive director at Natura for many years, served as NGO liaison for the Earth Summit in Rio.

Founders reported that Natura filled a need left unmet by the public sector that international donors were willing to support. Natura personnel also felt that NGOs could more efficiently manage international funds than could the public sector. Projects at Natura are carried out on a contract basis without hiring permanent personnel. Although USAID has encouraged long-term continuity, administrators felt that typically unreliable international funding made this approach much more practical. Outside of the cumbersome bureaucracy of the government, Natura could also address environmental problems more directly.

Within Natura all agreed that their success resulted from the high quality personnel committed to the organizational objectives. Kakabadse felt that the vision of a well-diversified group of founders in determining those objectives was also crucial. Others stressed stimulating working conditions and adequate salaries in contrast to the public sector.

Given the nature of the educational activities that Fundación Natura is involved in, close monitoring by the donors is difficult, but evaluations are nevertheless positive (Lieberman & Wood 1982; Wood 1988). Care is taken to comply with the auditing system of each donor, and yearly since 1988 an external audit by Price-Waterhouse is available to donors.

A concern for public image — domestically, within Latin America, and across the oceans — has also been a factor in maintaining accountability. Gonzalo Oviedo, an administrator of the debt swap projects with Natura, explained that Natura felt an enormous responsibility to public opinion because of its high visibility.

NATIONAL BIODIVERSITY INSTITUTE AND BIODIVERSITY PROSPECTING

Costa Rica has been called the "world's largest center of tropical research" (Umaña & Brandon 1992) and the National Biodiversity Institute (INBio), founded in 1989, supplements a tradition of scientifically oriented environmental NGOs. INBio is nonprofit, nongovernmental, and committed to economic development but unique among NGOs, principally because its primary objective is to inventory the biodiversity of Costa Rica and put the knowledge to work in further economic activity. In late 1991 INBio received international attention by announcing a two-year contract for more than $1 million with the pharmaceutical giant Merck & Co., Ltd. to support this effort. In exchange, INBio has provided Merck with chemical extracts from insects, plants, and microorganisms to be used for drug screening. INBio also receives a share of royalties on any resulting commercial products (Reid et al. 1993).[9]

The Beginning of the National Biodiversity Institute

INBio's birth followed the creation of the Ministry of Natural Resources, Energy, and Mines (MIRENEM) in 1986, which brought environmental concerns to the cabinet level of government. MIRENEM established a Biodiversity Office in 1987 with the support of a three-year grant from the MacArthur Foundation. The Biodiversity Office, under the responsibility of Rodrigo Gámez, determined to "save, know, and use" Costa Rica's biodiversity with a commitment to fostering economic and human capital development in the country and serving as a source of biodiversity management information internationally (Gámez et al. 1993: 58).

Spurred on by news of potential funding from the international community, INBio was created in October 1989 by a planning commission established by MIRENEM. The commission included representatives from other government ministries, universities, the National Museum, the National Scientific Research Council, and two scientific environmental NGOs.

A 15-member Assembly and a 6-member Board of Directors (drawn from many of the organizations represented in the planning commission) govern INBio. Thus, INBio is tightly linked to MIRENEM, to the university community, and to the scientifically oriented NGOs in Costa Rica. INBio enjoys tax-free status and receives grants and tax-free donations of specimens and other materials.

The National Biodiversity Inventory

Despite previous specialized inventories of Costa Rica's flora and fauna by national and international researchers, INBio's goal to complete the inventory is ambitious. After building a site for offices, management, and storage of biological specimens, making plans, and training personnel, INBio became firmly involved in inventorying the nation's biodiversity and building the database to manage the information. Through 1992 it was supported by $3 million in grants from a wide variety of private foundations, international environmental NGOs, and the governments of Costa Rica, the United States, Sweden, and Norway. During 1993 INBio's income totaled about $1.8 million, almost 20 percent of which resulted from commercial contracts (National Biodiversity Institute [hereafter INBio] 1994). An estimated $30 million was required over the next 10 years to conduct the national biodiversity inventory.

INBio uses Costa Rica's biodiversity and the knowledge of it to generate income to help preserve and maintain the wildlands and to increase human capital and economic development in Costa Rica. The use of biodiversity to generate income is referred to as biodiversity prospecting. The information generated at INBio is shared freely with noncommercial users, both national and international. Thus, the four main program areas at INBio are: the inventory, biodiversity prospecting, information management systems, and public relations.

INBio has a strong national orientation and a commitment to hiring Costa Rican citizens for positions at all levels. At the end of 1993 INBio had an administrative and scientific technical staff of 77 in addition to 34 parataxonomists who collect specimens from regional offices (INBio 1994). INBio has also benefited from short-term volunteers from Costa Rica and abroad. Dan Janzen and colleagues (1993: 223) explain the rationale for the approach:

Costa Rica does not have many decades and many millions of dollars to train a large number of university graduates to the Ph.D. level to inventory its biodiversity. Nor can it expect the international science community to drop everything and to conduct Costa Rica's inventory.

But the inventory is urgent, so INBio decided to tap an abundant underutilized resource — Costa Rica's rural populace — to collaborate with Costa Rican university graduates in biology and the taxonomic community to get the job done within a decade at a reasonable cost. The move makes sense from several perspectives. Rural Costa Rica is flush with highly capable under-employed adults, the international scientific community has long overestimated the training requirements for persons participating in a thorough biodiversity inventory, and Costa Rica's extraordinary biodiversity both makes the job inviting and attracts the international technical and training assistance needed to gradually empower Costa Rica to do much of the job itself.

INBio has also broadened participation among other organizations within Costa Rica. Sittenfeld and Gámez (1993: 85) note that, to increase national research capacity and to spread the new income around, "INBio also subcontracts as much as possible of the sample processing, extracting, chemical analysis, etc., to Costa Rican laboratories, and it aggressively seeks out university and hospital laboratories for in-country projects in blind screening and ecology-driven search."

INBio's public relations program has spread knowledge both nationally and internationally. Hundreds of visitors, including foreign and domestic dignitaries and students, come to learn about INBio every year. Staff members publish in international journals, speak at international conferences, and hold workshops for local groups and groups from all over Latin America (INBio 1994).

INNOVATION FOR THE ENVIRONMENT

Both Fundación Natura and INBio were created with the express intent of capturing international funds in large quantity. In neither did the financial incentive stifle innovation; on the contrary. The financial incentives reinforced the commitment of some of the finest talent available and encouraged them to put that talent to work in the provision of international public goods. In both cases the public goods they produce, while of decidedly more value to some than to others, are valued both at home and abroad. However, by serving as a flexible base of entrepreneurial talent, these NGOs have furthered innovative ways to provide environmental services.

Biodiversity Prospecting Contracts

The biodiversity prospecting contract between Merck and INBio revolutionized the way countries view property rights for genetic resources. By adding value to raw genetic material, Costa Rica, through INBio, gained property rights over it. Until Rio's Convention on Biodiversity, agreed to by more than 150 countries, raw genetic resources were internationally considered to be in the public domain. However, Northern pharmaceutical companies that patented drugs expected those patents to be respected in developing countries (Sedjo 1992). As developing countries recognize that their rainforests contain most of the world's remaining biological wealth, they are looking for ways to reap the rewards of investment in biodiversity. INBio's private contracts with Merck and others, further explored in the following chapter, embodied the concerns voiced in the international arena, namely North-South technology and resource transfers, and conservation and economic development in the South. The contracts also established mechanisms to address these concerns.

Debt-for-nature Swaps

International NGOs and NGOs in both Costa Rica and Ecuador provided entrepreneurial input for the development of debt-for-nature swaps. Costa Rica generated more than $40 million in funds for conservation through the nonprofit National Parks Foundation, which attracted funds from the Netherlands, Sweden, and a wide array of international NGOs (World Resources Institute 1992: Table 20.6). This represents about two-thirds of the amount generated in all debt-for-nature swaps worldwide during the same 1987–91 period. Alvaro Umaña, director of MIRENEM at the time, believed that donors "would be more likely to make long-term commitments to specific lands, where they could see both the challenges and the yearly progress," and that an NGO would offer donors increased "flexibility and responsiveness" over the public sector (Umaña & Brandon 1992: 95–96). Thus, MIRENEM and the Central Bank authorized the National Parks Foundation to carry out the swaps.

Roque Sevilla, an economist and then president of Fundación Natura in Ecuador, is credited with key innovations for the design of the debt-swap mechanism. A WWF newsletter states, "Debt-for-nature swaps took a great leap forward with the Sevilla proposal. . . . By issuing bonds rather than cash, Ecuador reduced the threat of inflationary impacts, a drawback of swaps. Furthermore, the use of bonds provides a dependable long-term means of support for local conservation" (World Wildlife Fund 1988: 6). The agreement among the Ecuadorian government, Natura, WWF, and The Nature Conservancy generated $10 million to be converted into local bonds.

Natura's debt-swap agreement was only the second that the international NGO community had negotiated. The first was negotiated by Conservation International with Bolivia in August 1987 and drew criticism for its inflationary impact and for the possible loss in sovereignty of the parkland under question (World Resources Institute 1992: Table 20.6; Burton 1990). However, international environmental NGOs learned quickly and their flexibility, their ability to raise money quickly, and their entrepreneurial contributions made debt-for-nature swaps possible (Burton 1990; Jakobeit 1996).

CONCLUSIONS

The experience of INBio and Fundación Natura shows no inherent inconsistencies between the reputed advantages of NGOs (commitment, flexibility, and innovation) and working on a large scale. Although these examples are obvious success stories and products of specific historical contexts and local entrepreneurial input, they demonstrate that economic entrepreneurship is a powerful side of NGOs neglected in a popular vision inspired by grass-roots action. Clearly, strong relationships with governments, the for-profit sector, and international donors alter the incentives that NGOs face. Moreover, the benefits of such NGO activity cannot be expected to be distributed equally. Nevertheless, while providing international public goods, Southern NGOs play valuable economic roles in developing countries.

The Economic Role of NGOs

The NGOs chosen as case studies are both environmental producers of international public goods. Each attracts a diversified portfolio of grants or contracts that might not otherwise head south. In so doing they effectively export environmental public goods, but the benefits, both in terms of production and public goods, are shared in the South. Like exporters of private goods they bring in foreign exchange, new technology, ideas, and international contacts. They contribute to economic production, employment, and increased human capital. They are also a flexible base of entrepreneurial talent and contribute innovations in both public goods and the institutional arrangements to provide them. Many of the managers trained in NGOs go on to work in the for-profit or public sectors, and many managers trained in Fundación Natura have gone on to initiate grass-roots environmental NGOs. INBio, as noted earlier, is particularly interested in training local personnel.

The fact that close relationships with governments, the for-profit sector, and international donors alter the role of NGOs vis-à-vis grass-roots action does not negate these economic benefits. Not all NGOs need to fight the government. Undoubtedly, many GONGOs and DONGOs are so closely aligned with the government or major donors that they have little independent personality. This does not mean that donors should pour money into public-sector projects instead or co-opt grass-roots groups with major donations. NGOs offer international donors and local governments a vehicle for the production of public goods more flexible and accountable than public sectors. Nevertheless, NGOs are not responsible to the public and cannot replace the public sector. If international donors are to complement local government provision of public goods effectively without destabilizing or replacing the proper role of government, close collaboration with the government sector is necessary.

Relationships Alter Incentives

Relationships with international donors, governments, and the private sector alter the incentives that NGOs face. However committed NGO management may be to the objectives of the organization, if the objectives of major donors differ from those of the NGO, conflicts of interest will arise and compromises may have to be made. The for-profit sector is interested in profits and a positive public image. Bilateral donors have their national interest at heart, for example, biological diversity for the biotechnology industry. International environmental donors may be most concerned with slowing population growth or protecting their bird of choice. Local environmental NGOs may be more concerned with local development and health issues as they relate to the environment. The national governments may be most interested in economic growth.

As pointed out earlier, Natura often took the side of local business against more radical environmental NGOs, reflecting their base of support. Natura personnel reported a conflictive relationship with some donors and differences in ideology with many but also found areas where they could agree and work together — or if not, projects were refused. INBio contracted with Merck only after substantial legal assistance and negotiation; and INBio's close relationship with the local government may preclude its serving as a critical voice.

As grass-roots NGOs scale up to work on major projects with large donors, because of these altered incentives, their political role will change. However, these NGOs may be no less committed than those who have not yet had the opportunity to turn down a major grant. Self-interest and altruism coexist. The fact that conflicts of interest are likely between parties need not keep them from working together productively.

Allocation of Benefits

Certainly, nothing here implies that the allocation of benefits from increased economic activity in the provision of environmental international public goods will be in any sense optimal or fair. NGOs, like governments, can only inefficiently provide public goods. However, as argued earlier, NGOs offer advantages over government provision, particularly when international donors are involved. Fairness is an even more difficult criterion and one that economists are ill equipped to address. Markets are not fair, but many would agree that economic growth is desirable despite its haphazard path.

Typically, NGOs are truly responsible only to their donors and management. They may also be regulated by government to some extent. The public goods produced should be those specified by the objectives of the organization, unless managers behave opportunistically. Thus, Southern NGOs funded by Northern donors will provide public goods in an uneven fashion — skewed toward international tastes and management objectives. Opportunists may use NGOs for purely private benefit if monitoring and enforcement are absent and reputation incentives fail.

The public goods produced are not equally valued by all parties even if they are fully available to all. National parks may only be enjoyed by those in a position to visit, and the mere preservation of biodiversity is not of equal value to all. Environmental education may be of little interest to some or unavailable to those without access to a television, for example.

The jobs, technology transfer, and foreign exchange brought in by the export of international public goods are likewise not distributed evenly. Also, as with for-profit investment relationships, international parties may benefit to a greater extent than parties in developing countries.

However, Southern NGOs reliant on external donors must be recognized as independent entrepreneurial economic entities, contributing to innovation, production, and technological transfer as they produce public goods for the international community. This role establishes them as members of the global community, part of the new fabric of international political-economic relationships. Although this chapter and the following are most concerned with the economic side of this political-economic role, Chapter 7 recognizes the essentially political nature of much NGO activity, and Chapter 8 more directly addresses the role of Southern NGOs in the global community.

NOTES

1. Of the $105 million from all U.S. sources in 1991, 41 percent was implemented through NGOs and an additional 25 percent went to other nonprofit nongovernmental organizations not defined as NGOs: botanical gardens and zoos, museums, and universities. Most were United States–based NGOs — only 22 percent of the total funding was implemented by local organizations. However, of that destined to local organizations, 63 percent went to local NGOs, 20 percent to governments, and the remaining 17 percent to nonprofit botanical gardens and zoos, museums, and universities (Abramovitz 1993).

2. Bebbington and Farrington (1993) make reference to yuppie NGOs. See Fisher (1993) on BINGOs.

3. Schumpeter refers to entrepreneurs exclusively in the male gender, but women take active entrepreneurial roles in NGOs, as the case studies demonstrate. More often than not "the entrepreneur" is a group of people, each apportioning unique entrepreneurial talents.

4.   See Kaimowitz (1993b) and Annis (1992) for explorations on the roles of NGOs in technology transfer in Latin America.

5.   See Kaimowitz (1993a), Carroll (1992), and Farrington and Bebbington (1993) on NGO relationships with the public sector.

6.   Experimental evidence demonstrates that economists behave more self-ishly than non-economists. Although some have argued economists self-select into their profession (Carter & Irons 1991), others warn that economic theory teaches economists to behave selfishly — perhaps to their long-run detriment (Frank, Gilovich, & Regan 1993).

7.   See, for example, Ben-Ner and Van Hoomissen (1993) and Atkinson (1990).

8.   Much of the information in this case study was obtained by the author in interviews in May and June 1990 with personnel from Natura, the public sector, other environmental NGOs in Ecuador, and USAID/Ecuador. Chapter 3, note 15 provides a list of many of the personnel and their affiliations. This chapter uses additional information and perspectives provided in interviews with the following persons: Luis Miguel Campos, coordinator, Acción Ecológica; Germanico Larriva B., administrative coordinator, Tierra Viva/Quito; Fernando Montesinos, president, Tierra Viva/Cuenca; Alan Moore, specialist in wildlands planning and management, formerly with the Food and Agriculture Organization in the Galápagos; Robert Mowbray, Office of Agriculture and Natural Resources, USAID; Gladys Rodríguez, ecologist and teacher, formerly manager in Fundación Fauna y Flora, in Guayaquil.

9.   This section relies heavily on *Biodiversity Prospecting* (Reid et al. 1993), produced by the World Resources Institute (WRI) in conjunction with INBio and others, to which the author contributed while at WRI. Walter Reid was a vice president at WRI and other principal contributors to the chapters here cited include the leadership of INBio: Rodrigo Gámez, director; Ana Sittenfeld, director of Biodiversity Prospecting; and Daniel Janzen, technical advisor and biology professor at the University of Pennsylvania.

6

Partnerships and Public Goods

Beginning in the 1980s, the notion of partnership has increasingly been linked to nongovernmental organizations (NGOs) and the struggle for sustainable development. The *Agenda 21* document that came out of Rio, for example, is permeated with calls for partnership between governments, industry, international organizations, NGOs, and academia to work toward the solution to development and environment goals (Sitarz 1993). Although U.S. Agency for International Development had worked in partnership with U.S. private voluntary organizations since World War II, in the 1980s and 1990s the buzzword became ubiquitous in donor rhetoric (Jordan 1996). As revealed in Chapter 2, not only is the Inter-American Foundation reorienting its efforts to focus on establishing partnerships between local communities, NGOs, and the private sector, but the International Development Bank is also moving in the same direction.

Partnership is a political-economic notion; and it is certainly part of the fabric of new relationships in Latin America. Partnership means joining hands and working together for a common goal. Some development professionals, fed up with donors preaching partnership, have implied that partnership may be nothing more than complicity in the donor paradigm (Fowler 1998). Others have conducted research to demonstrate under what conditions "intersectoral cooperation among public agencies, nongovernmental organizations, grassroots groups, and international donors" can help build social capital and solve modern problems (Brown

& Ashman 1996). However, partnership is also an economic concept about various parties each offering their comparative advantage or particular expertise. Vice President Gore's campaign to reinvent government, for example, hinged on the idea of partnership in the economic sense — using the private and nonprofit to streamline government and make it more efficient (Osborne & Gaebler 1992).

NGOs are frequently pivotal in partnerships with both the for-profit and public sectors for sustainable development (Long & Arnold 1995; *New Partnerships in the Americas* 1994). As discussed in the last chapter, it was environmental NGOs that had the initiative and the flexibility to innovate debt-for-nature swaps — a contractual arrangement, or partnership, involving private commercial banks, Latin American governments, and both Northern and Southern NGOs. The National Biodiversity Institute (INBio) of Costa Rica was also introduced as an NGO involved in a variety of contractual partnerships with the public and private sectors.

This chapter uses a case study of INBio and its relationships with the local government, the international for-profit sector, and other local and international nonprofit NGOs to examine the economics of partnerships. The economic complementarities of partnerships across the nonprofit, for-profit, and public sectors are illuminated. The chapter shows how relationships with both the public and for-profit sectors can enhance the ability of a nonprofit NGO to produce complex environmental goods that are both public and private.

Each partnership can be thought of as a unique economic arrangement to solve problems in the provision of public goods. Certainly INBio is an exceptional case; and the problem that INBio's partnerships have confronted is the difficulty of defining property rights to raw genetic material. Not all partnerships involving NGOs and the public and private sectors have the same characteristics, nor are they all successful; but a close-up analysis of this NGO and its partnerships helps illuminate the economics of the notion.

In this case, the nonprofit status of INBio offers flexibility to enter into innovative complex contracts with both the public and private for-profit sectors that provide partial solutions to public-goods problems when property rights over genetic resources are still too costly to define. In particular, INBio's special monopoly position legitimized by the government allows for the capture of economic rents in transactions with the international for-profit sector. These rents are not distributed as profit but are reinvested in the production of public and private goods.

The following section explains the distinct roles and complementarities of the nonprofit, for-profit, and public sectors and it suggests that partnerships between these sectors can provide additional public benefits. The subsequent section explains why the kind of complex contracts that INBio and other NGOs may form with their partners can be well suited to provide and protect the complex public and private goods that improved management of biodiversity requires, while private property rights cannot be expected to resolve the problem. The case of INBio and the particular contracts and partnerships there developed are explored in the penultimate section and conclusions are summarized in the final section.

POSSIBILITIES IN NONPROFIT PARTNERSHIPS

A Mixed Ecology of Nonprofit, Public, and Private Enterprise

Chapter 3 established the role of nonprofits as providers of public goods demanded by donors undersatisfied with the level of public goods being supplied by government. Nonprofits also have the advantage of avoiding the political entanglements of government and can respond flexibly to a changing environment. Donors may prefer to support the nonprofit sector, where they have more control over the quality of the public service, than to support the public sector. Thus, nonprofit firms can play important roles in the production and provision of public goods as long as transparency and accountability can be maintained.

The potential complementarity of the public and nonprofit sectors in providing public goods was also brought out in Chapter 3. The nonprofit sector is subject to free rider problems, but the government can tax and ensure provision. The nonprofit sector may leave gaps in social services or let these services be determined by the wealthy; the government can help fill gaps and broaden the decision-making base. Nonprofits contracted by government can operate on a smaller scale, personalize service provision, and invoke some of the advantages of competition by bidding for government contracts or grants.

Chapters 4 and 5 established the role of Southern NGOs in providing international public goods. Foreign aid, funneled through the public sectors of developing countries, can distort public institutions when the pressures of donor demands create institutions more responsive to donor funds than to domestic politics. Southern NGOs are free to search out areas where donor funds can complement domestic concerns and provide international public goods that are valued both at home and abroad. Development, democracy, and environmental protection jointly benefit people in both the North and the South, although certainly not all benefit to the same extent. In addition to filling gaps in local provision of public goods, Southern NGOs bring in foreign exchange, increase economic production and employment, and provide opportunities for technology transfer, human capital development, and international networking.

This chapter recognizes that the distinction between public and private goods is not so clear cut; and for this reason, nonprofits have further advantages in teaming with the private and public sectors in partnerships to provide complex public goods or goods that are jointly public and private. Hammack and Young (1993) brought together a number of papers that focus on the complex ecology of nonprofits in the marketplace as they interact with and depend on for-profit and government organizations. Sometimes nonprofit firms produce a variety of public and private goods that may cross-subsidize each other. With special tax provisions, the private goods of nonprofits are sometimes viewed as unfair competition to for-profit firms. The notion that nonprofit firms in monopoly positions can generate surpluses for the production of public goods is also introduced. The authors also note that nonprofit and for-profit business often team up, providing the nonprofit with revenues and the for-profit with favorable publicity.

The International Institutional Ecology

The full complexity of the new role for nonprofit NGOs blooms in the international arena. NGOs, such as INBio, have increasingly complex relationships with local governments, international donors, and the international and local marketplaces.

The burst of Southern NGO activity in the past two decades has resulted in increased interaction between NGOs and the local government. Latin America's NGOs were rooted in the Liberation Theology of the Catholic Church; they focused on empowering the poor and often questioned the political system. As Latin America entered an era characterized by democratization and an increased openness to international trade and foreign investment, the state, the market, and civil organizations — including NGOs — have formed new relationships and redefined their roles (de Janvry & Sadoulet 1993). NGOs started working alongside the states that they helped to democratize. Development practitioners and scholars began to emphasize the complementarities between the state and NGOs and the benefits of working together (Bebbington & Thiele 1993; Carroll 1992). The World Bank required cooperation between NGOs and the state so that NGOs could complement government provision of public goods without replacing or destabilizing the state (Kaimowitz 1993b; Paul & Israel 1991).

As NGOs modernize to accept more funds, more responsibility, and new relationships, their incentives change and old roles may be left behind. Southern NGOs are accountable to local objectives and membership but also to Northern donors. Modern, scaled-up NGOs, such as INBio, work closely with local governments and may have substantial financial and commercial objectives as well. Chapter 5 stressed the importance of allowing for complex motivations; self-interested behavior can and does coexist with loyalty, commitment, and altruism. Opportunism is also a possibility. However, particularly as relationships become more complex, Southern NGOs become accountable to a wider variety of actors.

The case of INBio has been chosen to analyze how a close relationship with the state can enhance the ability of a Southern nonprofit to provide public goods. The cooperation of the state gives INBio a certain monopoly privilege — akin to property rights — over the genetic resources in the national parks. This monopoly position in the production of joint public and private goods allows it to earn rents from commercial transactions that are then directed to the production of local and international public and private goods. Complex contracts between INBio, the state, domestic and international nonprofits, the international commercial sector, and external government organizations support the preservation of biodiversity, the production of biodiversity information, and increases in human capital and economic development in Costa Rica.

BIODIVERSITY AND PROPERTY RIGHTS

Costa Rica is a country less than half the size of England — only 19,575 square miles (about 5 million hectares) — but extremely rich in biological diversity. It contains at least 4 percent of the world's terrestrial species and is of great interest to scientists and conservationists. Some 27 percent of the land mass is now under protection, and Costa Rica already has a long tradition of scientifically oriented environmental NGOs. Some think of Costa Rica as the "world's largest center of tropical research" (Umaña & Brandon 1992).

INBio operates under a cooperative agreement, with the Ministry of Natural Resources, Energy, and Mines (MIRENEM) of the Costa Rican government, to inventory jointly the biological diversity in the protected areas of Costa Rica (Reid et al. 1993). INBio was founded with the objective of attracting international funds, increasing local human capital, and putting the knowledge and funding gained to work for economic development.

As a nonprofit, INBio accepts grants and tax-free donations of materials. However, as brought out in the previous chapter, it also received international attention for a contract arranged with Merck Chemical & Co. Merck provided more than $1 million over two years to support the inventory and in exchange received chemical extracts from insects, plants, and microorganisms to be used for drug screening. INBio also receives a share of royalties on any resulting commercial products. The contract was renewed in 1994, and INBio's commercial and noncommercial relationships continue to grow. In exchange for the exclusive position that MIRENEM has granted it to inventory the nation's biodiversity, INBio allocates a minimum portion of all project budgets to the National Parks Foundation and releases information produced to MIRENEM (Reid et al. 1993).

Public and Private Forest Goods

Biological diversity or biodiversity is only one of the various public goods that INBio protects or produces and only one of a wide variety of public and private goods that the forests of Costa Rica offer. When sustainably managed, forests can offer many private goods for harvest: timber and other plants as well as meat and fish from wildlife. Many of the goods offered are public or semi-public. National parks offer various leisure activities and attract domestic and international tourists; they also have educational value. Forests have important ecological functions as watersheds and carbon stores, and they have protection and waste assimilation functions and microclimatic functions. People may also attach value just to knowing that the forests exist as part of our culture and heritage (Swanson & Barbier 1992).

Biodiversity itself has complex public and private aspects. Ecologically, biodiversity is a pure public good, of benefit both domestically and internationally. The pharmaceutical value of genetic resources, on the other hand, once innovation justifies a patent, can become an exclusive good. National sovereignty to biodiversity would give states an exclusive right to raw genetic resources, except for the fact that the same genetic resources may be found in many different countries.

The complex public-private nature of forest and biodiversity goods offers opportunities for nonprofit NGOs to exploit partnerships with the public and private sectors toward the provision and production of the public and private goods associated. INBio, for example, receives domestic public and private support and international public and private support. It produces public goods that are shared freely domestically and internationally, and it produces private goods for international commercial contracts.

Property Rights and Genetic Resources

Environmental problems can often be alleviated with enforceable, tradeable property rights. Harold Demsetz (1967) argued that as natural resources become scarce and increase in value, property rights are defined over them. Although this holds true for land, mineral, and even water resources, for environmental public goods private property rights may be difficult or impossible to define. However, pressures have built to assign rights to genetic resources (Sedjo 1992). Developing countries claimed sovereign rights to genetic resources under the Convention on Biodiversity in 1992 (UN Environment Programme 1992). Simultaneously contracts between nonprofit organizations, industry, and other parties are emerging, particularly for pharmaceutical research (Laird 1993).

The pressures for property rights to genetic resources are based on an increase in their perceived value. For the pharmaceutical industry, developments in biotechnology increased the feasibility of screening large quantities of tropical species for potentially valuable, natural chemical compounds and thus increased the demand for samples to screen. Further, despite advances in genetic engineering, ethnopharmacology (the study of medicines used by traditional communities) is still leading to commercially valuable drugs. Reid and colleagues (1993) record 21 companies actively screening natural products — both with and without ethnopharmocological targeting. Fifteen of these companies began such screening only in the past decade.

Thus, demand for genetic variability has increased while the earth's primary reservoirs of genetic wealth — tropical forests — are being depleted at rates of 2–3 percent per year in many countries of Latin America and Asia (World Resources Institute 1994: Table 19.2). Pressures for property rights have naturally increased.

Pharmaceutical companies obtain property rights or patent protection for the value added to genetic resources through scientific innovation, and researchers have long questioned high profits in the pharmaceutical industry (Comanor 1986; Scherer 1993). Moreover, although patent protection for pharmaceutical developments (as well as for genetically engineered plants and for hybrid seeds) provides incentives for innovation at the commercial end,[1] few incentives exist to protect and maintain the biologically diverse environment to supply commercial needs (Barton 1991). Until the Convention on Biodiversity, genetic resources were considered the common heritage of mankind, and pharmaceutical companies freely tapped traditional knowledge and gathered raw genetic material for the development of new drugs. At the 1992 Earth Summit in Rio de Janeiro, the South demanded property rights, and it was agreed that states should hold sovereign rights to genetic resources. Now genetic materials should not be gathered without the informed consent of the government; yet national sovereignty is a long way from private property rights.

Countries in the South and their citizens and businesses, in order to protect habitat for diverse species, must forgo the economic benefits of developing these areas. National sovereignty over genetic resources gives some incentive to the state to protect natural areas, but not to individuals and businesses. Because politics and bureaucracy determine how the state makes decisions and acts, it is unclear a priori who would have incentives to do what. The likelihood of efficient incentives is negligible.[2]

The further definition of private property rights would be a costly and politically driven process, despite pleas by lawyers and economists for justice and appropriate incentives (Barton & Christensen 1988).[3] Those parties with the most at stake could be expected to maintain a strong political presence in the struggle for property rights (Libecap 1989). Particularly when it remains unclear what value property rights to genetic resources would have, the benefits of assigning such rights may not justify the costs.[4]

Because the same genetic material can be widely dispersed, potentially many different landowners, indigenous communities, and even countries could claim the same genetic resource that results in a commercially valuable product. When random scientific screening results in valuable discoveries, property rights might be allocated on the basis of where the material originated. However, because property rights for land may be poorly defined and poorly enforced, and because forest land may often belong to the state (or to indigenous groups), this would take us little beyond state sovereignty. Traditional knowledge has led to commercially valuable products for hundreds of years, but only recently has serious consideration been given to the question of property rights to that knowledge. Even if discovery by modern science of that knowledge could be traced to a particular tribe, place, or person, the question of allocating rights is still very difficult. Is a special right for the knowledge to be given, distinct from ownership rights for unidentified genetic resource? If so, is it the medicine man who has the knowledge that should be compensated or the entire community, and how should the boundaries of the community be drawn?

Complex Contracts in Lieu of Property Rights

Although property rights might be seen as a precondition to contracts over the use of genetic resources, INBio's contract with Merck preceded the Biodiversity Convention in Rio. Also, although INBio always functioned under authority of the state, as the following case study reveals, legislation concerning sovereignty came later.

Indeed, property rights can only serve to allocate resources efficiently when they are well defined, enforced, and trade in the marketplace. However, the achievement of well-defined rights for biodiversity that are both just and efficient is not possible. Contracts are an alternative to such market transactions; and, like property rights, contracts can also serve to make human interaction more efficient (Williamson 1985).

Certainly, the question of INBio's right as a private NGO to benefit from contracts over Costa Rica's biodiversity is not without controversy (Kloppenburg 1992; Martínez-Alier 1993). Kloppenburg (1992), for example, implies that INBio as a private organization has usurped rights from the public to Costa Rican biodiversity. However, as explained below, INBio has always functioned in close partnership with the national government and no profits are distributed. Nevertheless, the benefits from INBio's contracts are not distributed equally among Costa Rican citizens. Moreover, a relatively small portion of project budgets (10 percent in most cases) is invested back in conservation activities; as of 1995 INBio had directed $245,000 to the National Parks Foundation.[5]

Still, INBio has multiple public objectives. The public goods it supports extend beyond the preservation of biodiversity. It also produces biodiversity information that is shared freely domestically and internationally, and INBio enhances technology transfer, human capital development, and economic development. These benefits cannot be shared equally, but the country benefits substantially. As the country benefits with economic development and an increased appreciation for the biological wealth contained in the forests, pressure on the wildlands should be decreased.

THE INTERNATIONAL INSTITUTIONAL ECOLOGY OF RELATIONSHIPS

Before presenting the details of the case study, it should be emphasized that INBio's experience is unique and may remain so. In addition to rich genetic wealth and a local interest in conservation and tropical science, Costa Rica boasts stable democratic rule, a large middle class, and standards of health, education, and literacy that match those of industrial nations (Gámez et al. 1993). Although Merck and INBio renewed their initial contract, commercial contracts of this size for samples of natural chemical compounds are still uncommon. INBio may have a unique comparative advantage (Aylward 1993), and the marginal value of the additional hectare of species habitat to the pharmaceutical industry may be far too low to replicate this particular case around the world (Simpson, Sedjo, & Reid 1996). Nevertheless, the innovative combination of nonprofit, public, and international commercial and donor relationships deserves exploration.

Producing Public and Private Goods

INBio's current main objective is to inventory the biodiversity of the country — a project undertaken jointly with MIRENEM — and to use the knowledge produced to generate income for the preservation of the wildlands and for economic and human capital development in Costa Rica. For the most part, the knowledge produced is made freely available to noncommercial users. However, tied to chemical extracts, similar information adds value to raw genetic resources and is marketed to commercial users. Thus, INBio produces joint products — general and need-specific information on the biodiversity of the country — that are both public and private goods.[6] It also supports the protection of national parks directly in all project budgets.

INBio is funded both by international donor grants and with commercial contracts. From its founding in mid-1989 through 1992, INBio was supported by $3 million in public and private grants (private foundations, such as MacArthur, Pew, Alton Jones, and Noyes; international environmental NGOs like the World Wildlife Fund-United States and The Nature Conservancy; and the governments of Costa Rica, the United States, Sweden, and Norway) (Gámez et al. 1993: 60). INBio's income during 1993 came to $1.8 million, and almost 20 percent of that resulted from commercial contracts (National Biodiversity Institute [hereafter INBio] 1994).[7] All project budgets — both commercial and donor — include support for the national park protection, for human capital development and technology transfer, and for the inventory generally; thus public and private goods are indeed produced jointly.

In fact, INBio has four main program areas: the inventory, biodiversity prospecting, information management systems, and biodiversity information distribution. These programs are all mutually supportive and each interacts with public, nonprofit, and commercial interests. Biodiversity information is made freely available to the Costa Rican government for use in policy, conservation, education, and tourism. The production of that information, however, increases INBio's marketability in the private sector for consulting services and as a supplier of biological samples. INBio also develops marketable expertise in biodiversity information management, while at the same time its management system enhances the distribution of biodiversity information provided as a public good to the local, regional, and international communities. Mutually beneficial collaborative arrangements with other nonprofit organizations, such as museums and universities, also figure into INBio's input and output.

With such complex cross-subsidization of public and private goods, nonprofit status provides flexibility to arrange contracts and collaborative arrangements acceptable to all parties that would be impossible in the public sector. A private for-profit firm certainly could not receive the kinds of general grants that INBio has relied on. Nevertheless, both the public and for-profit sectors are essential to the success of INBio as a nonprofit.

Relations with the National Government

INBio was initiated by the government: it was created by a planning commission established by MIRENEM. Representatives from other government ministries, universities, the National Museum, the National Scientific Research Council, and two established scientific environmental NGOs made up the commission. Costa Rica has acted as a pioneer in creating nonprofit organizations to complement government activities by harnessing external private-sector contributions (Umaña & Brandon 1992). The National Parks Foundation (NPF) was created in 1978 to support the national parks system. Like the NPF, INBio has a unique status legitimized by the government.

INBio functions under a cooperative agreement with MIRENEM.[8] MIRENEM is responsible for administrating the national parks and biological reserves. INBio contributes to the preservation of Costa Rican biodiversity through the generation and use of biodiversity information.

INBio and MIRENEM jointly carry out the inventory: both provide personnel, installations, and equipment. INBio is granted an "official and specific recognition status" for the technical and scientific administration of the inventory (Sittenfeld & Gámez 1993: 87). INBio is also granted permission to collect samples of species for use in scientific research — commercial, nonprofit, and public — as long as the research program is communicated on an annual basis to the National Park System. INBio promises to include in all commercial research budgets (and other research budgets when possible) 10 percent for donation to the NPF to support the preservation of the parks. Fifty percent of economic returns, such as royalties from a valuable drug discovery, are likewise promised to the NPF. In addition, INBio agrees to provide MIRENEM with technical advice and to "Within its capacity . . . put at the disposition of MIRENEM, by the mechanisms established for the case, the pertinent information contained in its Data Bases for Conservation to be used for decision making on the management and conservation of biodiversity and other matters related to its jurisdiction" (Sittenfeld & Gámez 1993: 88).

Thus, INBio is granted a certain monopoly status within Costa Rica regarding biodiversity information, although it turns over much of what it produces with that privilege to the public domain.[9] The NPF was granted a monopoly status as the unique nonprofit designated to receive domestic and international funds for national parks. INBio's monopoly status is on a commercial level. As the sole organization designated to produce the information that adds value to Costa Rica's genetic resources and renders them particularly marketable to international commercial interests, INBio has gained property rights over this genetic wealth from and for Costa Rica. INBio does not have a monopoly over collections in the conservation areas of Costa Rica; only its status as an information producer is unique. New legislation in Costa Rica further specifies the sovereign national rights over biological diversity, vis-à-vis other potential collectors of species samples, recognized in Article 3 of the Convention on Biodiversity (Sittenfeld 1994).[10]

Contracts with the International Private Sector

INBio is using its special status to obtain monopoly rents from the international for-profit sector and redirect them back to the production of public goods.

INBio's contract with Merck & Co has received the widest attention. Under a two-year agreement recently renewed, Merck provided a project budget of $1 million (plus 13.5 percent overhead) to INBio. At least 30 percent of the budget supported the biodiversity inventory and 10 percent was directed to the NPF.[11] Direct support (including laboratory equipment) for the extraction of a limited number of identified and documented biological samples for Merck's exclusive use[12] during the two-year period involved about 30 percent of the budget. The remainder of the budget was directed to human capital development. Any royalties that result from successful products derived under the collaboration will be shared equally between INBio and the NPF.

INBio has also worked with the British Technology Group (BTG), a technology licensing company, and the Kew Royal Botanical Gardens in England to develop a nematicide from a plant compound. Ecologists had observed some ten years ago that field mice preferred starvation to eating the seed of a certain plant in Costa Rica. BTG contacted INBio after having researched and patented the compound for use as a biodegradable, nontoxic nematicide. INBio agreed to provide BTG with a specified amount of the compound, but first had to learn to isolate the compound from the leaves, instead of the seeds, for a more abundant supply. BTG funded the research with 30 percent of the project budget directed to the NPF, and INBio received rights to develop the nematicide commercially in Costa Rica. A local manufacturer has investigated producing the nematicide with royalties paid to the National Park System and to INBio. Because the natural nematicide holds promise for banana cultivation, local banana growers have supported field research (Sittenfeld 1994).

Bristol Myers Squibb Company and Cornell University have worked with INBio using chemical ecology to seek valuable pharmaceutical products from insects (INBio 1994). Much of the work is supported by a grant from a consortium composed of the U.S. Agency for International Development, the U.S. National Science Foundation, the U.S. National Institutes of Health, and the National Cancer Institute. As part of the agreement, Bristol Myers has donated to the NPF, contributed laboratory equipment, and provided training in its own labs for two Costa Rican scientists. Should valuable drug compounds be identified as a result of this research, both INBio and Cornell are guaranteed a share of future profits. As with all other royalties that INBio might receive, half of these potential royalties would be directed to the NPF (Sittenfeld 1994).

INBio's information management program also works with the international for-profit sector. Intergraph Corporation of Huntsville, Alabama, a supplier of integrated technical information management systems, has contributed $750,000 worth of hardware, software, and services to assist INBio in the development of a computerized Biodiversity Information

Management System. Intergraph shares the proceeds of any marketable software developed through the relationship.[13]

Obviously, the unwritten component of the commercial relationships is the positive advertising value the private profit-seeking companies receive as a result of an association with INBio. As an environment friendly organization pursuing state-of-the-art technology and pioneering property rights relationships that provide incentives to preserve tropical rainforests in a country well known for its ecotourism and its stable democracy, INBio provides a valuable boost to the public image of Northern commercial partners. Because many of these relationships were timed appropriately to take advantage of the publicity associated with the Earth Summit in Rio de Janeiro in June 1992, the advertising component should not be underestimated.

Collaborations in the Nonprofit Sector

Much of INBio's work is collaborative research alongside other nonprofit organizations. The Cornell-Bristol Myers project discussed earlier involves funding from nonprofits and government agencies in the United States for collaborative research between INBio (a nonprofit NGO), Cornell (a nonprofit university), and a for-profit corporation.

Another research project completed in December 1993 involved Cornell University, the University of Costa Rica, and the National University. The project evaluated a number of plant extracts for activity against malaria, coccidiosis, and snake bites. Scientists from the National Cancer Institute of the United States also assisted under this project in testing for anti-viral activity useful in the search for substances active against human immunodeficiency virus (INBio 1994: 31).

A substantial part of INBio's revenue for 1993 came from other nonprofits including conservation NGOs (7 percent), universities (10 percent), and foundations (10 percent). Twenty-three percent came from bilateral and multilateral government agencies, and, as noted previously, 19 percent came from commercial contracts. The balance came from interest on the principal of a debt-for-nature swap (10 percent)[14] and from other sources (19 percent), which included income on investments and exchange rate differentials as well as payments to personnel for international speeches and conferences (INBio 1994: 57).

Complex Contracts

INBio is thus characterized by a variety of relationships, all of which are mutually supportive. Most of these relationships are based on sharing information, a complex public good that can also be proprietary. The transfer of technology to INBio is exchanged for access to information about potentially valuable genetic resources and for advertising benefits. The complex contracts, which govern the relationships, economize on the costly definition of rights over the property involved.

In many cases INBio's supporting partners expect only public goods. These public goods include: the preservation of the tropical forests for their many values, the production of biodiversity information to be used locally and internationally, and economic and human capital development in Costa Rica. Yet, INBio also markets private goods commercially. Specific quantities of samples and related information are exchanged for determined project budgets. INBio provides advertising benefits to its commercial partners as well. This mix of goods complicates INBio's incentives. The need to be accountable to such a wide variety of parties makes transparency all the more important. Considerable controversy has resulted from the fact that Merck has required that the royalty rate remain private information (Kloppenburg 1992).[15]

Working with multiple public and private partners has benefits. Joint production of the complexity of public and private goods characterizes the entire process. Complementarities in production increase the final product of both public and private goods; that is, investments toward the production of commercial products increase the production of public goods and vice versa. Thus the production process takes advantage of both profit motives and donations to produce more public goods than would otherwise be possible.

An essential component in this case is INBio's unique monopoly position — essential because only a monopoly could extract rents from the international commercial sector. Martínez-Alier (1993: 115) argues that INBio and Costa Rica sold cheap, making the point that "the Poor sell cheap." Competitive "INBios" within Costa Rica would bid down prices and reduce the relatively minor rents now collected. INBio's privileged position is only partly created by its role, specifically designated by the government, in carrying out the inventory of species diversity. Costa Rica also has a comparative advantage relative to other tropical countries as a center for tropical research. High local standards of education, literacy, and health and stable democratic rule give Costa Rica's INBio a further advantage. This unique comparative advantage may allow INBio to continue to capture rents to the genetic diversity from the international commercial sector and reinvest them in the preservation of local biological diversity and other public goods.

CONCLUSIONS

The case of INBio and its complex political-economic partnerships provides an in-depth example of the new fabric of institutional relationships growing within Latin America — and between Latin America and the global community — as the for-profit, private sector expands and the public sector opens up space for nonprofit activity.

INBio's partnerships involve economic contracts with the public and private sectors, contracts that allow for more efficient provision of public goods than would be possible without the combined effort of these three sectors. In more detail than Chapter 5, this chapter has demonstrated how NGOs can provide a flexible, private-sector answer to the provision and production of international public goods. The superior flexibility of a nonprofit NGO over the public sector allows complex contracts with the international and domestic for-profit sectors as well as with domestic and international donors to support the production of both private goods and international public goods. The case illustrates how NGO partnerships with the public and for-profit sectors can enhance the production of public goods.

Nonprofit NGOs are arguably the natural providers of international public goods. Global governance structures lack power and are subject to grander public choice problems than national governments. Moreover, the nonprofit sector offers the flexibility to join commercial incentives together with the altruism of private foundations and the collective decision of public-sector governance in the provision, production, and protection of environmental public goods. As shown in this case, INBio has harnessed the power of the international commercial sector toward the provision of environmental goods that are jointly public and private.

Four key elements to INBio's success may be generalizable to other partnerships: a strong relationship with the public sector can provide a nonprofit with added legitimacy that facilitates relationships with international partners, be they other nonprofits, donors, or commercial partners; similarly, a government-designated nonprofit can more flexibly gather and coordinate international funds than the public sector; when private goods can be produced jointly with the public goods of the nonprofit NGO and successfully marketed, government-designated NGO monopolies may be able to earn rents for reinvestment in the production of public goods; and finally, the NGO in question must demonstrate commitment to the public goods objectives and maintain transparency and accountability to its many partners.

Although the experience of INBio's partnerships with the public and for-profit sectors demonstrates efficiency gains in the production of public goods, partnerships may also fail. Many examples of promising partnerships directed toward environmental benefits have been collected to encourage parties to work together for the public good. A healthy scepticism may be in order, however: working together can be costly, and good intentions can degenerate into free riding or opportunism when dealing with ordinary self-interested individuals. Partnerships will only be successful in providing public goods when mutual benefits can be achieved for the participants.

The political ramifications of such international partnerships are also complex, as is clear from the criticism that has been directed at INBio. Unlike Latin America's NGOs of the 1960s and 1970s, whose international relationships were perhaps less overt, INBio is clearly a participant in the global community and, thus, subject to some suspicion at home. Still, relative to the flood of foreign investment that has entered Latin America and Costa Rica specifically in the 1990s, INBio is only a small part of a dramatically changing political-economic relationship with the global community.

NOTES

1.   See Besen and Raskind (1991) on the economics of intellectual property protection. Sharing information also affords benefits in technology diffusion and increased production. Limiting the distribution of intellectual property thus has short-run costs but the resultant profits provide incentives for further innovation. Developing countries may weigh these costs and benefits differently than do developed countries (Siebeck 1990).

2.   The public choice literature attests to this; see Mueller (1989).

3.   Gollin (1993) discusses how intellectual property rights (trade secrets, copy, patents, etc.) might be applied to biological resources and related information.

4.   Studies by Simpson, Sedjo, and Reid (1994) and Aylward (1993) suggest that rents from property rights to genetic resources may be small.

5.   Direct communication with Ana Sittenfeld, June 28, 1995.

6.   See Posnett and Sandler (1986) on the efficiency of financing charitable activity with a jointly produced private good.

7.   Accounting is kept in colones and the income for fiscal year ended December 1993 was 275.27 million colones. The exchange rate used is 155

colones/$.

8.   The agreement is translated and reprinted in Sittenfeld and Gámez (1993: 86–89).

9.   Aylward and colleagues (1993) suggest that economic efficiency would improve if INBio charged noncommercial users as well as commercial users for the use of database information.

10.   Sittenfeld (1994: 5–6) explains that,

Under the new law [December 1992], any entity that wants to collect or manage biodiversity samples from a Conservation Area for research or other uses must obtain a permit or sign a concession agreement with the Ministry of Natural Resources. This legislation declares all wild animals (including invertebrates) to be "public domain" and "national patrimony," regardless of whose property they inhabit. Non-timber, wild plants are viewed as "public interest," as well as the conservation, research and development of genetic resources. Those things which are of public utility are defined by law as "public interest," the use of which is governed by a specific by-law. The by-law regulates the conditions related to the production, management, extraction, commercialization, industrialization and use of genetic resources.

11.   See Laird (1993: Box IV.3) for a breakdown of the budget.

12.   "Exclusive" means that INBio could not circulate samples of the same species to other commercial clients. Other collectors, however, might well gather these samples. See Aylward and colleagues (1993: 49).

13.   See Gámez and colleagues (1993: Box II.2) for more on the project between INBio and Intergraph.

14.   The debt was originally purchased at a discount by private foundations. In exchange, local government bonds now provide a constant source of interest income to INBio and the NPF (Umaña & Brandon 1992).

15.   It is known, however, that royalties on this kind of early stage research, which contributes to a valuable product, are typically in the range of 1–5 percent (Laird 1993).

7

Sharing Information:
Politics and Economics

The explosion of nongovernmental organizations (NGOs) in the global community and the globalization of the world economy have at least one root in common: the information revolution. The costs of transmitting information have fallen sharply in the past two decades, during the same period when both NGOs and international investment have expanded rapidly. By the mid-1980s fax machine use was growing exponentially globally. International telephone traffic expanded over threefold between 1983 and 1993 (Commission on Global Government 1995). Internet hosts were estimated at 9.4 million in January 1996 — 85 percent more than the year before, a rate maintained over the previous five years (*The Economist* 1996: 110).

The widespread use of communication satellites combined with computer modems, televisions, faxes, and phones has facilitated international business dealings (Carnoy et al. 1993); it has also facilitated the organization of those who work for common causes (Salamon 1995). Annis (1992) was among the first to suggest "informational empowerment" because of increased connectedness of grass-roots organizations, domestic urban professional NGOs, and NGOs at the international level. He pointed to increased possibilities in Latin America for electronic mail, access to Web sites, and computer conferencing in urban centers, with faxes reaching even rural areas.

Modern business is increasingly information intensive; but many NGOs are in the business of sharing information. In addition to advocacy, networking, and awareness raising, NGOs conduct research, educate, train, and build capacity. Information and communication are key to their production processes, both as input and output. The decreased costs of information transmission have a major impact on the economics of NGOs.

Because the economic activity of most NGOs is sharing information, it is difficult to separate economics from politics. Certainly NGOs are both political and economic entities; and the political implications of information technology on NGOs has received increasing attention. Scholars find that newly empowered and connected NGOs are taking a larger role in world politics (Mathews 1997). Some link communications technologies specifically to successful democratic uprisings (Jones 1994; Chatfield 1991). Many see a growing "global community" based on NGOs and improved communications technology while the role of the state changes (Commission on Global Governance 1995; McCarthy, Hodgkinson, & Sumariwalla 1992; Princen & Finger 1994).

This chapter builds a political-economic framework to illuminate the effects of falling communication costs on information-intensive NGOs in Latin America. The following section introduces the economics of information goods and why they are suitable to NGOs. Two subsequent sections draw on case descriptions of NGOs in Latin America to analyze the inputs and outputs of the production processes of NGOs involved in information-sharing activities. These sections also illustrate that because of the nature of information, the line between economics and politics must blur. The next section describes participation as the technology employed by NGOs and analyzes how this participatory process changes both economic and political environments; it predicts an expanding role for NGOs as states and markets in Latin America realign. Concluding implications of the decreasing costs of information-sharing on the NGO sector are summarized in the final section.

THE ECONOMICS OF INFORMATION-INTENSIVE NGOs

An understanding of the economics of information-intensive NGOs enhances the discussion among social scientists of the significance and implications of the information revolution and the concurrent explosion of NGOs. However, because information is a political good as well as a public good, the tools of economics have certain limitations. Earlier chapters have described the role of NGOs as producers of public goods. The purpose of this section is to illuminate the particular complexities that result because those public goods are also information goods. The remainder of the chapter demonstrates the insights to be gained by thinking of NGO information-sharing activity in terms of the classical economic production function, where technology is applied to transform inputs into outputs. In this case, however, the technology is participation — a concept still foreign to most economists.

The Economics of Information Goods

Information goods are among the public goods most commonly produced or disseminated by NGOs in developing countries, but unfortunately economists have made little progress in the study of information as a public good (Cowen 1992). Stigler (1961: 213) complained that at the time of his writing, information occupied "a slum dwelling in the town of economics." Most economic models still assume the best technology to be known, and the role of advertising demands far less attention from economists than expenditures on it by producers would require. Progress has been made in some areas: incentives for research and development, decision making under uncertainty, human capital, and search costs; but many gaps remain. Perhaps because of what Boulding (1966: 2) calls "the intrinsic heterogeneity of its substance" most economists have avoided systematic study of sticky areas of information, including the analytical microeconomics of the externalities of information and information as a public good. Nevertheless, more than 35 years ago Fritz Machlup estimated, from the macroeconomic perspective, that "knowledge industries" made up 29 percent of adjusted GNP in the United States.[1] In the 1980s in countries who are members of the Organisation for Economic Co-operation and Development, the information sector accounted for between one-third and one-half of gross domestic product and by the year 2000 the figure should reach 60 percent for European Communities (Saunders, Warford, & Wellenius 1994).

Pure public goods are both nonrival and nonexclusive, and, thus, information is an impure public good. Although information is completely nonrival (to share information with an additional consumer imposes no cost on those already consuming it), the high costs of transmitting information mean that exclusion of persons from its benefits is possible. Information can be sold as a private good, yet its benefits are not entirely appropriable either. Arrow (1984: 142) explains:

Information is inappropriable because an individual who has some can never lose it by transmitting it. It is frequently noted in connection with the economics of research and development that information acquired by research at great cost may be transmitted much more cheaply. If the information is, therefore, transmitted to one buyer, he can in turn sell it very cheaply, so that the market price is well below the cost of production. But if the transmission costs are high, then it is also true that there is inappropriability, since the seller cannot realize the social value of the information. Both cases occur in practice with different kinds of information.

But then according to well-known principles of welfare economics, the inappropriability of a commodity means that its production will be far from optimal. It may be below optimal; it may also induce costly protective measures outside the usual property system.

Another characteristic, pointed out by Stuart Macdonald (1992: 55), that makes information awkward to buy and sell is the fact that "it cannot be displayed to a potential buyer, otherwise he will possess without having to buy. So those who buy information are always uncertain of precisely what it is they are buying."

Because of this inappropriability, the nonprofit NGO sector, rather than the for-profit sector, is particularly involved in those information transfer activities characterized by wide public benefits and few alternatives to appropriate returns. The for-profit sector is active in media areas where potential consumers can be excluded or where advertisers willingly foot the bill for consumers' access.

Several other characteristics of information as a public good are worth noting in the context of NGOs. In the first place, information misused — misinformation or the transmission of overly selective information — can be considered a public bad. What is a public good for some might be a public bad in the eyes of others: information and its interpretation are political and the reliability of information is always subject to question. Moreover, information may be available only in packages or lumps (O'Brien & Helleiner 1982). Some of it may be useful while other is not; some of it may be considered of public benefit while other may not. The usefulness of information may also be tied to time and place.[2] Information may become rapidly obsolete and need to be updated. For this reason, the information-sharing relationships among NGOs, or between NGOs and their target groups, may be of more interest than the particular information shared.

An Information-Intensive Production Process

This section has described NGOs as producers of information goods. Because information is a complex public good, the private sector is usually not the best provider from an economic standpoint. Thus, governments and NGOs are particularly involved in information activities. Yet the nonprofit sector has several advantages over the public sector in providing public goods, particularly at the international level where global governance is weak.

Because NGOs are producers of information goods, their activities can be described in economic terms as transforming inputs into outputs by means of technology. This is the objective of the next three sections. A description of the information-sharing outputs of NGO activity follows.

THE INFORMATION-SHARING OUTPUTS OF NGO PRODUCTION

Information is a difficult commodity for economists to come to grips with; it is intrinsically heterogeneous in substance, neither entirely public nor private, and typically, at least partially, political. Thus, rather than attempt a rigorous analytical discussion of the information-sharing production process of NGOs, this chapter appeals to accounts of how NGOs themselves describe their work. The discussion reveals both the economic value of the activities that NGOs engage in and the difficulty of separating the economic from the political activity.

Most NGOs are involved in a combination of information-sharing activities including two or more of the following: education and training, research, capacity building, networking, awareness raising, and social change. These six related and overlapping activity areas are described by drawing on six NGO case accounts written by representatives of the relevant organizations.

Education and Training

For economists, education and training increase human capital. Within the past 30 years, it has become common (for economists and policymakers generally) to view education and training as investments in human capital — activities that will increase future production or pleasure (Becker 1993). Investments in human capital provide a direct return to the person educated, and the positive externalities of a more educated populace provide additional social returns as well. Increases in human capital are also recognized as a powerful prerequisite to economic development.

Many NGOs educate and train. For example, the Institute of Education for Rural Development (INEDER) is based in Cochabamba, Bolivia and has worked since 1975 to improve living standards for local farmers.[3] INEDER works in the province of Carrasco with approximately 100 farming families. Program areas in education and training include agriculture, animal husbandry, and health. Clearly INEDER works to increase human capital and rural productivity.

However, is education really confined to human capital as economists understand it? It is not, according to the educators of INEDER. They state, "Producers of wheat, while producing their crops to satisfy their immediate needs, are also 'producing' awareness, and the social organization that uses that awareness to influence the world. The seeds of 'raised awareness' are to be found at all levels of everyday life. It is the task of INEDER's educators to help the peasants associate social conflicts with the individual conflicts to which their situation subjects them" (Theunis 1992: 241). Education does increase human capital — this investment may result in increased wheat production; but clearly NGOs also educate to build social capital — an investment for social and political ends.[4] Indeed, representatives of INEDER claim, "An explicit aim of INEDER is to contribute to the macroeconomic and political change of the national society. It is hoped that such change will ultimately be carried out by the target groups and mobilized, via the intermediary groups, by INEDER" (Theunis 1992: 239).

Complementing their research and training activities, INEDER directs programs in peasant organization, promotion of women, and communication through radio and television. The radio and television programs are described as cultural, rather than explicitly educational.

Research

Research is also viewed by economists as an economically productive investment activity. Private firms may undertake research that they keep secret and on which they collect private returns. Public investments also fund basic research to be used as a public input to enhance production generally. The research and development of the Internet communications system is an example of public investment in research that increases productivity in the private and public sectors, and not least in the private, nonprofit sector. Research made available publicly is considered a public good.

Research is produced by many NGOs in developing countries and is the primary activity of the National Biodiversity Institute (INBio), the Costa Rican NGO cataloging the biodiversity of the country, discussed at length in Chapter 6. INBio is intensely involved in the production, management, private sale, and public distribution of biodiversity information at a highly professional level. It has identified and documented biological samples for Merck Chemical & Co. to screen for potentially valuable commercial chemical compounds and has worked with the for-profit Intergraph Corporation of Huntsville, Alabama to develop a computerized Biodiversity Information Management System. This developing-country NGO conducts research suitable for private sale to multinational corporations. It also makes similar information freely available to the Costa Rican government and other nonprofit organizations.

INBio's stated objectives are much less political than, for example, INEDER's; they address human capital and economic development directly. INBio was created to carry out the tasks of "determining what biodiversity lies in [Costa Rica's] protected areas . . . and integrating the non-destructive use of this biodiversity into the intellectual and economic fabric of national and international society" (Gámez et al. 1993: 56). INBio is specifically committed to training local personnel to carry out the inventory at all levels.

Another NGO that sees itself as primarily involved in research is the National Forum for Colombia (FORO), founded in 1982 in Bogota.[5] FORO's mission is not so precisely defined, however. Representatives of FORO comment that, "A number of years ago some of our consultants said FORO 'is like jelly held in the hand. If you open your hand the jelly slides off. If you squeeze tightly it escapes through your fingers'" (Theunis 1992: 173). Yet FORO persisted in its goal to "initiate programs of research, advocacy, communication and advisory support — based on the needs of the people of Colombia . . . with . . . organizations [that] seek to encourage all Colombians to take an interest." These same representatives comment that although research is key to their work, they have found that for some Northern partners "'research' is synonymous with wasting paper, time and resources" (Theunis 1992: 181). Research, of course, is not of uniformly high quality and its usefulness as a public good or as an investment good may be quite difficult to evaluate.

Capacity Building and Institutional Strengthening

The terms "capacity building" and "institutional strengthening" are often used to describe what NGOs do. The language itself implies an investment that might increase output, but these terms do not belong to economists. The goals attributed to capacity building or institutional strengthening typically include increasing participation, transparency, and accountability. Improving technical and managerial abilities is also part of the package, as is promoting self sufficiency (Carroll 1992; Haas, Keohane, & Levy 1993). Capacity building is a form of information sharing; it may involve the kind of education and training referred to earlier as human capital, but it also involves helping local people "achieve a sense of self-confidence and pride" (*New Partnerships in the Americas* 1994: 92).

Concertación is an umbrella NGO in San José, Costa Rica, founded in 1988, that serves as a forum for NGOs supporting grass-roots organizations in Central America.[6] It works to build capacity in member NGOs. Representatives explain the role of Concertación: "What is intended with Concertación in Central America is for participating NGOs [to] be able to strengthen each other in order to confront the challenges of thinking and acting in Central America as a region, and to support the democratization and participation processes of grassroots initiatives" (Theunis 1992: 124). Member NGOs of Concertación likewise engage in capacity-building activities with grass-roots organizations. Concertación representatives counsel, "NGOs should aim to help strengthen grassroots organizations' capabilities and skills for mobilizing local, public or private economic and institutional resources and for negotiating conditions favoring their consolidation. In this sense, foreign resources should be used to develop skills that can assure a popular groups' stronger bargaining power in their relationships with the State" (Theunis 1992: 126).

The work of FORO in Colombia, noted earlier, is also in the capacity building and institutional strengthening tradition; so is the work of INEDER in Bolivia. Representatives of INEDER describe their capacity-building role, distinguishing it from training: "Dialogue with the NGO may enable the target [peasant] group to know itself better and to define its aspirations more precisely" (Theunis 1992: 239). As Fisher (1993: 7) emphasizes, capacity building is not a one-way street, something that NGOs do for their target groups. Rather, it is something that happens between them.

Networking

The primary means that Concertación uses in efforts to strengthen the institutions it works with is networking at the regional level. Representatives of Concertación state, "Today, the network concept stands out as one of the most adequate proposals for institutional strengthening and development in that it allows organizations to articulate by means of a network in order to confront growing challenges without having to enlarge the institution's formal structure. Individual weakness may be overcome inherent to the network's member institutions" (Theunis 1992: 124). They characterize a network saying: "A network is more than just an institution. It constitute[s] a space for organizing a permanent flow of ideas and resources between the group of institutions participating in the network" (Theunis 1992: 124). The network facilitates the sharing of information but also transforms the member institution into a part of a larger entity.

Such networks have both economic and political roles. Ronald Burt (1992) considers a network to be "social capital" — valuable to profit-seeking firms as well. Unlike human capital, however, Burt points out that social capital is jointly rather than privately held, yet social capital provides opportunities for economic advancement. Job seekers are well aware of the need to invest in building a network (Granovetter 1995). Nevertheless, the kind of connectedness that the representatives of Concertación describe as an outcome of the network is more than an economic investment, it is also a political transformation — a political empowerment of the parties concerned (Annis 1992).

Of the other NGOs described above, FORO in Colombia is also particularly concerned with networking activities.

Awareness Raising

The term "awareness raising" has a distinctly political ring to it, but how does it differ from education? Awareness raising is one of the primary outputs of NGO activity. INEDER, the Bolivian NGO described earlier, raises awareness to prepare for eventual macroeconomic and political change, while educating and training for rural development.

Teatro Popular ICTUS is an NGO founded in 1956 in Santiago, Chile.[7] Although ICTUS now uses theatre, video, and television to raise cultural and critical awareness, during the military dictatorship its access to national television was denied. Target groups for presentations are those involved with social change — including unions, students, women's groups, intellectuals, and other grass-roots organizations. Representatives of ICTUS emphasize the power of their medium: "The video has the ability to combine, powerfully and credibly, areas of affect and rationality, emotionality with the transmission of ideas and information. . . . Video programs unite people and inspire them to express themselves. Therefore, besides the winning of the right to meet and talk, we also represent the right to discuss, listen to, question, change and communicate ideas" (Theunis 1992: 226, 229). ICTUS is concerned with education and research as well as networking, but representatives state, "Our most outstanding achievement has been the creation, introduction and legitimization in Chile of a special language and medium: video as an educative instrument, a liberator of communication. And through it the possibility for social organizations and agents of change to develop processes of communication, training and organization" (Theunis 1992: 232). Clearly the output of ICTUS contributes to human and social capital, and sharing ideas increases public goods. Yet all of this is inextricably intertwined with essentially political processes.

The Research Center for Feminist Action (CIPAF) in Santo Domingo, Dominican Republic[8] is also concerned with raising awareness in pursuit of change. Management claims, "The concept that best captures our *raison d'être* is the commitment to achieving lasting social change" (Theunis 1992: 108). Activities, "take place in three closely-related yet distinct areas: research, education/training and public information. . . . The goal is to empower women by providing them with access to reliable, scientific knowledge about the society we live in and the place accorded to women in it, so that they may undertake whatever action they deem necessary for its transformation" (Theunis 1992: 107). CIPAF appeals more to scientific knowledge than does ICTUS, which openly appeals to emotion in their presentations to popular groups and students. CIPAF representatives note that, "Although CIPAF is pleased and proud of the close working links that have developed over the years with numerous *popular sector* women's groups, we do not consider ourselves as a grass-roots organization but a research/education institution" (Theunis 1992: 109).

CIPAF has a middle-class staff and does not shy from establishment relationships. Although founded in 1980 under a social-democratic government, the new right-wing government "has generally maintained good relations, requesting information, sending representatives to our meetings, and even consulting us on several occasions. We attribute this to our policy of visibility, accessibility and scientific responsibility" (Theunis 1992: 109). CIPAF also boasts "the largest feminist documentation center in the Caribbean, receiving ten to fourteen requests daily" (Theunis 1992: 111).

Despite their different approaches — one scientific and the other theatrical — both CIPAF and ICTUS are committed to awareness raising for social change.

Social Change

Social change can also be considered an economic output, the result of NGO production. Social change is an information-sharing output. Effective social change that brings sustainable solutions requires discussions between stakeholders and government and citizen participation in decision making and engagement in political processes (Uphoff 1986). Social change is information and communication intensive.

All of the NGOs discussed earlier participate in social change or aspire to it. CIPAF directly advises the Dominican government on women's issues. Concertación is intimately involved with the process of democratization in Central America; it has developed negotiating and lobbying operations with foreign and international NGOs and governments. FORO seeks out and finds "opportunities within the state apparatus for projects aimed at social change" (Theunis 1992: 178). INEDER and ICTUS work to raise awareness as preparation for eventual social change. INBio's work is research, but it seeks to strengthen Costa Rica by increasing human capital and economic potential.

THE INFORMATION-SHARING
INPUTS OF NGO PRODUCTION

NGOs produce and share information as the output of much of their activity. This is the public good that donor contributions support. This same information is destined to be a public input[9] — an input that many can use simultaneously — toward the productive activity of the grassroots organizations that NGOs target.

Information, however, is also a primary input to NGO production. NGOs obtain information inputs in a variety of forms. Many of the donations that Southern NGOs receive arrive in kind as training or technical assistance. Like most inputs, information inputs may also require cost outlays, especially in terms of transaction costs. Obtaining feedback from target groups is an important input to effective NGO production that requires a transaction cost outlay. By investing in networking, NGOs exchange information and strengthen each other's production process. Information may also be exchanged between NGOs in a kind of barter transaction or pooled as they jointly undertake a project.

Donations of Information

Donors share information, technical assistance, and training with nonprofit NGOs for some of the same reasons they give monetary donations: this in-kind contribution is expected to increase the quality of the public good produced and will not increase profits. Just as Southern NGOs engage in capacity building with local target groups, they are themselves often the recipients of training and technical assistance from Northern partners, sometimes at considerable cost.

INBio, for example, to further the biodiversity inventory, receives technical expertise from Northern partners. Although "All of INBio's directorate and staff are Costa Rican, . . . foreign researchers will continue to play a highly significant role in technology transfer at INBio for some time" (Sittenfeld & Gámez 1993: 88). Indeed, INBio consciously fosters an environment attractive to foreign taxonomists who wish to come, study, and share their expertise (Janzen et al. 1993).

INEDER devotes 30 percent of staff working days (and hence 30 percent of donor contributions) to in-house development of this input to production, which includes experience-based self-instruction as well as theoretical and practical training (Theunis 1992: 243). ICTUS also stresses the importance of research and training for the development of NGO personnel and laments the reluctance of Northern partners to fund such research and training programs (Theunis 1992: 231).

Sharing Information Inputs through Networks

Donors, however, have found ways to cut training costs by encouraging partnership among Southern NGOs — specifically networks — so NGOs can learn from each other rather than depending on donors for training (*New Partnerships in the Americas* 1994).

Concertación, for example, is designed as a "permanent flow of ideas and resources" between NGOs in Central America. It is a formal network whose purpose is institutional strengthening — an input to other NGOs. Some scholars have noted that networking may be donor driven (Clark 1995). Others note that although donors have targeted funding on formal NGO networks, "informal networking often evolves as organizations discover they have good reasons to cooperate" (Fisher 1994).[10] Such informal service networks strengthen internal management through the exchange of ideas, leadership skills, and administrative techniques. NGOs also link into networks through the Internet, particularly in such fields as public health and the environment.[11]

FORO consciously engages in networking both as an output activity and as an input. Representatives explain, "FORO has sought to pursue a policy of generous linkage in an effort to allow the newer and smaller NGDOs [nongovernmental development organizations] to learn from our successes and mistakes, and in the certainty . . . that it is necessary to improve contacts, coordination and interchange" (Theunis 1992: 179). FORO has also worked to form a network of NGOs throughout Latin America to deal with urban problems in major cities.

Perhaps revealingly, INEDER and ICTUS, those NGOs of the cases here presented most eager to receive training from donors, also appear to be the least involved with networking activities. An effective information network can provide continual updates of time sensitive information as well as local knowledge gained through practical experience (Macdonald 1992). The same kind of information is not available in one-time training activities.

Private for-profit firms also engage in networking for the exchange of some forms of information (Macdonald 1992), but profit-making goals may have mixed effects on incentives to share information (Kirby 1988). Because of the peculiar characteristics of information as a commodity, for-profit firms may also benefit from sharing or trading information rather than engaging in market transactions. Yet for-profit firms may protect information to increase profits; this may result in wasteful duplication of research and development, costly investments in maintaining secrecy, and losses of potential synergies from sharing information (Macdonald 1992). Nonprofit NGOs can freely share information without concern to protect profits — the information public goods they produce usually cannot be bought and sold anyway. NGOs do not compete for market share like for-profit producers do. They do, however, compete for donor funds, and this may partially explain cases of isolationism among NGOs (Clark 1995). However, NGOs also share similar objectives, such as raised awareness, increased citizen participation, and other kinds of social change. Ultimately they have more reasons to share information than do profit-seeking firms.

Barter Relationships

Networking activities can lead to barter between NGOs (Fisher 1994), often for information goods. Ben-Ner (1993) concludes that the conditions for barter are more easily met between nonprofit firms than between for-profit firms, largely because nonprofits may share similar goals and trust each other. Economists question the existence of barter because the purpose of money is to reduce transaction costs in trade — finding double coincidence of wants is generally costly. However, the barter transaction is social and political as well as economic; it enhances trust and builds relationships. Moreover, information is a difficult good to trade for money; to do so, one must invest in keeping it private. The transaction costs of marketing information may be high; and such activity may build distrust when nonprofits need a trustworthy reputation. Thus, information sharing among NGOs can be expected, whether in simple networking exchanges or in delayed barter exchange.

Joint Projects

NGOs also share information when they engage in joint projects. Private for-profit firms that engage in joint research need to juggle antitrust laws and may or may not invest in keeping results private (Grossman & Shapiro 1986; Katz 1986). Nonprofit NGOs generally have neither concern and frequently pool information when they work together on projects.

INBio, for example, undertakes projects in cooperation with other nonprofit organizations including universities and research institutes. One project involving Cornell University, the University of Costa Rica, and the National University evaluated plant extracts for activity against coccidiosis, malaria, and snake bites (National Biodiversity Institute 1994).

CIPAF also engages in joint research with other nonprofits. It has worked with a national trade union federation on a research project on women in the trade union movement, particularly in the industrial free zones. In a second project, at the request and with the participation of a rural women's confederation, it has built a data bank (Theunis 1992).

Communication Feedback

Finally, a most important input for NGOs is direct feedback from the capacity-building activities in which they engage. Although education, training, capacity building, and awareness raising may be the output of NGO production, communication is a two-way street, an output-input activity. The dialogue that NGOs engage in provides an immediate and lasting return both from the benefits of self expression and from the additional insights gained.

The research of CIPAF, for example, is inspired by their contacts with target groups. Representatives state that, "Research topics generally emerge from the experiences of particular social groups. They may be identified by us or brought to our attention by the very women concerned" (Theunis 1992: 108). Representatives of ICTUS also explicitly recognize the importance of systematic dialogue with and feedback from target groups. "The purpose of 'feedback' is to obtain systematic knowledge, awareness of the direct and indirect effects of the videos on organized groups, the ways in which they are viewed, the discussions they inspire, any requirements which are not met, possibilities of improving key aspects of production, distribution, use, and so forth" (Theunis 1992: 227).

Clearly NGOs are information-intensive producers: their economic outputs are information-sharing activities, and for many economic reasons, NGOs are also the recipients of shared information as well. The next section posits that the technology employed to transform inputs into outputs is participation. However, participation is a more slippery concept than the technology found in most economic production functions.

PARTICIPATION, POLITICS, AND ECONOMICS IN A NEW LATIN AMERICA

Participation is the word that donors and NGOs use to describe the process (the technology) of these information-sharing activities here described. Although it is undoubtedly true that in the 1990s, "the mantra of participation has become more sacred than its practice" (Najam 1996: 136), still, many of Latin America's NGOs are actively engaged in partic- ipatory processes. Participation implies not merely sharing information but true dialogue where participants learn from each other and together emerge with solutions (Galtung 1982). Synergies of information and skills come together and both participants and process itself benefit. Economists usually hold technology fixed during the production period, but participa- tion is a dynamic technology: the participants interact with and shape the process.

This section examines how the participatory process of information sharing by and among NGOs can enhance both the political and the economic environment by strengthening the foundations of democracy in civil society and controlling opportunism. The surge of NGO activity in Latin America coincides with dramatic changes in the roles of the public and private sectors and ushers in a new political and economic balance.

The Process of Participation

Participation as process does not translate particularly well into economics. Here it is defined as a dynamic technology, but other economists have also struggled with the concept.[12] Thinking as an economist, Hirschman (1970) originally conceived of "voice" as costly. Economists view participation as costly: the time-consuming meeting, the difficult negotiation; they see participation as transaction costs. McCloskey and Klamer (1995) moved beyond the usual sterile economic conception when they estimated that "One Quarter of GDP is Persuasion." However, those costs — input costs — are only half the story.

Participation also carries a benefit. Hirschman (1971: 6) amended his argument in *Exit, Voice, and Loyalty*, noting, "My case for the potential superiority of voice over exit would have been considerably strengthened had I realized that in certain situations the use of voice becomes acutely pleasurable and should therefore no longer be computed as a cost, but as a benefit." Even when it may not be acutely pleasurable, the exercise of voice or the act of participation results in both learning and new social and political relationships — an inevitable increase in human and social capital, so to speak, but also a political empowerment.

Indeed, participation can even be viewed as an ideal — a democratic ideal (Boswell 1990). Many scholars of democratic processes look to participation the way economists look to efficiency. For economists, the more efficient a policy is, the better, all else equal. Political analysts have suggested that public policies should also be evaluated as to whether they elicit greater citizen participation (Ingram & Smith 1993). Long ago de Tocqueville argued that active participation of voluntary associations vitalized democracy (Boswell 1990). Jonathan Fox (1992) also claims that leadership accountability depends critically on participatory subgroups.

Strategies of major donors, such as the U.S. Agency for International Development, explicitly involve NGOs to encourage greater citizen participation and strengthen the foundation for democracy. Many of the Southern NGOs supported with international funds have become active participants in newly democratic states in Latin America (*New Partnerships in the Americas* 1994). De Janvry and Sadoulet (1993: 670) state that "the joint happening of proliferation of grassroots movements and NGOs and return to democracy is probably the most important occurrence in Latin America from the standpoint of institutional change." Thus, donors may be partially responsible for furthering these forces of participatory democracy.

Controlling Opportunism

Although the participatory process can be seen as a means to enhance the environment for democracy, others argue that it also enhances the "contractual environment" and the institutions that support a market economy (Boswell 1990; Haas, Keohane, & Levy 1993). Participation, information sharing, and networking by NGOs and other voluntary associations support social monitoring that ensures greater transparency of institutions and organizations, improved accountability, and contract compliance. For economic systems, this translates into more efficient use of scarce resources.

Transparency is important for NGOs themselves, because nonprofit organizations lack incentives to minimize costs and produce public goods that are difficult to monitor. As argued in Chapter 5, as an organizational form, NGOs are certainly vulnerable to opportunism. Although examples of it abound, observers find that the norm among NGO personnel is a high degree of commitment (Fisher 1993). Nonprofit NGOs need a trustworthy reputation to continue receiving donor funds and from a long-run standpoint, their best interest rests in maintaining an honest, open environment.

By sharing information — through networks or barter — NGOs build external relationships that depend on trust and often on shared commitments. By encouraging greater citizen participation, NGOs may strengthen consensus building in civil society. Both activities contribute to a cultural environment that tolerates less corruption and opportunism. This kind of cultural environment can have the added payoff of reinforcing compliance of economic contracts and controlling corruption (Granovetter 1985).[13]

CONCLUSIONS

The rapid changes in technology, which have slashed costs of communication and information transmission, add new dimensions to the changing balance among public, for-profit, and NGO sectors in Latin America. Human rights NGOs successfully limited Mexican government response to the rebellion in Chiapas by alerting human rights groups worldwide and focusing media attention, according to Mathews (1997). She quotes Mexico's Foreign Minister José Angel Gurría, as remarking, "The shots lasted ten days, and ever since, the war has been . . . a war on the Internet" (Mathews 1997: 54). Moreover, the contacts with Northern donors provide access to new technology, ideas, and information. As intensive consumers and disseminators of information, NGOs have developed human and social capital that can provide a flow of trained leaders for both the public and for-profit sectors and open up spaces for dialogue among parties shaping change.

Indeed, not only is Latin America at a critical juncture, but new communications technologies have changed social and economic relationships around the world. Antonelli (1992: 6) compares telecommunications networks to "motorways in the fifties, electricity at the beginning of the century, railways in the nineteenth century, canals in mid eighteenth century," calling them the "basic infrastructure of the *modern* economic system." Other analysts have measured social rates of return to telecommunications infrastructure to range between 20 and 40 percent (Saunders, Warford, & Wellenius 1994).

Unquestionably, changes in communications technology have affected political and economic processes enormously, and the effects are not unambiguously positive.[14] Political campaigns can be waged over the airwaves instead of in town meetings, and interested citizens can cheaply be contacted by fax or e-mail networks and alerted to contact congressional representatives for key votes. Economic activity has become increasingly information-intensive and new communications technologies have changed the shape of financial services, media, transportation, tourism, commodities, and marketing generally (Saunders, Warford, & Wellenius 1994). The modern economy is suddenly a global economy, due primarily to the new ease of communicating globally. Those not linked to global markets are increasingly disadvantaged.

NGOs play active roles in both political and economic realms. The reduced costs of communication and information transmission have enormous implications for their information-intensive production processes and for their potential political roles.

As the costs of communication and information transmission and manipulation fall, the costs of production fall for NGOs and productivity increases. For the same costs, their information-sharing activities can be more effective and can command a wider reach. Research becomes more efficient for CIPAF, INBio, and FORO with the help of cheaper and more portable computers and ever improving information management systems. Education and training are facilitated for INEDER and CIPAF with new economical possibilities in desk-top publishing for the largely literate Latin American target groups. Capacity-building activities may involve sharing new information technologies to empower target groups. Old-fashioned face-to-face communication may diminish but need not fall by the wayside. New technologies can be used to expand and enrich the modes of communication and strengthen relationships without replacing the human contact integral to the subtle dimensions of capacity building. ICTUS exemplifies the ability of NGOs to use new information technologies, such as video and television, to raise awareness and ultimately change society.

Likewise, information-sharing inputs to NGO production are also facilitated. The costs of donations of information from Northern partners drop substantially, and networking is simpler when cohorts are connected by faxes or e-mail. The ability to share information cheaply through barter or joint projects is also substantially enhanced.

As costs fall and productivity increases in information-intensive NGOs, they also become a more attractive investment for potential donor funds vis-à-vis alternative, less information-intensive opportunities. Moreover, information technologies could be used to improve the transparency of internal NGO management, rendering them more trustworthy recipients of funds.

However, not all NGOs benefit equally from the falling costs of communication, and extending powerful new technology to NGOs will have mixed effects. Some grass-roots groups in developing countries still lack access to telephones and in some cases the technological advances may tend to widen the gap between the haves and the have-nots (Comor 1994). The World Bank has recently placed new priority on extending information technology in developing countries (Talero & Gaudette 1996) but Saunders, Warford, and Wellenius (1994: 20, 34 n.18) explain that previous low priority among multilaterals for telecommunications infrastructure in developing countries may have reflected fears that "in some countries rapid two-way communication among the population could facilitate political instability." Upsetting an entrenched political system may not be a bad thing, but certainly the possibilities for manipulating information to political advantage are also enhanced.[15] New technologies can be used for either the lofty goals of education and participation or toward the less desirable ends of deception and political exploitation.[16] Informational empowerment may explain some of the power of yuppie NGOs in Latin America and some of the resentment as well.

To what extent is the informational empowerment of Southern NGOs by Northern donors a form of what some might call imperialism? Petras (1997: 19) claims that the leaders of Southern NGOs dependent on Northern donors are being turned into "apologists for the neoliberal system." Unquestionably, lower communication costs have facilitated the inclusion of Southern NGOs into a new "global community" (Commission on Global Governance 1995; McCarthy, Hodgkinson, & Sumariwalla 1992). Although global media with Western filters and profit motives may be cause for worry, the anticipated effects of an increasingly globally-networked NGO community also offer considerable hope. NGOs interacting across North-South borders and South-South borders are finding considerable common ground and sharing information to increase the impact of their work. The facilitation of communication and information exchange relationships has already enhanced the trust across borders that results in community building. Committed members of NGOs around the world can potentially contribute to the establishment of healthy global cultural norms and greater participation, transparency, and accountability.

NOTES

1.   Machlup (1962) as cited in Lamberton (1982).

2.   Hayek (1945) is quoted on time and place information in Ostrom, Schroeder, and Wynne (1993: 51).

3.   This and several of the following NGO cases are taken from Theunis (1992), an edited collection authored by representatives of the developing-country NGOs, with kind permission from Kluwer Law International. For the complete case description of INEDER, see Theunis (1992: 235–48).

4.   Social capital is also useful for economic ends; see Burt (1992).

5.   See Theunis (1992: 171–85).

6.   See Theunis (1992: 117–29).

7.   See Theunis (1992: 223–34).

8.   See Theunis (1992: 105–15).

9.   See Sandler (1992: 136–41) for an economic analysis of public inputs.

10.   Fisher (1994: 135) is skeptical of donor-funded networks: "International donors tend to concentrate their assistance on the more formal, easily recognizable GRSO [NGOs that are grass-roots support organizations] networks, thus strengthening any oligarchical tendencies that umbrella organizations may have to siphon off foreign assistance rather than strengthening ties among GRSOs."

11.   See New Partnerships in the Americas (1994) for an annotated listing of some environment-related Internet networks in which NGOs participate.

12.   See Carroll (1992) on participation as both input and output. See Boswell (1990) on the inadequacies of the economic rationale that regards participation merely as a cost.

13.   It is not clear that democratic governance is the most direct route to economic growth. That is a much broader claim. Observers of Asian development experience often argue the opposite (Overholt 1993).

14.   See The Economist (1995: 21–23) for a concise survey of related literature.

15.   Indeed, as communications costs fall, so do the costs of organizing large interest groups relative to the costs of organizing small interest groups. Thus the

pessimistic conclusions of Olson (1982), that special interests will tend to dominate broader interests, may also be diminished.

    16.   See Weiss (1993) on public information campaigns.

8

Contributions to Compromise and Global Community

The information revolution in the past 15 years has furthered the rapid rise of the global economy; it has also allowed for the building of global community. Multinational organizations and intergovernmental organizations are part of that global community; so, too, are nongovernmental organizations (NGOs). Mathews (1997), referring primarily to NGOs, calls the post–Cold War era "The Age of Nonstate Actors." Numerous other scholars have called attention to the growing role of NGOs in international politics (Princen & Finger 1994; Spiro 1995; Weiss & Gordenker 1996).

At the national level, some have used NGOs and other voluntary organizations as indicators of the vibrancy of civil society (Putnam 1993). The rapid growth of NGOs in the developing world has coincided with an era of democratization, and many scholars have credited Southern NGOs with strengthening the bonds of civil society in developing countries generally and in Latin America in particular (Annis 1992; Clark 1991; de Janvry & Sadoulet 1993; Fisher 1998; Fox 1990). Julie Fisher argues that Southern NGOs, particularly those that support grass-roots organizations, have helped to nurture viable civil societies in a variety of ways: NGOs help pluralize civil society — they increase the number of intermediary organizations between the citizen and the state; NGOs target the poor and help sustain their local institutions; many NGOs are specifically dedicated to human rights activities; by empowering local communities, NGOs work on bottom-up democratization; NGOs work with and may activate the broader independent sector, including church groups and university programs; and, finally, NGOs interface with the for-profit sector, especially in their work on microenterprise development, and create viable linkages between local civil society units and for-profit activities (Fisher 1998: 13–17). For the most part, the case studies in this book support Fisher's claims, despite repeated emphasis that many NGOs do not support grass-roots groups and that international donor aid distorts NGO activity.

Since the mid-1990s, however, scholars are increasingly circumspect about the role of Southern NGOs in civil society. Macdonald's research in Central America led her to question the effect of neoliberal NGOs on civil society (Macdonald 1995). Fowler (1998) likewise raises concern for the accountability and legitimacy of Southern NGOs that use international leverage in local political processes, but also notes their increasing influence in international circles. Edwards and Hulme (1996) blame official funding for weakening the legitimacy of NGOs and distorting their accountability.

Indeed, the identity crisis in the NGO community that began in the 1980s has yet to be resolved. Fisher (1998) is certainly not blind to the accountability and legitimacy concerns, but suggests that NGOs can work to avoid overreliance on a single donor or excessive domination by government. Bebbington (1997: 1756) suggests that shrinking aid levels in Latin America offer hope of "rerooting civil society institutions back into their own societies . . . less distorted by the incentives and agendas fostered by foreign aid." Nonetheless, successful NGOs must be accountable to their donors, and international donors, even a diversified set, distort the activities of Southern NGOs. Thus, it seems that international donors both distort and energize civil society in Latin America.

This chapter focuses on the more positive aspects of this dilemma by addressing the questions of compromise and global community. Southern NGOs are active at local, national, and international levels. They have energized civil society in Latin America, and they are also participants in a process of globalization of civil society. Southern NGOs have been instrumental in resolving North-South conflicts and facilitating global change. Key to conflict resolution is the incentive to compromise. Financial interests often underlie successful conflict resolution. Compromise that allows progress is another side of the coin to the issue of cooptation of Southern NGO agendas by Northern grants. Along a wide spectrum of issues, Northern and Southern partners have negotiated compromise, as Northern donors match their agendas for international public goods with Southern NGOs willing to produce those public goods and eager to receive funds that further their own agendas as well.

Particularly at the global and international levels, NGOs are building blocks in civil society. NGOs, their partners, and their networks enrich the basis of global social capital — the fiber of international relationships, where mutual trust and understanding grow and the ability to solve problems cooperatively is fostered. As communication costs fall, NGOs representing various concerns — human rights, women, and the environment — have united across borders with others who have similar interests. The independent sector aid provided through NGOs may provide a basis of improved understanding for tackling the more difficult country-to-country conflicts inevitable in today's rapidly changing global environment.

This chapter uses case studies of environmental NGOs in Ecuador and national environmental funds (NEFs) in Latin America to explore the process of compromise between Northern donors and Southern NGOs and the building of global community.

NORTH-SOUTH CONFLICTS ON SUSTAINABLE DEVELOPMENT

The 1992 UN Conference on Environment and Development in Rio de Janeiro and the process of dialogue leading up to it highlighted often sharp ideological divisions between the North and the South in regard to how environmental problems should be handled and financed (Porter & Brown 1996).

Early Northern interest in environmental concerns in the South had focused on endangered species and population control (Kaimowitz 1996). Influential studies, such as Paul Ehrlich's *The Population Bomb* (1968) and the Club of Rome's *The Limits to Growth* (Meadows et al. 1972), directed attention to the potential of rapid population growth in the South and consequent increased resource use to stress the earth beyond its limits. In the 1980s issues of global change increasingly came to the fore: depletion of the ozone layer, global warming, the loss of biodiversity, and the loss of the world's forests. The North began to regard jealously the disappearing tropical forests in the South as global public goods. Population growth in the South and slash and burn agriculture were still seen as primary threats to tropical forests, their abundant species diversity, and their potential to stabilize or destabilize the earth's climate.

Developing countries have often reacted angrily by pointing the finger back at the North, initially for excessive per capita consumption and resource use, and later for responsibility for current damage to the ozone layer and contributions to global warming. The debate has traditionally polarized to population versus consumption, with jealousy, suspicion, and sometimes racist fears exacerbating the misunderstanding.

Before the Earth Summit developing countries, and not least Brazil, still viewed national forests as resources to be used for national development. Their overriding concern was (and is) the need for economic development to increase employment and improve living standards. Financial resources in the South were extremely scarce even for urgently needed public goods to serve local development, and countries were demanding debt relief (New World Dialogue 1991). One of the achievements of the Rio conference was the general agreement that development in the South is consistent with, and indeed necessary for, sustainable global systems. Countries were able to get past the sensitive cries that rich countries were blaming the poor for population increases and slash and burn agriculture. Developing countries also came to understand better the value of their forests to the entire world.

Frequently North-South differences on sustainable development are based on differences of emphasis or priority rather than outright opposing interests. Needs for clean water and sanitation facilities are far more immediate concerns in the South than the ozone layer or biodiversity. Northern concerns with pesticide use may seem excessive in the South, especially in light of needs to increase agricultural production for food and rural employment.

The South also views suspiciously Northern environmental agendas that appear to be driven by economic interests. The biotechnology industry, for example, can profit from biological diversity in the South — turning Southern genetic wealth into patented pharmaceuticals sold worldwide (Scherer 1993). The issue of intellectual property rights for genetic resources has also become an important point of conflict (Gollin 1993).

Rio also pointed out the many areas where sharp differences of opinion exist within the North on sustainable development issues. For example, the United States, under the Bush administration, refused to sign the Convention on Biodiversity, arguing that it did not adequately protect intellectual property rights for the biotechnology industry. The United States also opposed targets and deadlines for reducing greenhouse gas emissions. Al Gore and Tim Wirth, then congressional members of the U.S. delegation, criticized the Bush administration's positions. Members of U.S. environmental NGOs voiced their opposition to the U.S. position by staging demonstrations on Rio beaches in protest (Soroos 1994).

Some of the most controversial issues at Rio related to questions of financing sustainable development and the transfer of environmentally sound technology from the North to the South (Sitarz 1993). Obviously the South feels that the North is responsible for most of the environmental degradation and should bear the burden of the cost of repair.

Despite the many conflicts, the *Agenda 21* document that resulted from Rio managed to achieve significant agreement along a broad spectrum of issues, agreement that relationships between Northern donors and Southern NGOs had helped to build.

The following section analyzes the environmental NGO community in Ecuador as of 1990. Northern donors and Southern NGOs in Ecuador confronted many of the same conflicts that preceded the Rio convention. Struggles to resolve such conflicts at the local level undoubtedly have contributed to greater understanding globally.

ENVIRONMENTAL NGOs IN ECUADOR

Ecuador presents an interesting case study of environmental NGOs because it developed a strong and diverse community early on.[1] Fundación Natura, the powerful and well-connected NGO introduced in Chapter 3 and discussed in Chapter 5, was certainly a lead player. Ecuador's environmental community, however, included a variety of other actors.

The Range and Growth of NGOs

The number and strength of environmental NGOs in Ecuador started to expand rapidly in the mid to late 1980s, but Ecuador's environmental community was rooted in the establishment of the Galápagos Islands as a national park in 1959. At this time the Charles Darwin Foundation for the Galápagos Islands, an international NGO, was founded, and Ecuador started to recognize its unique environmental riches. Fundación Natura was established in 1978 and grew rapidly in the 1980s. Between 1984 and 1990 approximately 24 domestic environmental NGOs, plus additional chapters of Natura, were founded in Ecuador.[2]

More than many countries in South America in the 1980s, Ecuador attracted donors interested in protecting biodiversity. From the Galápagos Islands and their Pacific Coast through the Andes mountains and the Amazon rainforest, Ecuador is a small country rich in biological diversity. Yolanda Kakabadse, executive director of Natura in 1990, pointed out additional reasons that donors preferred Ecuador to many of its neighbors.

Ecuador had avoided the guerrilla groups in rural areas that plagued Peru and Colombia at the time; and the political stakes with regard to the environment were not so difficult as they were in Brazil. Moreover, the national attention given to the Galápagos Islands and the efforts made to acquaint school children with the park helped to develop an environmental consciousness that was only beginning to grow in other countries of Latin America.

Many of the new environmental NGOs that were founded from 1984 to 1990 were splinter groups of Natura and had a more radical orientation than did this mainstream environmental NGO. Tierra Viva was the first environmental NGO to form, in 1984, from a splinter group of Fundación Natura. This chapter of Natura in Cuenca developed major differences with Natura over an industrial park to be constructed on agricultural land in Cuenca. In the end Fundación Natura sided with industry. The local group sided with the peasants and split from Natura to become Tierra Viva.[3] Although Tierra Viva also had a chapter in the capital (founded in 1986) that was more politically oriented, Tierra Viva/Cuenca focused on local projects. The German Service of Social and Technical Cooperation, as of 1990, provided most of Tierra Viva/Cuenca's administrative and project support. The U.S. Agency for International Development (USAID) has also provided some financial and technical support and U.S. Peace Corps volunteers have provided assistance. Tierra Viva was cooperating with a number of other international organizations and had membership in Friends of the Earth International (Tierra Viva 1990).

Acción Ecológica in Quito was another, even more radical, environmental NGO that split from Natura in 1985 and was founded in 1987 under this name. Acción Ecológica was funded from European NGOs as of 1990 and refused donations from U.S. organizations and from the private business sector on principle, according to the coordinator.

Other smaller groups include a group of lawyers that focus on environmental law, Corporation for the Defense of Life (CORDAVI); a group of biologists trained in the Galápagos (Conservación Semilla de la Vida), another group of biologists in Quito (Ecociencia), and a variety of local groups dedicated to specific issues from the various regions of the country.

Finally, among the range of environmental and natural resource-related NGOs in Ecuador is the Institute for Agricultural Strategies (IDEA) introduced briefly in Chapter 3. IDEA conducts research on natural resource management and sustainable agriculture issues. Founded in 1985 with the help of USAID, as of 1990 most of IDEA's funding came from USAID.

Conflicts, Compromise, and
Participation: Fundación Natura

The relationship of Fundación Natura with its one-time major donor, USAID, was full of both conflict and compromise, as revealed in interviews in mid-1990. As stated earlier in Chapter 3, 85 percent of international grants in Natura's first four years of operation were from USAID, and from 1978 to 1988 this figure remained over 60 percent (Fundación Natura 1989a). However, particularly in these early years of operation, Natura consciously maintained independence from USAID by covering all administrative costs with membership fees and other income sources. The executive director noted that USAID had created many NGOs completely dependent on USAID, citing an example of an NGO in Costa Rica that failed when USAID pulled out. She emphasized that this was not the case with Fundación Natura.

Natura management stated that despite the professional and cordial relationship between USAID and Natura, contention often surfaced over ideological issues and difficult compromises were necessary. Some in management were critical of the degree to which USAID tried to impose a political agenda on Natura, noting that USAID was never completely successful in these efforts.

One of Natura's basic objectives, when founded, was to promote environmental education in Ecuador; USAID was interested in supporting this objective. Officials from USAID and project evaluations credit the early strong support from USAID as a key factor in the success of Fundación Natura as an organization.[4] Lieberman and Wood (1982: 54) state that the USAID–financed Country Environmental Profile "significantly increased Natura's stature in the eyes of both the public and professional communities of Ecuador." Their evaluation of the first USAID-Natura environmental education project (EDUNAT I) states, "EDUNAT I involves the majority of Natura's time, finances and personnel. It is the dominant project and Natura's prime institutional motivation. EDUNAT I gives Natura a high profile both nationally and internationally" (Lieberman & Wood 1982: 97).

Natura documents show sharp contrast with statements of in-country USAID personnel. Natura's first four-year-anniversary presentation describing the education project neglected to mention USAID's donor role. Likewise when reviewing Natura's relationships with international agencies, the World Wildlife Fund (WWF) and the International Union for the Conservation of Nature (IUCN) stand out, but USAID is not mentioned. USAID is mentioned, however, in relation to some relatively small project donations (Fundación Natura 1983). The role of USAID relative to other donors is also minimized in several of Natura's other reports to its membership. Clearly Fundación Natura and USAID have viewed, or wished to depict, the prominence of USAID's role in Natura very differently. Presumably these documents were sensitive to a negative perception within Ecuador of USAID.

However, Natura continued to accept USAID grants that increased Natura's visibility and supported its basic goal of environmental education. EDUNAT I, completed in 1982, was followed by EDUNAT II in 1983–88, aimed primarily at institutionalizing environmental education in the school system. Evaluators describe it as the "largest and most comprehensive environmental education program undertaken by a conservation NGO in Latin America" (Wood 1988: 5–6). USAID also financed, in 1987, an update of the environmental profile. In August 1988 EDUNAT III began with a budget of approximately $1 million, to last 5 years.[5] The objective of EDUNAT III was to solidify the former phases and to extend environmental education to informal community education channels.

The increased stature and visibility attracted additional members. Membership increased from the original 43 members to approximately 1,200 by 1983 and 6,000 by 1989 (Fundación Natura 1983, 1989a). In 1989 just half of the membership was from Quito, the capital city (Fundación Natura 1989b). Domestic support from both membership fees (approximately $5 per adult or $6.50 per family) and from the local private sector was significant enough to cover all administrative expenses (in early years) without charging overhead — a policy intended to avoid dependence on foreign donors. The first local chapter of Natura was established in Cuenca in 1982. Other chapters were established in Quito in 1983, in Guayaquil in 1984, and in Azogues in 1988 (Fundación Natura 1989a). Local chapters manage local projects often with private sector support and rely heavily on volunteer labor.

Even while their total membership grew, Natura lost some members for ideological reasons connected to their major foreign donor as evidenced by the splinter groups. These groups include the chapter in Cuenca that separated to become Tierra Viva, and Acción Ecológica, which refused to work with U.S. organizations. However, Natura's increased portfolio allowed for increases in both full-time staff and part-time consultants and employees, who received training and sometimes went on to form other environmental NGOs.

Natura's relationship with its major Northern donor, USAID, reveals both the depth of North-South conflict and the potential for compromise and common ground. Clearly the opportunity to receive large grants that would expand the productive capacity of Natura encouraged the search for common ground with USAID. Despite continued differences, the relationship was mutually beneficial. Both USAID and Natura were able to pursue the objectives of their organizations. In the process each developed greater understanding of the other.

The Natura–USAID relationship also enhanced environmental participation to a significant extent in Ecuador, both within and outside of Natura membership. Ultimately this made for a richer, more diversified environmental community. This is significant and ironic given the criticism that yuppie NGOs, like Natura, are often subject to from their compatriots. The case of Natura shows how the work of NGOs, which some may scorn as illegitimate, can in fact contribute to a richer civil society in Latin America.[6]

A Spectrum of Donors for Ecuador's NGOs

Certainly USAID was not the only donor that Natura compromised with. Natura, by 1990, had received substantial support from many foreign and international agencies. Since its founding, Fundación Natura had been supported with technical assistance and grants from WWF and the IUCN. The Inter-American Foundation has been another major donor, representing about 15 percent of international donations over the 1978–88 period. Other principal donors include the MacArthur Foundation and The Nature Conservancy (TNC).[7]

Despite the relative abundance of environmental donors for Ecuador and despite the ability of Natura, as a financially stable NGO, to pick and choose among donors, Kakabadse stated that some compromise was inevitable in the determination of Natura's programs. She said it was necessary to adapt to the reality of the availability of funds for particular areas. Although Natura's main priority was environmental education, according to Kakabadse, foreign interests focused on biodiversity, the Amazon, and pesticides. Natura either refused grants (which sometimes happened) or compromised. Kakabadse also felt that Fundación Natura, especially relative to younger and less financially stable NGOs, had significant negotiating power vis-à-vis donors.

Gonzalo Oviedo saw the availability of donor funds along an ideological spectrum. From his point of view, on one end were the governmental agencies of developed countries, such as USAID, with an agenda to promote the interests of their own governments. At the other end of the spectrum were the radical international environmental NGOs, such as Greenpeace, who were insensitive to the needs of a country, like Ecuador, to develop economically. Somewhere in between were the more politically neutral donors that could be dealt with more easily. Kakabadse noted that Natura's mainstream position was appropriate to its national stature and funding sources, including USAID.

Natura also compromised with domestic donors and maintained a close relationship with the public sector. The board of directors and the membership of Natura are described as well connected in the public sector, able to elicit support, and also willing to support public sector initiatives.[8] Thus, Natura's relationship with the public sector is mutually supportive and constructive. Natura also received significant financial support from private corporations and reflected mainstream positions on issues where private-sector interests and concern for the environment might be at odds. USAID personnel mentioned several occasions where Natura had been criticized for taking the industry side of issues.

The debt-for-nature swaps negotiated in 1987 and 1989 certainly increased Natura's ability to choose its own agenda but also caused conflicts with other environmental NGOs concerned about how the money was spent. Natura was chosen to manage the proceeds of a debt swap worth $10 million in face value. That amount of Ecuador's external debt was purchased at a substantial discount by WWF and TNC and converted into local bonds. Natura uses the interest on the bonds to finance conservation projects. When the bonds mature, the principal becomes an endowment for Natura.

NGOs that objected to Natura's mainstream positions were very critical of the debt swap. Fernando Montesinos of Tierra Viva/Cuenca said that some debt-swap funds were used by Natura to neutralize efforts of other groups to halt oil exploration in protected areas. Certainly he objected to this, especially because the Ecuadorian public were paying the *sucres* to Natura for the cancellation of the debt.[9] Acción Ecológica condemned the debt swap on the grounds that the first world had already impoverished the third world — economically and environmentally — and there was no debt to be paid. Acción Ecológica also felt the swap represented a loss of sovereignty to donor will and a sale of Ecuadorian biodiversity to the first world multinationals who would use it to keep the third world in a continued state of dependence (Acción Ecológica 1990).

A wide range of ideological opinion exists within Ecuador and a wide range of environmental NGOs developed, supported by the spectrum of donors to which Oviedo alluded. The more radical environmental NGOs in Ecuador have quite different funding sources than Natura. Their donors are almost always foreign and also radical in orientation. Oviedo worried that radical U.S. or European international NGOs had beguiled

Ecuadorian youth into fighting for causes they did not properly understand. Representatives of these NGOs, however, felt that although available funding may have influenced in part their choice of activities, they had been able to find donors with interests compatible to their own.

The more radical environmental NGOs in Ecuador were far less financially stable than was Natura in 1990, and administrative support was a stumbling block. Luis Miguel Campos, coordinator of Acción Ecológica, said that donors would no longer support administrative costs. He suggested that Acción Ecológica might have to sell plants or start an ecological restaurant to cover these costs. Tierra Viva expressed similar concerns about administrative costs. These two groups were perhaps the most financially stable of the radical NGOs. Many were reportedly run almost without funds on the basis of volunteer labor alone and occasional project funds.

The radical groups essentially eschewed support from likely domestic sources. The domestic private business sector helped Natura with administrative costs. The more radical groups played the offensive with modern business, often because of anti-consumption ideology, and waived this domestic source of financial support. Many radical environmental NGOs also avoided working with the public sector. Germanico Larriva, administrative coordinator of Tierra Viva/Quito, explained that the government sector, like much of the private business sector, worked against the environment. Consequently, Tierra Viva/Quito worked in opposition to the government sector, rather than alongside it.

Conflicts often arose between Natura and the more radical NGOs. The issue of oil drilling in protected areas divided the environmental community in the early 1990s. Fundación Natura, from a mainstream pro-government and pro-private sector perspective, supported the oil exploration while most other environmental NGOs denounced it. The issue of oil exploration in the Yazoni National Park and Natura's pro-exploration stand elicits the most severe criticism.[10] Natura's lack of action to protect the national forest of Pinchincha from development was also criticized. Some thought that investors had connections in Natura. Similarly, Natura was criticized for upholding industrial interests in opposing the cultivation of eucalyptus wood for export.[11]

Some from Natura thought the youth of many of the newer environmental NGOs were being seduced by radical donor concerns; the radical NGOs thought Natura's favor was bought by industry and the public sector. Some personnel in radical NGOs commented that Natura's success with achieving grants indicated a willingness to bow to international donors. However, for Natura and for the other NGOs, the reality is more complex.

Relationships require compromise and donor–NGO relationships are no exception. Many of the radical NGOs had only minimal local support (with the exception of volunteer labor) and thus were free of the obligations to the private and public sectors that Fundación Natura bore. Natura received substantial support from the Ecuadorian private sector for administrative costs and consequently considered its perspective. Likewise, compromises were made to maintain a supportive relationship with the public sector. Although the radical NGOs believed Natura compromised environmental ideals to private and government interests, the radical NGO managers were relatively free to pursue personal interests, supported by foreign funds and unencumbered with domestic responsibilities.

Despite the conflicts, personnel from Natura believed the work of the more radical groups to be supportive to that of Natura in general. Neptali Bonifasc said that "the 'ecoguerrillas' — the activists — are absolutely necessary."[12] Their role, he explained, was to hit the press with demonstrations and radical actions. Natura, as a mainstream organization, was unable to do this.

Oviedo, administrator of Natura's debt swap, argued that Natura felt an enormous responsibility to public opinion. He stated, "Fundación Natura has become, in the eyes of the public, a basic reference institution of the people." He explained that Natura received suggestions, demands, and requests from all kinds of people, from all over the country, about anything and everything related to the environment. He felt that Natura's visibility made it vulnerable to public opinion and thus responsible to public opinion in order to maintain a positive image. Oviedo expressed concern not only for Natura's domestic image but also its international image, particularly within Latin America.

Building Compromise, Understanding, and Global Community

Unquestionably foreign donors distorted and intensified the environmental debate in the Ecuadorian community. To some extent, international debates were brought to life in the context of Ecuador's environment. Environmental NGOs funded by Northern donors are not democratic representatives of local civil society, but they do participate in it and enliven it. Foreign donors intensify the voices of the membership of Southern environmental NGOs. These members are clearly part of local civil society. Further, NGOs like Natura have struggled to retain a voice independent of their donors. They are much more than mere representatives of donors' interests in Ecuador; they also represent Ecuador's and Latin America's interests.

The spectrum of environmental NGOs in Ecuador and its associated spectrum of donors illustrates the range of positions both within Ecuador's environmental community and within the donor community. As the process of matching donors and recipient NGOs proceeds, so does a process of education both within Ecuador and among donors. Ecuador is educated to the wide range of issues and positions with which the international environmental community is concerned, and the donor community is educated to the various perspectives and priorities within Ecuador. As a large NGO with relationships with many donors, Natura has an intense learning process. Each compromise achieved requires a better understanding of donor objectives. Perhaps for the donors the learning is most intense when grants are rejected. As NGOs and donors interact over longer periods of time, common ground across borders and divisions within them are made plain to all. This must ultimately strengthen bonds of global community.

The effort to decide which of Ecuador's environmental NGOs are legitimate in the local context seems dubious at best. A reasonable indicator of legitimacy might be the proportion of volunteer labor used in the NGO. This would make the underfunded radical NGOs more legitimate. However, with a single radical donor, they might also be the more easily co-opted. Natura's supportive relationships with the local public and private sector also argue for a measure of local legitimacy. The public sector, although it may be dominated by elites, is the legitimate representative of the people. Also, it is hard to argue that the local private sector is not a legitimate part of local civil society. Moreover, although volunteer labor might be measured in hours, it is more difficult to measure the volunteer energy that Natura has invested in maintaining independence from international donors.

During the 1990s the attention of foreign donors has focused more directly on democracy-building activities. The environmental NGO community is a frequent target of such efforts. The NEFs described below are essentially financial transfer mechanisms with democracy-building goals.

NATIONAL ENVIRONMENTAL FUNDS
IN LATIN AMERICA

Earlier chapters have drawn attention to donor proclivity for building new institutions in developing countries according to current fads.

Certainly then, legacies of the 1990s are the national funds with links to NGOs that have proliferated around a variety of themes (Bebbington 1997; Jordan 1996). The pain of structural adjustment spurred the innovation of the Bolivian Emergency Social Fund, which soon found imitators throughout Latin America and then the world. At approximately the same time that social funds swept Latin America, so too did NEFs.

The NEFs were born of the experience of debt-for-nature swaps and social funds. Like the social funds, the NEFs first took root in Bolivia: the National Fund for the Environment (FONAMA) was established in 1990, just four years after Bolivia's Emergency Social Fund was founded. Control over debt-swap funds by Fundación Natura in Ecuador caused considerable jealousy on the part of other environmental NGOs. The NEFs, however, are a mechanism to channel long-term funds for the environment to the environmental community at large in each country. Early debt-for-nature swaps in Latin America (for example, in Bolivia, Ecuador, and Costa Rica)[13] were based on commercial debt. The NEFs have been based primarily on the reduction of bilateral debt, much of it under the Enterprise for the Americas Initiative (EAI) announced by President Bush in June 1990.[14] By mid-1994, 17 countries in Latin America had NEFs.[15] Most NEFs in Latin America focus on park management, biodiversity, and natural resource management issues. In 1998 additional U.S. bilateral government debt was authorized for trust funds of this type, now more narrowly focused on tropical forest protection than was the original EAI legislation.[16]

Unlike the social funds, which were designed to be temporary, the NEFs were designed for the long term; they were also designed with the intent of promoting civil society and democratic processes within Latin American countries. Like the social funds, the NEFs work in partnership with national and local governments.

Gathering Long-Term Funds from Various Donors

With various ultimate financiers, many of them international, the NEFs finance environmental services, but rarely undertake management of specific environmental projects. Fund managers agreed on the following definition when they met in a mid-1994 forum in Bolivia: "A fund organizes environmental funding by coordinating a portfolio of projects and programs and by facilitating communication among donors. It creates a broad and diverse fund-raising program to support both start-up and long-term implementation. It manages funding through an investment strategy aimed at influencing government and private spending and by providing transparent, effective, service-oriented management of grant programs and project funding" (Starke 1995: 3–4). Although recipients of project funds from NEFs tend to be local environmental NGOs, public agencies are also funded, as in, for example, the case of FONAMA in Bolivia. The specific management structure of the funds varies from trusts to foundations to nonprofit corporations. Although not all Latin American NEFs are establishing endowments, the long-term nature of project funding is considered one of the primary advantages of the NEFs.

Although a variety of donors have contributed to the NEFs, international debt reductions have provided well over half of funds committed between 1990 and 1994 — primarily from funds generated under the EAI. Commercial debt-for-nature swaps have also played a role, as have additional funding and technical assistance from Northern governments, foundations, Northern NGOs, and the Global Environment Facility (GEF). In some cases local national governments have provided significant complementary funding and the local private sector has also contributed.

EAI-generated funds were responsible for the inception of NEFs in Argentina, Bolivia, Chile, Colombia, El Salvador, Jamaica, and Uruguay and provided approximately $160 million of the $333 million of funds committed in Latin America (for which information was available) by mid-1994.[17] Other U.S. government sources, especially the USAID, have committed an additional $56 million. Canada offered debt reductions in Colombia, El Salvador, Nicaragua, Honduras, and Peru totaling more than $20 million. The Puerto Rican Conservation Trust financed commercial debt swaps that provided funding for NEFs in Jamaica and the Dominican Republic. WWF-US worked with a U.S. commercial bank for a debt donation for a NEF in Guatemala. The German Agency for Technical Cooperation actively supported the formation of the National Fund for Protected Areas of the State (PROFONANPE) in Peru and many other European countries have been negotiating donations or debt cancellations. The GEF has also provided funding and support for the design of trust funds in Bolivia, Brazil, and Peru. Further, an informal working group of international donors, the Interagency Planning Group (IPG), was formed in the fall of 1993 and planned the First Global Forum on Environmental Funds, held in Santa Cruz, Bolivia in mid-1994 to share experience and further progress. Twenty-three agencies comprised the IPG at the time of this meeting, including NGOs like TNC and WWF; official donors like USAID, the World Bank, and the GEF; the European Commission; and a number of private foundations (Starke 1995).

A Forum for Local and International Participation

In addition to providing funds over the long term, a key objective of the NEF, according to the IPG, is a participatory operating style that promotes civil society and democratic processes in the host country (Interagency Planning Group 1995). USAID, for example, will only provide endowment funds to privately managed organizations and encourages broad participation (USAID 1994a). By "including a wide range of 'stakeholders' in the governance and management" donors intend to "promote democracy, strong civil societies, accountability, and consensus-building" (Starke 1995: 1).

Frequently, "participation" translates to "NGOs"; and NGOs funded by foreign donors may not be the best representatives of local civil society. However, to a greater or lesser extent, the NEFs are governed democratically and may, nevertheless, encourage a more vibrant local civil society. ECOFONDO in Colombia, for example, as of July 1994, had the largest NGO membership of any NEF in Latin America and operated under the democratic control of the member NGOs. At that time 226 NGOs and 27 government organizations were represented as members; and membership was growing — 180 new NGOs had applied for membership. ECOFONDO was established as a private NGO that functions administratively outside of the government sector, although 2 of the 7 board members are from the government. The other 5 board members are NGO representatives, elected by the General Assembly (in which all 253 members participate). Projects are assigned to NGOs or NGOs working with the government (Ruiz 1994).

In the case of FONAMA in Bolivia, the public sector has retained control of the fund. FONAMA is within the administrative structure of the Ministry of Sustainable Development and Environment. Grants are distributed to government agencies as well as to NGOs. To accomodate the concerns of various donors, FONAMA has established multiple subaccounts, each with an administrative council that includes a representative of the relevant donor's agency. Only the EAI account has majority representation from the NGO community, as required by U.S. law. As of 1994 FONAMA was the largest NEF in Latin America, with $80.5 million in funds committed (International Union for the Conservation of Nature, The Nature Conservancy, & World Wildlife Fund 1994).

One of the most striking aspects of the NEFs in Latin America, evidenced in these two cases, is the degree to which specific circumstances have infuenced the institutional design of the funds and how they are ultimately controlled.[18] Both local and international politics are clearly at work. Local vested interests and elites, marginalized voices supported by external donor funds, and specific donor demands and requirements all interact and ultimately result in an institution that governs how a new stream of resources will be spent. Designed to strengthen civil society, clearly the NEFs and the funds at stake encourage new kinds of interactions among interested parties.

Whatever the local political outcome, the funds serve as a global forum for communication.[19] The various donors, international and local, most often have particular objectives for their donations. The NEF is like a financial clearinghouse, matching donor objectives with NGOs able to carry out those projects. The process should result in improved coordination between donors and recipients and should reduce the costs of project planning and implementation over the long term. The funds attempt to align the desires of national and international donors with local needs, as represented by the local environmental NGO community and in coordination with the public sector.

The role of the NEF as a forum can potentially further the building of global community beyond the bilateral donor-NGO relationships described in the study of Ecuadorian NGOs. The various donors and NGOs with their many differences in objectives and priorities come to the forum, exchange ideas, compromise, learn, and coordinate environmental activities. The NEF offers the opportunity for dialogue among grant recipients and among donors; ultimately the North-South interaction is more complex and richer than isolated bilateral donor-NGO relationships.

Although the NEFs are intended as a tool to strengthen local civil society, they are arguably better tools to strengthen global civil society. The heavy hand of donors in local civil society processes is beginning to cause offense; Bolivia is a case in point. Bebbington (1997: 1758) reports on the "barrage of criticism dealt out in 1996 by the Bolivian press over charges that NGOs earn large wages from international funds, are unaccountable to society, and engage in subversive activites." The charges have merit — international NGOs funded by foreign donors are primarily accountable to their donors and to objectives of the organization itself. Donors have intended to change civil society — to make it more participatory, more inclusive of those who may have been left out of the process. Undoubtedly in some cases donor intentions were more subversive than those ideals. However, the participatory process that Northern donors and energetic and committed Southern NGOs have unleashed in Latin America is not something that either side has control over; it is more properly a globalization of civil society in Latin America.

Global Governance versus Independent-Sector Aid

The experience of the NEFs in Latin America also provides a constructive example of global public good provision to be contrasted with the experience of the GEF. Most of the NEFs in Latin America are focused on forest preservation activities to slow global warming and maintain biological diversity — environmental services that benefit the entire global community. NEFs thus provide global public goods. National governments are frequently assumed to be the natural providers of public goods, as explained in Chapter 3; global governance mechanisms might, for the same reasons, be invoked to provide global public goods.

Indeed, the GEF is such a global mechanism. The GEF was established just prior to the UN Conference on Environment and Development as a multilateral thee-year pilot initiative intended to help the South provide environmental services needed by the whole world. At Rio it was agreed that the GEF be used as an interim facility for the climate change and biological diversity conventions. In March 1994 it was established as the official permanent facility (El-Ashry 1994; Fairman 1996).

In its short life, the GEF has been a lightning rod for controversy (Bowles 1996; Fairman 1996; Wells 1994). Because of its status as the prospective official mechanism for large-scale global environmental financing, both developed and developing countries felt that stakes were high in determining the rules of operation for the GEF. Moreover, the initial ambiguous mandate and interim nature of the facility prolonged the period of controversy. Fairman found that rather than acting as a forum for positive communication and consensus building, the GEF has hindered agreement (Fairman 1996: 77).

NEFs, in contrast, began their work much more quietly, although funding levels have compared favorably to GEF projects. The active project portfolio in Latin America for both the GEF and the Montreal Protocol Multilateral Fund (both managed under the World Bank) was only $162 million in FY 1996 (World Bank Environment Department 1996). This represents less than half of the funds committed to Latin American NEFs between 1991 and 1994, the period for which aggregate data are available (Dillenbeck 1994). Most of the funds generated to support NEFs, however, have gone toward establishing endowments; so the actual project spending by the NEFs is much less than the funds committed to them.

The quiet success of the NEFs contrasts sharply with the controversy surrounding the GEF and further illustrates advantages of aid through NGO mechanisms. The NEFs avoid high profile international conflicts and allow local compromise. Keohane (1996: 25) concludes, "Because international financial transfers involve the provision of funds by one set of countries in order to alter the operational priorities of others, conflicts of interest are endemic. . . . Financial transfer institutions can only work well when the interests of powerful actors intersect." However, not all international financial transfers need be country-to-country. NGOs offer the possibility of lower profile, independent-sector transactions. The interests of the minor actors may intersect much more easily that those of the powerful.

Southern NGOs can produce international and global public goods and skirt the difficulties of global governance and financial mechanisms. They can also complement global financial mechanisms. Just as NGOs and government often work as complements in the domestic context, the activity of environmental NGOs complements the role of the GEF. Although the GEF cannot tax, governments make contributions. The GEF broadens the decision-making base to include Southern perspectives and fills gaps in environmental priorities left by independent organizations by eliciting comprehensive analyses and setting global priorities. Independent NGOs produce many of the services provided for by GEF funding. Much like independent nonprofits working on domestic problems, Southern environmental NGOs can better target service provision with personal knowledge of clientele. The bureaucratic burden on the GEF is lightened and competition among service providers is introduced. The NEFs described in this chapter work in partnership with governments, but they are much closer to the NGO complement than to the official multilateral GEF.

Working independently of global mechanisms, Southern NGOs can be expected to provide international public goods that are skewed toward donor interests, in most cases Northern donors. This may mean that the local compromises achieved are typically made to the benefit of the North. The new exclusive focus of EAI monies on tropical forest conservation attests to that fact. Public sectors in Latin America and domestic donors must be responsible for providing those public goods desired domestically.

NORTHERN DONORS, SOUTHERN DEMOCRACY, AND GLOBAL COMMUNITY

The agenda of Northern donors is clearly visible on a broad scale in the environmental NGOs of Latin America. The emphasis on green issues, on preserving biodiversity and slowing climate change, is not what it would be in the absence of donor funds. Clean air and water and soil erosion are environmental issues that more directly impact Latin American citizens and the productivity of their economies. The North-South differences and ideological compromises need not be exaggerated; evidence shows that some foreign grants are rejected. However, on many issues compromise is possible; and on these issues, Northern funds can encourage substantial Southern cooperation.

Southern environmental NGOs provide these global public goods for those Northern donors willing to contribute. Effective global governance and financial mechanisms are lacking; and, as argued in Chapter 4, Latin America's public sectors should not be designed to serve the international community. Southern NGOs are in a position to respond to both donor and local demands for environmental services — they can provide environmental services that jointly benefit both the North and the South. Working in partnerships with global financial mechanisms and with public-sector partners, NGOs, including the NEFs, can complement the activity of official global mechanisms, such as the GEF, with greater flexibility and less bureaucracy. They can also complement domestic public-sector activity.

As Southern NGOs and Northern donors find common ground toward the provision of environmental services, a process of community building on a global scale is begun. As individual donors and Southern NGOs come to agreement on joint projects, each develops a better understanding and appreciation for the concerns of the other party. Compromises between such partners can provide the basis of understanding for the more difficult compromises that become necessary between governments. Donors and Southern NGOs alike come to appreciate more fully the wide range and complexity of perspectives and priorities in both the North and the South, as donors along a spectrum of ideological positions match up with like minded Southern NGOs. The global community is expanded as parties find common ground abroad for positions that are perhaps not widely shared at home.

Financial pooling mechanisms like the NEFs can provide further information-sharing nexus for global community as various donor representatives from around the world interact with each other and with representatives of the host public sector and civil society. Democratic processes are called on to reconcile the objectives of the various donors, NGOs, and governments — all stakeholders in the global community. Whether the excessive proliferation of such funds is desirable, however, is another story.

In many cases, Southern democracy is also enhanced by the NGO activity. Northern grants — even those from large donors to yuppie NGOs

— can encourage increased citizen participation in Latin America, as in the case of the Natura–USAID relationship in Ecuador and in the case of ECOFONDO in Colombia. In Ecuador as awareness built, so did the variety of Southern perspectives represented, and civil society was enriched. ECOFONDO provided the opportunity for democratic participation among hundreds of environmental NGOs along a wide spectrum of interests.

Domestic civil society in these cases was also distorted, but certainly no more than the Latin American business environment is distorted by foreign investment. In both cases the power of the foreign money may be offensive to some and dangerous; but it brings with it new ideas, perspectives, technology, employment, training, and links to the global community.

NOTES

1. See Meyer (1993) for a more detailed review of the environmental community in Ecuador as of 1990.

2. According to Gonzalo Oviedo of Fundación Natura as of May 1990. This section draws on the interviews mentioned in Chapter 3, note 15. Interviews in June 1990 with the managers of environmental NGOs in Ecuador, other than Natura, are also drawn on in this chapter. These individuals are: Luis Miguel Campos, coordinator, Acción Ecológica, Quito; Germanico Larriva B., administrative coordinator, Tierra Viva, Quito; Fernando Montesinos, president, Tierra Viva, Cuenca; Gladys Rodríguez, ecologist and teacher, formerly manager of Fundación Fauna y Flora, Guayaquil.

3. Interview with Fernando Montesinos, president of Tierra Viva, Cuenca.

4. USAID personnel interviewed who made such comments include Robert Mowbray and Fausto Maldonado.

5. Gonzalo Oviedo in interview with the author.

6. Meyer (1995b) makes a stronger case for this point with the help of an analytical model.

7. Estimated from graphic in Fundación Natura (1989a): pp. (not numbered).

8. See Wood (1988). Neptali Bonifasc, Yolanda Kakabadse, Angel Paucar, and Arturo Ponce also described the Natura-public sector relationship as consciously supportive.

9. The Central Bank of Ecuador, instead of repaying debt in dollars to international banks, repays it to Natura in sucres as a result of the debt swap. Nevertheless, on international markets, the debt at the time of the purchase was worth much less than what the Central Bank will have to pay Natura.

10. Natura maintained that oil exploration was absolutely essential to the developing Ecuadorian economy. Robert Mowbray from USAID felt that the oil

company under question, Conoco, was acting in an environmentally conscious manner.

11.   Fausto Maldonado of USAID explained that because eucalyptus is not native to Ecuador, it need not be protected from extinction. Furthermore, its cultivation would help to hold the soil on hillsides where more temporary crops would cause erosion. Prohibiting the export merely kept wood prices low for the domestic furniture industry.

12.   This quote and subsequent quotes are translated from the Spanish by the author.

13.   World Resources Institute (1992: Table 20.6) lists early debt for nature swaps.

14.   In addition to calling for the reduction of bilateral debt, with residual funds directed to support sustainable development, the EAI also encouraged the promotion of international investment in Latin America. It also offered the vision of Latin America as a free-trade area (Hakim 1992).

15.   See Meyer (1997b) for a more in-depth study of Latin America's NEFs. In addition to those countries reviewed in Chapter 2, Jamaica and Belize also started NEFs before 1994 and are included in this case. Unless otherwise documented, information on the NEFs here presented is taken from the profiles contained in the Report of the First Global Forum on Environmental Funds (International Union for the Conservation of Nature, The Nature Conservancy, & World Wildlife Fund 1994) and from Meyer (1997b).

16.   Personal communication, William Millan, The Nature Conservancy, July 1998.

17.   The 1998 legislation authorized an additional $325 million over three years to be distributed between Latin America, Asia, and Africa, ibid.

18.   Meyer (1997b) analyzes how both efficient and inefficient forces of institutional change are at work on the NEFs.

19.   See Haas, Keohane, and Levy (1993) on the role of global environmental institutions in providing bargaining forums and reducing transactions costs. Boswell (1990) finds the "public cooperation" fostered by forums more important than economic considerations.

9

Conclusions

The explosion of nongovernmental organizations (NGOs) in the international community is yet another indication of our shrinking globe. Representing the energy of global civil society, developing country NGOs are responding to demands to provide international public goods. Although their appearance on the world's stage seems quite sudden, their roots are easily traced back to World War II and even earlier. The United States–based international NGOs established to coordinate war relief showed the first strong presence in developing countries with food aid. Relief work turned to development efforts as Europe and Canada joined forces with growing private and official aid. By the early 1970s NGOs were making major inroads at the United Nations. By the end of the 1990s they had secured the World Bank.

Rooted in traditions of the Catholic Church, Latin America's NGOs have challenged authoritarian states and are now working alongside more democratic governments. NGOs have both catalyzed and responded to change. However, it has not always been possible to maintain balance between indigenous energy and foreign funding. The early support of private donors like the Ford Foundation and even public donors like the Inter-American Foundation gently empowered voices that might otherwise have been squelched by authoritarian regimes. Heavy conservative USAID funding in the 1980s in Central America, however, produced NGOs that had little indigenous color. In the 1990s, with democracy taking hold and the private sector taking over, Latin America's NGOs represent a strong, diverse, and supportive community, which, like the new economy, is closely tied to the global community.

Scaling up was not easy for Latin America's NGOs — the 1980s were a time of identity crisis amid confusion regarding the realms of the public and private sectors. As the international aid community pushed downsizing public sectors in Latin America in the 1980s, NGOs were called on to pick up the slack. As part of the private sector, donors found NGOs to be more efficient and less encumbered by bureaucracy and politics than were public institutions. However, locals learned that NGOs were more accountable to foreign donors than to domestic beneficiaries. Although NGOs may efficiently provide public goods that the public sector is not providing, it is the government that is responsible to the citizens.

Yet, while many fads come and go in the international aid community, Latin America's NGOs endured. Some endured much better in fact than did public institutions, such as the Dominican extension service, that were subjected to decades of buffeting by tides of development assistance.

Although to suspicious governments NGO activities were sometimes seen as subversive, NGOs endured in part because they brought in needed foreign exchange. They provided employment, ideas, and innovation, and they brought in new technology. They contributed to economic production while at the same time producing public goods that helped satisfy neglected segments of the population. This was true for the yuppie NGOs, and it was also true for those NGOs more closely connected to grass-roots groups. Separating committed from commercial NGOs may be of little use, when both essentially provide public goods for the international community.

The professionalization of NGOs certainly encouraged observers to categorize NGOs; many found the new partnerships among NGOs, the state, and the private sector offensive. The institutional fabric of an NGO like the National Biodiversity Institute (INBio), with close ties to both the government and to multinational corporations, differed radically from that of the NGOs that nurtured community leaders in the tradition of Paulo Freire. INBio's partnerships, although based on trust, also involved written contracts — complex contracts that allowed INBio to subsidize the production of public goods with private good production. Partnerships are political-economic relationships, however, and although the economics might be efficient, the politics bothered some.

Generally, for many NGOs, separating politics from economics is difficult; as information producers and transmitters, they are active in both realms. Many NGOs conduct research, provide training and education, and attempt to build capacity in grass-roots groups. Others are more overtly political, engaging in advocacy, networking, and awareness raising. NGOs are information intensive, and for them the information revolution is particularly poignant because it decreases their costs and improves their productivity. NGOs are empowered by the information revolution and much more closely connected to the global community.

Economically and politically, Latin America's NGOs are part of the global community. They produce public goods desired by international donors and by local clientele as well. Environmental NGOs in Latin America are much more concerned with biodiversity, global warming, and forest preservation than they would be if funded domestically. Northern contributions have elicited compromise, but they have also elicited greater understanding. Northern contributions have distorted civil society in Latin America, and they have also energized it. Latin America plunged headlong into the global economy in the 1990s. As members of global civil society, Latin America's NGOs should help ease the transition into the global community.

References

Abramovitz, Janet N. 1993. *Trends in Biodiversity Investments: U.S. Based Funding for Research and Conservation in Developing Countries, 1987–1991*. Washington, D.C.: World Resources Institute.

Acción Ecológica. 1990. "Y Sin Embargo Se Mueve. . ." *ALEPH* 4, pp. 4–6.

Agricultural Enterprise Board of Consulting and Co-investment. 1989. *Memoria 1989*. Santo Domingo: Agricultural Enterprise Board of Consulting and Co-investment.

Agricultural Policy Studies Unit. 1989a. "Programa Nacional de Apoyo a la Agricultura Bajo Riego." Santo Domingo. Draft.

Agricultural Policy Studies Unit. 1989b. "Datos de Bolsillo Sobre la Agricultura Dominicana." Santo Domingo: Agricultural Policy Studies Unit.

Agricultural Policy Studies Unit. 1987. "Reorganizacion Institucional del Sector Agropecuario." In *Compendio de Estudios Sobre Políticas Agropecuarias en República Dominicana 1985–1988*. Santo Domingo: Editora Corripio, C. por A.

Akerlof, George A. 1983. "Loyalty Filters." *American Economic Review* 73, pp. 54–63.

American Consortium for International Public Administration. 1986. "Institutional Development: Improving Management in Developing Countries." Washington, D.C.: American Consortium for International Public Administration.

Annis, Sheldon. 1992. "Evolving Connectedness Among Environmental Groups and Grassroots Organizations in Protected Areas of Central America." *World Development* 20, pp. 587–95.

Annis, Sheldon. 1987. "Can Small-scale Development be a Large-scale Policy? The Case of Latin America." *World Development* 15 (Supplement), pp. 129–34.

Antonelli, Cristiano. 1992. *The Economics of Information Networks*. Amsterdam: Elsevier Science Publishers.

Aquino González, Carlos. 1978. *Fundamentos Para una Estrategia de Desarrollo Agrícola*. Santiago: Centro de Investigaciones Económicas y Alimenticias, Instituto Superior de Agricultura.

Arellano-López, Sonia and James F. Petras. 1994. "Non-Governmental Organizations and Poverty Alleviation in Bolivia." *Development and Change* 25 (July): 555–68.

Arrow, Kenneth J. 1984. *Collected Papers of Kenneth J. Arrow*. Vol 4, *The Economics of Information*. Cambridge, Mass.: Belnkap Press of Harvard University Press.

Atkinson, Rob. 1990. "Altruism in Nonprofit Organizations." *Boston College Law Review* 31 (May): 501–639.

Aylward, Bruce A. 1993. "The Economic Value of Pharmaceutical Prospecting and its Role in Biodiversity Conservation," Paper No. DP 93-05. London: London Environmental Economics Center.

Aylward, Bruce A., J. Echeverría, L. Fendt, and Edward B. Barbier. 1993. "The Economic Value of Species Information and its Role in Biodiversity Conservation," Paper No. DP 93-06. London: London Environmental Economics Center.

Baloyra, Enrique. 1990. "El Salvador." In Howard J. Wiarda and Harvey F. Kline (Eds.), *Latin American Politics and Development*, 3rd ed., pp. 483–97. Boulder, Colo.: Westview Press.

Barton, John H. 1991. "Patenting Life." *Scientific American* 264, pp. 40–46.

Barton, John H. and E. Christensen. 1988. "Diversity Compensation Systems: Ways to Compensate Developing Nations for Providing Genetic Materials." In Jack R. Kloppenburg (Ed.), *Seeds and Sovereignty: The Use and Control of Plant Genetic Resources*, pp. 338–55. Durham, N.C.: Duke University Press.

Bebbington, Anthony. 1997. "New States, New NGOs? Crises and Transitions among Rural Development NGOs in the Andean Region." *World Development* 25, pp. 1755–65.

Bebbington, Anthony and John Farrington. 1993. "Governments, NGOs and Agricultural Development: Perspectives on Changing Inter-Organisational Relationships." *Journal of Development Studies* 29 (January): 199–219.

Bebbington, Anthony and Graham Thiele with Penelope Davies, Martin Prager, and Hernando Riveros. 1993. *Non-Governmental Organizations and the State in Latin America: Rethinking Roles in Sustainable Agricultural Development*. New York: Routledge.

Becker, Gary S. 1993. *Human Capital,* 3rd ed. Chicago, Ill.: University of Chicago Press.

Ben-Ner, Avner. 1993. "Obtaining Resources Using Barter Trade: Benefits and Drawbacks." In David C. Hammack and Dennis R. Young (Eds.), *Nonprofit Organizations in a Market Economy*, pp. 278–93. San Francisco, Calif.: Jossey-Bass Publishers.

Ben-Ner, Avner and Theresa Van Hoomissen. 1993. "The Governance of Nonprofit Organizations: Law and Public Policy," PONPO Working Paper No. 195, December. New Haven, Conn.: Yale University Program on Non-Profit Organizations.

Berman, Edward H. 1985. *The Ideology of Philanthropy*. Albany: State University of New York.

Besen, Stanley M. and Leo J. Raskind. 1991. "An Introduction to the Law and Economics of Intellectual Property." *Journal of Economic Perspectives* 5, pp. 2–27.

Betances, Emelio and Hobart Spalding. 1997. "The Dominican Republic — After the Caudillos." *NACLA Report on the Americas* 30 (March–April): 16–42.

Blase, Melvin G. 1986. *Institution Building: A Source Book*, rev. ed. Columbia: University of Missouri Press.

Blumel, Wolfang, Rudiger Pethig, and Oskar von dem Hagen. 1986. "The Theory of Public Goods: A Survey of Recent Issues." *Journal of Institutional and Theoretical Economics* 142, pp. 241–309.

Booth, John A. 1990. "Nicaragua: Revolution Under Siege." In Howard J. Wiarda and Harvey F. Kline (Eds.), *Latin American Politics and Development*, 3rd ed. Boulder, Colo.: Westview Press.

Boswell, Jonathan. 1990. *Community and the Economy: The Theory of Public Co-operation*. New York: Routledge.

Boulding, Kenneth E. 1966. "The Economics of Knowledge and the Knowledge of Economics." *American Economic Review*, 56 (May): 1–13.

Bowles, Ian A. 1996. "The Global Environment Facility: New Progress on Development Bank Governance." *Environment* 38, pp. 38–40.

Bratton, Michael. 1989. "The Politics of Government–NGO Relations in Africa." *World Development* 17 (April): 569–87.

Brodhead, Tim. 1987. "NGOs: In One Year, Out the Other?" *World Development* 15 (Supplement), pp. 1–6.

Brown, L. David and Darcy Ashman. 1996. "Participation, Social Capital, and Intersectoral Problem Solving: African and Asian Cases." *World Development* 24, pp. 1467–79.

Brown, L. David and David C. Korten. 1991. "Working More Effectively with Nongovernmental Organizations." In Samuel Paul and Arturo Israel (Eds.), *Nongovernmental Organizations and the World Bank*, pp. 44–93. Washington, D.C.: World Bank.

Burt, Ronald S. 1992. *Structural Holes: The Social Structure of Competition*. Cambridge, Mass.: Harvard University Press.

Burton, Eve. 1990. "Debt for Development: A New Opportunity for Nonprofits, Commercial Banks, and Developing States." *Harvard International Law*

Journal 31 (Winter): 233–56.

Caravedo M., Baltazar. 1995. "NGOs, State, and Society in Peru: Anchors of the Utopian Vision." In Charles Reilly (Ed.), *New Paths to Democratic Development in Latin America: The Rise of NGO–Municipal Collaboration.* Boulder, Colo.: Lynne Rienner.

Carnoy, Martin, Manuel Castells, Stephen S. Cohen, and Fernando Henrique Cardoso. 1993. *The New Global Economy in the Information Age: Reflections on our Changing World.* University Park: Pennsylvania State University Press.

Carothers, Thomas. 1997. "Democracy without Illusions." *Foreign Affairs* 76, pp. 85–99.

Carroll, Thomas F. 1992. *Intermediary NGOs: The Supporting Link in Grassroots Development.* West Hartford, Conn.: Kumarian Press.

Carter, John R. and Michael D. Irons. 1991. "Are Economists Different, and If So, Why?" *Journal of Economic Perspectives* 5 (Spring): 171–77.

Carvajal, Rafael T. 1982. "El Servicio de Extensión y Organización Rural." In Fernando Durán (Ed.), *Alcances y Posibilidades del Sistema de Extensión "Capacitación y Visitas" en República Dominicana*, pp. 63–69. Santo Domingo: Departamento de Extensión y Capacitación Agropecuarias.

Cassen, Robert and Associates. 1994. *Does Aid Work? Report to an Intergovernmental Task Force*, 2d ed. Oxford: Clarendon Press.

Cernea, Michael M. 1988. *Nongovernmental Organizations and Local Development* Washington, D.C.: World Bank Discussion Papers.

Cesar Fernandes, Rubem and Leandro Piquet Carneiro. 1995. "Brazilian NGOs in the 1990s: A Survey." In Charles Reilly (Ed.), *New Paths to Democratic Development in Latin America: The Rise of NGO-Municipal Collaboration*, pp. 71–84. Boulder, Colo.: Lynne Rienner.

Chanlatte, Marino. 1986. "Informe de Actividades del Proyecto Apoyo a la Organización del Instituto Dominicano de Investigaciones Agropecuarias (IDIA) del 2 de Octubre de 1985 al 15 de Julio de 1986." Santo Domingo: Comite de Analysis de Políticas Agropecuerias, Consejo Nacional de Agricultura. Mimeograph.

Charnovitz, Steve. 1997. "Two Centuries of Participation: NGOs and International Governance." *Michigan Journal of International Law* 18 (Winter): 183–286.

Chatfield, D. 1991. "The Information Revolution and the Shaping of a Democratic Global Order." In Neal Riemer (Ed.), *New Thinking and Development in International Politics: Opportunities and Dangers.* Lanham, Md.: University Press of America.

Clark, John. 1995. "The State, Popular Participation, and the Voluntary Sector." *World Development* 23, pp. 593–601.

Clark, John. 1991. *Democratizing Development: The Role of Voluntary Organizations.* West Hartford, Conn.: Kumarian Press.

Cleary, Seamus. 1996. "The World Bank and NGOs." In P. Willetts (Ed.), *'The Conscience of the World': The Influence of Non-Governmental Organisations in the UN System*. Washington, D.C.: Brookings Institution.

Comanor, William S. 1986. "The Political Economy of the Pharmaceutical Industry." *Journal of Economic Literature* 24 (September): 1178–217.

Commission on Global Governance. 1995. *Our Global Neighborhood*. New York: Oxford University Press.

Comor, Edward A. 1994. *The Global Political Economy of Communication*. New York: St. Martin's Press.

Connections. 1995. "The NGO Explosion." Alliance for a Global Community, 1 (April): 1–4.

Cowen, Tyler, ed. 1992. *Public Goods and Market Failures: A Critical Examination*. New Brunswick, N.J.: Transaction Publishers.

Crouch, Luis B. 1986. "The Institutionalization of the Agricultural Research System in the Dominican Republic." Paper presented at the Agricultural Research Policy Seminar, University of Minnesota, St. Paul, April.

Cueto, Marcos, ed. 1994. *Missionaries of Science: The Rockefeller Foundation and Latin America*. Bloomington: Indiana University Press.

de Janvry, Alain and Elisabeth Sadoulet. 1993. "Market, State, and Civil Organizations in Latin America Beyond the Debt Crisis: The Context for Rural Development." *World Development* 21, pp. 659–74.

de León, Rodolfo. 1982. "Capacitación y Extensión." In Fernando Durán, (Ed.), *Alcances y Posibilidades del Sistema de Extensión "Capacitación y Visitas" en República Dominicana*, pp. 47–51. Santo Domingo: Departamento de Extensión y Capacitación Agropecuarias.

"Democracy and Technology." 1995. *The Economist*, June 17, pp. 21–23.

Demsetz, Harold. 1967. "Toward a Theory of Property Rights." *American Economic Review* 57, pp. 347–59.

Diamond, Larry, Juan J. Linz, and Seymour Martin Lipset. 1995. *Politics in Developing Countries: Comparing Experiences with Democracy*, 2d ed. Boulder, Colo.: Lynne Rienner.

Díaz-Albertini, Javier. 1993. "Nonprofit Advocacy in Weakly Institutionalized Political Systems: The Case of NGDOs in Lima, Peru." *Nonprofit and Voluntary Sector Quarterly* 22, pp. 317–37.

Dillenbeck, Mark. 1994. "National Environmental Funds: A New Mechanism for Conservation Finance." *Parks* 4, pp. 39–46.

Dominican Development Foundation. 1989. *Informe Anual 1988–1989*. Santo Domingo: Dominican Development Foundation.

Dominican Development Foundation. 1986. *20 Años al Servicio de la Comunidad*. Santo Domingo: Dominican Development Foundation.

Doorman, Frans. 1986. "Qué Pasa? Evaluación del Sistema de Generación y Transferencia de Tecnología en la Producción Arrocera en la República Dominicana." Santiago: Superior Institute of Agriculture.

Dore y Cabral, Carlos. 1982. "Posibilidades y Límites de la Reforma Agraria en la República Dominicana." *Los Problemas del Sector Rural en la República Dominicana* FORUM 3, pp. 151–73, Santo Domingo.

Dorner, Peter and Don Kanel. 1971. "The Economic Case for Land Reform: Employment, Income Distribution and Productivity." In Peter Dorner (Ed.), *Land Reform in Latin America*, pp. 41–56. Land Economics Monograph No. 3. Madison: University of Wisconsin Press.

Dovring, Folke. 1970. "Economic Results of Land Reform." Washington, D.C.: U.S. Agency for International Development.

Drabek, Ann Gordon, ed. 1987. "The Challenge for NGOs." *World Development* 15 (Supplement), pp. 1–262.

Durán, Fernando, ed. 1982. *Alcances y Posibilidades del Sistema de Extensión "Capacitación y Visitas" en República Dominicana*. Santo Domingo: Departamento de Extensión y Capacitación Agropecuarias.

Easley, David and Maureen O'Hara. 1983. "The Economic Role of Nonprofit Firms." *Bell Journal of Economics* 14 (Autumn): 531–38.

Ebel, Roland. 1990. "Guatemala: The Politics of Unstable Stability." In Howard J. Wiarda and Harvey F. Kline (Eds.), *Latin American Politics and Development*, 3rd ed., pp. 498–518. Boulder, Colo.: Westview Press.

Economist Intelligence Unit. 1995. *Haiti: Country Profile*. London: Economist Intelligence Unit.

Edwards, Michael and David Hulme. 1996. "Too Close for Comfort? The Impact of Official Aid on Nongovernmental Organizations." *World Development* 24, pp. 961–73.

Edwards, Sebastian. 1995. *Crisis and Reform in Latin America: From Despair to Hope*. New York: Oxford University Press.

Ehrlich, Paul R. 1968. *The Population Bomb: Population Control or Race to Oblivion*. New York: Ballantine.

El-Ashry, Mohamed. 1994. "The New Global Environment Facility." *Finance and Development* 31 (June): 48.

Elliot, Charles. 1987. "Some Aspects of Relations between the North and South in the NGO Sector." *World Development* 15 (Supplement), pp. 57–68.

Ensminger, Jean. 1992. *Making a Market: The Institutional Transformation of an African Society*. Cambridge: Cambridge University Press.

Fairman, David. 1996. "The Global Environment Facility: Haunted by the Shadow of the Future." In Robert O. Keohane and Marc A. Levy (Eds.), *Institutions for Environmental Aid*, pp. 55–87. Cambridge, Mass: MIT Press.

Fairman, David and Michael Ross. 1996. "Old Fads, New Lessons: Learning from Economic Development Assistance." In Robert O. Keohane and Marc A. Levy (Eds.), *Institutions for Environmental Aid*, pp. 29–51. Cambridge, Mass.: MIT Press.

Fama, Eugene F. and Michael C. Jensen. 1983. "Agency Problems and Residual Claims." *Journal of Law and Economics* 26 (June): 327–49.

Farrington, John and Anthony Bebbington with Kate Wellard and David J.

Lewis. 1993. *Reluctant Partners?: Nongovernmental Organizations, the State and Sustainable Agricultural Development.* New York: Routledge.

Fisher, Julie. 1998. *NonGovernments: NGOs and the Political Development of the Third World.* West Hartford, Conn.: Kumarian Press.

Fisher, Julie. 1994. "Is the Iron Law of Oligarchy Rusting Away in the Third World?" *World Development* 22, pp. 129–43.

Fisher, Julie. 1993. *The Road from Rio: Sustainable Development and the Nongovernmental Movement in the Third World.* Westport, Conn.: Praeger.

Fowler, Alan. 1998. "Assessing the Performance of Non-Governmental Organisations in Sustainable Development: The Case for Quality Not Quantity in International Aid." Paper presented at the Third International Conference of the International Society for Third Sector Research, Geneva, July.

Fowler, Alan. 1997. *Striking a Balance: A Guide to Enhancing the Effectiveness of Non-Governmental Organisations in International Development.* London: Earthscan Publications.

Fox, Jonathan. 1992. "Democratic Rural Development: Leadership Accountability in Regional Peasant Organizations." *Development and Change* 23, pp. 1–36.

Fox, Jonathan, ed. 1990. *The Challenge of Rural Democratization: Perspectives from Latin America and the Philippines.* London: Frank Cass.

Fox, Thomas H. 1987. "NGOs from the United States." *World Development* 15 (Supplement), pp. 11–19.

Frank, Robert H., Thomas Gilovich, and Dennis T. Regan. 1993. "Does Studying Economics Inhibit Cooperation?" *Journal of Economic Perspectives* 7 (Spring): 159–71.

Fundación Natura. 1989a. "10 Year Anniversary Folder." Quito: Fundación Natura. Mimeograph.

Fundación Natura. 1989b. "Informe de Labores del Periodo 1988–1989." Paper presented to the Asamblea General Ordinaria, Quito, November 14.

Fundación Natura. 1983. *Fundación Natura: 1978–1983.* Quito: Fundación Natura. Mimeograph.

Galtung, Johan. 1982. "The New International Order: Economics and Communication." In Meheroo Jussawalla and Donald M. Lamberton (Eds.), *Communication Economics and Development*, pp. 133–43. Oxford: Pergamon Press.

Gamarra, Eduardo A. and James M. Malloy. 1990. "Bolivia: Revolution and Reaction." In Howard J. Wiarda and Harvey F. Kline (Eds.), *Latin American Politics and Development*, 3rd ed. Boulder, Colo.: Westview Press.

Gámez, Rodrigo, Alfio Piva, Ana Sittenfeld, Eugenia Leon, Jorge Jimenez, and Gerardo Mirabelli. 1993. "Costa Rica's Conservation Program and National Biodiversity Institute." In Walter V. Reid, Sarah A. Laird, Carrie

A. Meyer, Rodrigo Gámez, Ana Sittenfeld, Daniel H. Janzen, Michael A. Gollin, and Calestous Juma (Eds.), *Biodiversity Prospecting: Using Genetic Resources for Sustainable Development*, pp. 53–68. Washington, D.C.: World Resources Institute.

Garilao, Ernesto D. 1987. "Indigenous NGOs as Strategic Institutions: Managing the Relationship with Government and Resource Agencies." *World Development* 15 (Supplement), pp. 113–20.

General Accounting Office. 1995. *Foreign Assistance: Private Voluntary Organizations' Contributions and Limitations*. Washington, D.C.: General Accounting Office.

Gollin, Michael A. 1993. "An Intellectual Property Rights Framework for Biodiversity Prospecting." In Walter V. Reid, Sarah A. Laird, Carrie A. Meyer, Rodrigo Gámez, Ana Sittenfeld, Daniel H. Janzen, Michael A. Gollin, and Calestous Juma (Eds.), *Biodiversity Prospecting: Using Genetic Resources for Sustainable Development*, pp. 159–98. Washington, D.C.: World Resources Institute.

Goodman, Margaret, Samuel Morley, Gabriel Siri, and Elaine Zuckerman. 1997. *Social Investment Funds in Latin America: Past Performance and Future Role*. Washington, D.C.: Inter-American Development Bank.

Granovetter, Mark. 1995. *Getting a Job: A Study of Contacts and Careers*, 2d ed. Chicago, Ill.: University of Chicago Press.

Granovetter, Mark. 1985. "Economic Action and Social Structure: The Problem of Embeddedness." *American Journal of Sociology* 91 (November): 481–510.

Grindle, Merilee S. 1986. *State and Countryside: Development Policy and Agrarian Politics in Latin America*. Baltimore, Md.: Johns Hopkins University Press.

Grossman, Gene M. and Carl Shapiro. 1986. "Research Joint Ventures: An Antitrust Analysis." *Journal of Law, Economics, and Organization* 2, pp. 315–37.

Haas, Peter M., Robert O. Keohane, and Marc A. Levy, eds. 1993. *Institutions for the Earth: Sources of Effective International Protection*. Cambridge, Mass.: MIT Press.

Hakim, Peter. 1992. "President Bush's Southern Strategy: The Enterprise for the Americas Initiative." *Washington Quarterly* 15, pp. 93–106.

Hammack, David C. and Dennis R. Young, eds. 1993. *Nonprofit Organizations in a Market Economy*. San Francisco, Calif.: Jossey-Bass.

Hansmann, Henry B. 1980. "The Role of Nonprofit Enterprise." *Yale Law Journal* 89 (April): 835–98.

Hayek, Friedrich A. 1945. "The Use of Knowledge in Society." *American Economic Review* 35, pp. 519–30.

Hernández, Luis and Jonathan Fox. 1995. "Mexico's Difficult Democracy: Grassroots Movements, NGOs, and Local Government." In Charles Reilly (Ed.), *New Paths to Democratic Development in Latin America: The Rise of NGO-Municipal Collaboration*, pp. 179–210. Boulder, Colo.: Lynne Rienner.

Hirschman, Albert O. 1971. *A Bias for Hope: Essays on Development and Latin America*. New Haven, Conn.: Yale University Press.

Hirschman, Albert O. 1970. *Exit, Voice, and Loyalty: Responses to Decline in Firms, Organizations, and States*. Cambridge, Mass.: Harvard University Press.

Honadle, George and Jerry VanSant. 1985. *Implementation for Sustainability: Lessons from Integrated Rural Development*. West Hartford, Conn.: Kumarian Press.

Hudock, Ann. 1997. "Setting the Development Agenda: Development vs Democracy." Washington, D.C.: School of Advanced International Studies, Program on Social Change and Development.

Hulme, David and Michael Edwards. 1997. *NGOs, States and Donors: Too Close for Comfort?* New York: St. Martin's Press.

Ingram, Helen and Steven R. Smith, eds. 1993. *Public Policy for Democracy*. Washington, D.C.: Brookings Institution.

Institute for Agricultural Strategies. 1989. "Research Training and Dialogue on Agricultural Policy." Quito: Institute for Agricultural Strategies. Mimeograph.

Interamerican Institute of Cooperation in Agriculture. 1989. "Estudio para el Análisis y Fortalecimiento Institucional y Operacional de la Secretaría del Estado de Agricultura (SEA)." Santo Domingo: Interamerican Institute of Cooperation in Agriculture. Mimeograph.

Inter-American Development Bank. 1997a. *Latin America After a Decade of Reforms: Economic and Social Progress, 1997 Report*. Washington, D.C.: Inter-American Development Bank.

Inter-American Development Bank. 1997b. *Resource Book on Participation*. Washington, D.C.: Inter-American Development Bank.

Inter-American Development Bank and Together Foundation. 1997. *Informatics 2000 Initiative: Civil-Society Task-Force Report*. Washington, D.C.: Inter-American Development Bank.

Inter-American Foundation. 1998. *Grassroots Development* 21:2.

Inter-American Foundation. 1996. *Annual Report*. Arlington, Va.: Inter-American Foundation.

Inter-American Foundation. 1995. *A Guide to NGO Directories*, 2d ed. Arlington, Va.: Inter-American Foundation.

Inter-American Foundation. 1992. *Annual Report*. Arlington, Va.: Inter-American Foundation.

Inter-American Foundation. 1986. *The Inter-American Foundation in Numbers: 1971–1985*. Arlington, Va.: The Inter-American Foundation.

Inter-American Foundation. 1983. *Annual Report*. Arlington, Va.: Inter-American Foundation.

Inter-American Foundation. 1981. *Annual Report.* Arlington, Va.: Inter-American Foundation.

Interagency Planning Group. 1995. "Environmental Funds: A New Approach to Sustainable Development." Report of a briefing, Paris, April 26.

International Union for the Conservation of Nature, The Nature Conservancy, and World Wildlife Fund. 1994. *Report of the First Global Forum on Environmental Funds.* Washington, D.C.: International Union for the Conservation of Nature.

"The Internet." 1996. *The Economist*, February 24, p. 110.

Israel, Arturo. 1987. *Institutional Development: Incentives to Performance.* Baltimore, Md.: Johns Hopkins University Press.

Jakobeit, Cord. 1996. "Nonstate Actors Leading the Way: Debt-for-Nature Swaps." In Robert O. Keohane and Marc A. Levy (Eds.), *Institutions for Environmental Aid*, pp. 127–66. Cambridge, Mass.: MIT Press.

Janzen, Daniel A., Winnie Hallwachs, Rodrigo Gámez, Ana Sittenfeld, and Jorge Jimenez. 1993. "The Role of the Parataxonomists, Inventory Managers, and Taxonomists in Costa Rica's National Biodiversity Inventory." In Walter V. Reid, Sarah A. Laird, Carrie A. Meyer, Rodrigo Gámez, Ana Sittenfeld, Daniel H. Janzen, Michael A. Gollin, and Calestous Juma (Eds.), *Biodiversity Prospecting: Using Genetic Resources for Sustainable Development*, pp. 223–54. Washington, D.C.: World Resources Institute.

Jones, Adam. 1994. "Wired World: Communications Technology, Governance and the Democratic Uprising." In Edward A. Comor (Ed.), *The Global Political Economy of Communication*, pp. 145–64. New York: St. Martin's Press.

Jordan, Patricia L. 1996. *Strengthening the Public-Private Partnership: An Assessment of USAID's Management of PVO and NGO Activities.* USAID Program and Operations Assessment Report No. 13. Washington, D.C.: U.S. Agency for International Development.

Kaimowitz, David. 1996. "The Political Economy of Environmental Policy Reform in Latin America." *Development and Change* 27 (July): 433–52.

Kaimowitz, David. 1993a. "NGOs, the State and Agriculture in Central America." In A. Bebbington and G. Thiele (Eds.) with P. Davies, M. Prager, and H. Riveros, *Non-Governmental Organizations and the State in Latin America: Rethinking Roles in Sustainable Agricultural Development*, pp. 178–98. New York: Routledge.

Kaimowitz, David. 1993b. "The Role of Nongovernmental Organizations in Agricultural Research and Technology Transfer in Latin America." *World Development* 21, pp. 1139–50.

Katz, Michael L. 1986. "An Analysis of Cooperative Research and Development." *Rand Journal of Economics* 17 (Winter): 527–43.

Keohane, Robert O. 1996. "Analyzing the Effectiveness of International Environmental Institutions." In Robert O. Keohane and Marc A. Levy (Eds.), *Institutions for Environmental Aid*, pp. 3–27. Cambridge, Mass.:

MIT Press.

Keohane, Robert O. and Marc A. Levy, eds. 1996. *Institutions for Environmental Aid*. Cambridge, Mass.: MIT Press.

Kirby, Alison J. 1988. "Trade Association as Information Exchange Mechanisms." *Rand Journal of Economics* 19 (Spring): 138–46.

Kline, Harvey F. 1990. "Colombia: The Struggle between Traditional 'Stability' and New Visions." In Howard J. Wiarda and Harvey F. Kline (Eds.), *Latin American Politics and Development*, 3rd ed., pp. 231–57. Boulder, Colo.: Westview Press.

Kloppenburg, Jack with Silvia Rodriguez. 1992. "Conservationists or Corsairs?" *Seedling* June–July, pp. 12–17.

Korten, David C. 1995. *When Corporations Rule the World*. West Hartford, Conn.: Kumarian Press.

Korten, David C. 1990. *Getting to the Twenty-First Century: Voluntary Action and the Global Agenda*. West Hartford, Conn.: Kumarian Press.

Korten, David C. 1987. "Third Generation NGO Strategies: A Key to People-centered Development." *World Development* 15 (Supplement), pp. 145–59.

Korten, David C. 1980. "Community Organization and Rural Development: A Learning Process Approach." *Public Administration Review* 40, pp. 480–511.

Kramer, Ralph M. 1985. "The Future of the Voluntary Agency in a Mixed Economy." *The Journal of Applied Behavioral Science* 21, pp. 377–91.

Lacroix, Richard. 1985. "Integrated Rural Development in Latin America." World Bank Staff Working Paper No. 716. Washington, D.C.: World Bank.

Laird, Sarah A. 1993. "Contracts for Biodiversity Prospecting." In Walter V. Reid, Sarah A. Laird, Carrie A. Meyer, Rodrigo Gámez, Ana Sittenfeld, Daniel H. Janzen, Michael A. Gollin, and Calestous Juma (Eds.), *Biodiversity Prospecting: Using Genetic Resources for Sustainable Development*, pp. 99–130. Washington, D.C.: World Resources Institute.

Lamberton, Donald M. 1982. "The Theoretical Implications of Measuring the Communication Sector." In Meheroo Jussawalla and Donald M. Lamberton (Eds.), *Communication Economics and Development*, pp. 133–43. Oxford: Pergamon Press.

Lamounier, Bolívar. 1995. "Brazil: Inequality Against Democracy." In Larry Diamond, Juan José Linz, and Seymour Martin Lipset (Eds.), *Politics in Developing Countries: Comparing Experiences with Democracy*, 2d ed., pp. 119–69. Boulder, Colo.: Lynne Rienner.

Lehmann, David. 1990. *Democracy and Development in Latin America: Economics, Politics and Religion in the Post-War Period*. Philadelphia, Pa.: Temple University Press.

Lele, Uma and Arthur A. Goldsmith. 1989. "The Development of National Agricultural Research Capacity: India's Experience with the Rockefeller

Foundation and its Significance for Africa." *Economic Development and Cultural Change* 13 (January): 305–43.

Levy, Daniel C. 1996. *Latin America's Private Research Centers and Nonprofit Development: Building the Third Sector.* Pittsburgh, Pa.: University of Pittsburgh Press.

Levy, Daniel C. and Kathleen Bruhn. 1995. "Mexico: Sustained Civilian Rule without Democracy." In Larry Diamond, Juan José Linz, and Seymour Martin Lipset (Eds.), *Politics in Developing Countries: Comparing Experiences with Democracy,* 2d ed., pp. 171–219. Boulder, Colo.: Lynne Rienner.

Libecap, Gary D. 1989. "Distributional Issues in Contracting for Property Rights." *Journal of Institutional and Theoretical Economics* 145, pp. 6–24.

Lieberman, Gerald A. and Diane Walton Wood. 1982. "Evaluation of Operational Program Grant to Fundación Natura in Ecuador." Quito: U.S. Agency for International Development. Mimeograph.

Long, Frederick J. and Mathew B. Arnold. 1995. *The Power of Environmental Partnerships.* Fort Worth, Tex.: Dryden Press.

Loveman, Brian. 1995. "Chilean NGOs: Forging a Role in the Transition to Democracy." In Charles Reilly (Ed.), *New Paths to Democratic Development in Latin America: The Rise of NGO–Municipal Collaboration,* pp. 119–44. Boulder, Colo.: Lynne Rienner.

Macdonald, Laura. 1997. *Supporting Civil Society: The Political Role of Non-Governmental Organizations in Central America.* New York: St. Martin's Press.

Macdonald, Laura. 1995. "A Mixed Blessing: The NGO Boom in Latin America." *NACLA Report on the Americas* 28 (March–April): 30–35.

Macdonald, Stuart. 1992. "Information Networks and the Exchange of Information." In C. Antonelli (Ed.), *The Economics of Information Networks.* Amsterdam: Elsevier Science Publishers.

Machlup, Fritz. 1962. *The Production and Distribution of Knowledge in the United States.* Princeton, N.J.: Princeton University Press.

Magat, Richard. 1979. *The Ford Foundation at Work: Philanthropic Choices, Methods, and Styles.* New York: Plenum Press.

Malena, Carmen. 1997. "NGO Involvement in World Bank-Financed Social Funds: Lessons Learned." World Bank Environment Department Paper No. 052. Washington, D.C.: World Bank.

Mansbridge, Jane J., ed. 1990. *Beyond Self-Interest.* Chicago, Ill.: University of Chicago Press.

Martínez-Alier, Juan. 1993. "Distributional Obstacles to International Environmental Policy." *Environmental Values* 2, pp. 97–124.

Mathews, Jessica T. 1997. "The Age of Nonstate Actors." *Foreign Affairs* 76, pp. 50–66.

Mazara, Freddy and José Nova M. 1982. "Aspectos Organizativos y Administrativos del Sistema de Extensión 'Capacitación y Visitas'." In Fernando Durán (Ed.), *Alcances y Posibilidades del Sistema de Extensión "Capacitación y Visitas" en República Dominicana*, pp. 33–36. Santo Domingo: Departamento de Extensión y Capacitación Agropecuarias.

McCarthy, Kathleen D., Virginia A. Hodgkinson, and Russy D. Sumariwalla, eds. 1992. *The Nonprofit Sector in the Global Community: Voices from Many Nations*. San Francisco, Calif.: Jossey-Bass Publishers.

McCloskey, Donald and Arjo Klamer. 1995. "One Quarter of GDP is Persuasion." *American Economic Review* 85 (May): 191–95.

Meadows, Donella H., Dennis L. Meadows, Jorgen Randers, and William W. Behrens, III. 1972. *The Limits to Growth*. New York: Universe Books.

Meyer, Carrie A. 1997a. "The Political Economy of NGOs and Information Sharing." *World Development* 25, pp. 1127–40.

Meyer, Carrie A. 1997b. "Public-Nonprofit Partnerships and North-South Green Finance." *Journal of Environment and Development* 6, pp. 123–46.

Meyer, Carrie A. 1996. "NGOs and Environmental Public Goods: Institutional Alternatives to Property Rights." *Development and Change* 27, pp. 453–74.

Meyer, Carrie A. 1995a. "Opportunism and NGOs: Entrepreneurship and Green North-South Transfers." *World Development* 23, pp. 1277–89.

Meyer, Carrie A. 1995b. "Northern Donors for Southern NGOs: Consequences in Local Participation and Production." *Journal of Economic Development* 20 (December): 7–22.

Meyer, Carrie A. 1993. "Environmental Nongovernmental Organizations in Ecuador: An Economic Analysis of Institutional Change." *Journal of Developing Areas* 27 (January): 191–210.

Meyer, Carrie A. 1992a. "The Irony of Donor Efforts to Build Institutions: A Case Study from the Dominican Republic." *Journal of Institutional and Theoretical Economics*, 148 (December): 628–44.

Meyer, Carrie A. 1992b. "A Step Back as Donors Shift Institution Building from the Public to the 'Private' Sector." *World Development* 20, pp. 1115–26.

Meyer, Carrie A. 1989. *Land Reform in Latin America: The Dominican Case*. New York: Praeger.

Montgomery, John D. 1979. "The Populist Front in Rural Development: or Shall We Eliminate the Bureaucrats and Get on with the Job?" *Public Administration Review* 39 (January–February): 58–65.

Mueller, Dennis C. 1989. *Public Choice II*. Cambridge: Cambridge University Press.

Myers, David J. 1990. "Venezuela: The Politics of Liberty, Justice and Distribution." In Howard J. Wiarda and Harvey F. Kline (Eds.), *Latin American Politics and Development*, 3rd ed. Boulder: Westview Press.

Najam, Adil. 1996. "NGO Accountability: A Conceptual Framework." *Development Policy Review* 14, pp. 339–53.

National Biodiversity Institute. 1994. *Memoria Anual 1993*. Heredia: National Biodiversity Institute.

National Planning Office. 1983. "Estudio de Base del Sector Agropecuario y Forestal." Santo Domingo: National Planning Office.

Naut, Carlos Amilcar. 1984. "Reseña Histórica de la Extensión en la República Dominicana," preliminary ed. Santiago: Centro de Desarrollo Agropecuario, Zona Norte.

New Partnerships in the Americas: The Spirit of Río. 1994. Washington D.C.: U.S. Agency for International Development, World Resources Institute, and New Partnerships Working Group.

New World Dialogue. 1991. *Compact for a New World*. Washington, D.C.: World Resources Institute.

NGO Group, World Bank. 1997. *Cooperation between the World Bank and NGOs FY96 Progress Report*. Washington, D.C.: World Bank.

Nielsen, Waldemar A. 1972. *The Big Foundations*. New York: Columbia University Press.

Nolasco, Joaquín. 1982. "La Comercialización Agrícola en la República Dominicana." *Los Problemas de Sector Rural en la República Dominicana* FORUM 3, Santo Domingo, pp. 47–72.

O'Brien, Rita C. and Gerald K. Helleiner. 1982. "The Political Economy of Information in a Changing International Economic Order." In Meheroo Jussawalla and Donald M. Lamberton (Eds.), *Communication Economics and Development*, pp. 100–32. Oxford: Pergamon Press.

Olson, Mancur. 1982. *The Rise and Decline of Nations*. New Haven, Conn.: Yale University Press.

Organisation for Economic Co-operation and Development. 1997. *Development Co-operation*. Paris: Organisation for Economic Co-operation and Development.

Organisation for Economic Co-operation and Development. 1996. *Development Co-operation*. Paris: Organisation for Economic Co-operation and Development.

Organisation for Economic Co-operation and Development. 1995. *Development Co-operation*. Paris: Organisation for Economic Co-operation and Development.

Organisation for Economic Co-operation and Development. 1994. *Development Co-operation*. Paris: Organisation for Economic Co-operation and Development.

Organisation for Economic Co-operation and Development. 1974. *Development Co-operation*. Paris: Organisation for Economic Co-operation and Development.

Osborne, David and Ted Gaebler. 1992. *Reinventing Government: How the Entrepreneurial Spirit is Transforming the Public Sector*. Reading, Mass.: Addison Wesley.

Ostrom, Elinor, Larry Schroeder, and Susan Wynne. 1993. *Institutional Incentives and Sustainable Development: Infrastructure Policies in Perspective*. Boulder, Colo.: Westview Press.

"The Other Government in Bangladesh." 1998. *The Economist*, July 25, p. 42.

Otto, Dianne. 1996. "Nongovernmental Organizations in the United Nations System: The Emerging Role of International Civil Society." *Human Rights Quarterly* 18, pp. 107–41.

Overholt, William H. 1993. *The Rise of China*. New York: W. W. Norton & Co.

Participation and NGO Group, The World Bank. 1996. *The World Bank's Partnership with Nongovernmental Organizations*. Washington, D.C.: World Bank.

Paul, Samuel and Arturo Israel, eds. 1991. *Nongovernmental Organizations and the World Bank: Cooperation for Development*. Washington, D.C.: World Bank.

Pérez Luna, Agapito. 1989. "Elementos Principales del Subsistema Institucional para la Generación y Transferencia Tecnológica en el Cultivo del Arroz en la República Dominicana." Santo Domingo: Interamerican Institute of Cooperation in Agriculture and International Service for National Agricultural Research.

Petras, James. 1997. "Imperialism and NGOs in Latin America." *Monthly Review* 49 (December): 10–27.

Porter, Gareth and Janet Welsh Brown. 1996. *Global Environmental Politics*, 2d ed. Boulder, Colo.: Westview Press.

Posnett, John and Todd Sandler. 1986. "Joint Supply and the Finance of Charitable Activity." *Public Finance Quarterly* 14 (April): 209–22.

Powell, Walter W., ed. 1987. *The Nonprofit Sector: A Research Handbook*. New Haven, Conn.: Yale University Press.

Princen, Thomas and Matthias Finger. 1994. *Environmental NGOs in World Politics: Linking the Local and the Global*. New York: Routledge.

Putnam, Robert D. 1993. *Making Democracy Work: Civic Traditions in Modern Italy*. Princeton, N.J.: Princeton University Press.

Reid, Walter V., Sarah A. Laird, Carrie A. Meyer, Rodrigo Gámez, Ana Sittenfeld, Daniel H. Janzen, Michael A. Gollin, and Calestous Juma, eds. 1993. *Biodiversity Prospecting: Using Genetic Resources for Sustainable Development*. Washington, D.C.: World Resources Institute.

Reilly, Charles A. 1995. *New Paths to Democratic Development in Latin America: The Rise of NGO-Municipal Collaboration*. Boulder, Colo.: Lynne Rienner.

Reilly, Charles A. 1993. "NGO Policy Makers and the Social Ecology of Development." *Grassroots Development* 17, pp. 25–35.

Rich, Bruce. 1994. *Mortgaging the Earth*. Boston, Mass.: Beacon Press.

Roett, Riordan and Richard S. Sacks. 1990. "Authoritarian Paraguay: The Personalist Tradition." In Howard J. Wiarda and Harvey F. Kline (Eds.), *Latin American Politics and Development*, 3rd ed., pp. 335–58. Boulder,

Colo.: Westview Press.

Rose-Ackerman, Susan, ed. 1986. *The Economics of Nonprofit Institutions: Studies in Structure and Policy.* New York: Oxford University Press.

Rosenberg, Mark B. 1990. "Honduras." In Howard J. Wiarda and Harvey F. Kline (Eds.), *Latin American Politics and Development*, 3rd ed. Boulder, Colo.: Westview Press.

Roth, Gabriel. 1987. *The Private Provision of Public Services in Developing Countries.* New York: Oxford University Press.

Ruiz, Juan Pablo. 1994. "Fondos Ambientales: La Experiencia Colombiana en el Contexto Internacional." Background paper for *New Partnerships in the Americas*. Unpublished.

Ruttan, Vernon. 1996. *United States Development Assistance Policy.* Baltimore, Md.: Johns Hopkins University Press.

Ruttan, Vernon. 1984. "Integrated Rural Development Programmes: A Historical Perspective." *World Development* 12, pp. 393–401.

Sachs, Jeffrey. 1989. *Development Country Debt and the World Economy.* Chicago, Ill.: University of Chicago Press.

Salamon, Lester M. 1995. *Partners in Public Service.* Baltimore, Md.: Johns Hopkins University Press.

Salamon, Lester M. 1987. "Partners in Public Service: The Scope and Theory of Government-nonprofit Relations." In Walter W. Powell (Ed.), *The Nonprofit Sector: A Research Handbook*, pp. 99–117. New Haven, Conn.: Yale University Press.

Samuelson, Paul A. 1954. "The Pure Theory of Public Expenditure." *Review of Economics and Statistics* 36 (November): 387–89.

Sanchez, Peter M. and David K. Jesuit. 1996. "Development and Democratic Consolidation: The Dominican Republic, Guatemala, and Peru in Comparative Perspective." *The Journal of Developing Areas* 31 (Fall): 1–24.

Sandler, Todd. 1992. *Collective Action: Theory and Applications.* Ann Arbor: The University of Michigan Press.

Sarles, Margaret. 1987. "Recommendation for Supporting Agricultural Research Institution-Building in Latin America and the Caribbean." Washington, D.C.: U.S. Agency for International Development, Bureau for Latin America and the Caribbean, Division of Agriculture and Rural Development.

Saunders, Robert J., Jeremy J. Warford, and Bjorn Wellenius. 1994. *Telecommunications and Economic Development*, 2d ed. Baltimore, Md.: Johns Hopkins University Press.

Scherer, Frederic M. 1993. "Pricing, Profits, and Technological Progress in the Pharmaceutical Industry." *Journal of Economic Perspectives* 7, pp. 97–115.

Schumpeter, Joseph A. 1942. *Capitalism Socialism and Democracy.* New York: Harper and Brothers.

Sedjo, Roger. 1992. "Property Rights, Genetic Resources, and Biotechnological Change." *Journal of Law and Economics* 35 (April): 199–213.

Seligson, Mitchell A. 1990. "Costa Rica." In Howard J. Wiarda and Harvey F. Kline (Eds.), *Latin American Politics and Development*, 3rd ed. Boulder, Colo.: Westview Press.

Siebeck, Wolfang, ed. 1990. "Strengthening Protection of Intellectual Property in Developing Countries: A Survey of the Literature," World Bank Discussion Paper No. 112. Washington, D.C.: World Bank.

Sigmund, Paul E. 1990. "Chile." In Howard J. Wiarda and Harvey F. Kline (Eds.), *Latin American Politics and Development*, 3rd ed. Boulder, Colo.: Westview Press.

Simon, Herbert A. 1993. "Altruism and Economics." *American Economic Review* 83 (May): 156–61.

Simon, Herbert A. 1991. "Organizations and Markets." *Journal of Economic Perspectives* 5 (Spring): 25–44.

Simpson, R. David., Roger A. Sedjo, and John W. Reid. 1996. "Valuing Biodiversity for Use in Pharmaceutical Research." *Journal of Political Economy* 104, pp. 163–85.

Siri, Gabriel. 1996. "Social Investment Funds in Latin America." *CEPAL Review* 59 (August): 73–82.

Sitarz, Daniel, ed. 1993. *Agenda 21: The Earth Summit Strategy to Save Our Planet*. Boulder, Colo.: EarthPress.

Sittenfeld, Ana. 1994. "Biodiversity Prospecting Frameworks: The INBio Experience in Costa Rica." Heredia: National Biodiversity Institute. Mimeograph.

Sittenfeld, Ana and Rodrigo Gámez. 1993. "Biodiversity Prospecting by INBio." In Walter V. Reid, Sarah A. Laird, Carrie A. Meyer, Rodrigo Gámez, Ana Sittenfeld, Daniel H. Janzen, Michael A. Gollin, and Calestous Juma (Eds.), *Biodiversity Prospecting: Using Genetic Resources for Sustainable Development*, pp. 69–98. Washington, D.C.: World Resources Institute.

Smith, Brian H. 1990. *More than Altruism: The Politics of Private Foreign Aid*. Princeton, N.J.: Princeton University Press.

Snow, Peter G. and Gary W. Wynia. 1990. "Argentina: Politics in a Conflict Society." In Howard J. Wiarda and Harvey F. Kline (Eds.), *Latin American Politics and Development*, 3rd ed., pp. 129–66. Boulder, Colo.: Westview Press.

Sollis, Peter. 1995. "Partners in Development? The State, Nongovernmental Organisations and the UN in Central America." *Third World Quarterly* 16, pp. 525–42.

Sollis, Peter. 1992. "Multilateral Agencies, NGOs, and Policy Reform." *Development in Practice* 2, pp. 163–78.

Soroos, Marvin S. 1994. "From Stockholm to Río: The Evolution of Global Environmental Governance." In Norman J. Vig and Michael E. Kraft (Eds.), *Environmental Policy in the 1990s*, 2d ed., pp. 299–321.

Washington, D.C.: CQ Press.

Spiro, Peter J. 1995. "New Global Communities: Nongovernmental Organizations in International Decision-making Institutions." *The Washington Quarterly* 18, pp. 45–56.

Starke, Linda. 1995. "Environmental Funds: The First Five Years." Commissioned by the UN Development Programme/Global Environment Facility for the Interagency Planning Group on Environmental Funds. New York: Interagency Planning Group.

Stigler, George. 1961. "The Economics of Information." *The Journal of Political Economy* 64 (June): 213–25.

Swanson, Timothy M. and Edward B. Barbier. 1992. *Economics for the Wilds: Wildlife, Diversity and Development.* Washington, D.C.: Island Press.

Talero, Eduardo and Philip Gaudette. 1996. "Harnessing Information for Development." World Bank Discussion Paper No. 313. Washington, D.C.: World Bank.

Tendler, Judith. 1982. "Turning Private Voluntary Organizations into Development Agencies: Questions for Evaluation." AID Program Evaluation Discussion Paper No. 12. Washington, D.C.: U.S. Agency for International Development.

Theunis, Sjef, ed. 1992. *Non-Governmental Development Organizations of Developing Countries.* Dordrecht: Martinus Nijhoff.

Tierra Viva. 1990. "Grupo Ecológico Tierra Viva: Presentación General." Cuenca: Tierra Viva.

Umaña, Alvaro and Katrina Brandon. 1992. "Inventing Institutions for Conservation: Lessons from Costa Rica." In Sheldon Annis (Ed.), *Poverty, Natural Resources, and Public Policy in Central America*, pp. 85–107. New Brunswick, N.J.: Transaction Publishers.

United Nations Environment Programme. 1992. "Convention on Biological Diversity." Nairobi: United Nations Environment Programme.

Uphoff, Norman. 1993. "Grassroots Organizations and NGOs in Rural Development: Opportunities with Diminishing States and Expanding Markets." *World Development* 21 (April): 607–22.

Uphoff, Norman. 1986. *Local Institutional Development: An Analytical Sourcebook with Cases.* West Hartford, Conn.: Kumarian Press.

U.S. Agency for International Development. 1996. "USAID Assistance by Region: Central America." February 11, 1998, at www.lanic.utexas.edu/la/region/aid/aid96/Assistance/cen.html.

U.S. Agency for International Development. 1989. *Development and the National Interest: U.S. Economic Assistance into the 21st Century.* Washington, D.C.: U.S. Agency for International Development.

U.S. Agency for International Development. 1988. "Sustainability of Development Programs: A Compendium of Donor Experience," USAID Program Evaluation Discussion Paper No. 24. Washington, D.C.: U.S. Agency for International Development.

U.S. Agency for International Development/Dominican Republic. 1989. "Program and Project Semester Report as of September 1989." Santo Domingo: U.S. Agency for International Development.

Uvin, Peter and David Miller. 1996. "Paths to Scaling-up: Alternative Strategies for Local Nongovernmental Organizations." *Human Organization* 55, pp 344–54.

van der Heijden, Hendrik. 1987. "The Reconciliation of NGO Autonomy, Program Integrity and Operational Effectiveness with Accountability to Donors." *World Development* 15 (Supplement), pp. 103–12.

Weisbrod, Burton A. 1988. *The Nonprofit Economy.* Cambridge, Mass: Harvard University Press.

Weisbrod, Burton A. 1977. "Toward a Theory of the Voluntary Nonprofit Sector in a Three-Sector Economy." In Burton A. Weisbrod (Ed.), *The Voluntary Nonprofit Sector,* pp. 51–76. Lexington, Mass: D. C. Heath.

Weiss, Janet A. 1993. "Policy Design for Democracy: A Look at Public Information Campaigns." In Helen Ingram and Steven R. Smith (Eds.), *Public Policy for Democracy,* pp. 99–118. Washington, D.C.: Brookings Institution.

Weiss, Thomas G. and Leon Gordenker, eds. 1996. *NGOs, the UN, and Global Governance.* Boulder, Colo.: Lynne Rienner.

Wells, Michael P. 1994. "The Global Environment Facility and Prospects for Biodiversity Conservation." *International Environmental Affairs* 6, pp. 69–92.

Wiarda, Howard J. and Michael Kryzanek. 1982. *The Dominican Republic: A Caribbean Crucible.* Boulder, Colo.: Westview Press.

Wiarda, Ieda Siqueira. 1990. "Brazil: The Politics of Order and Progress?" In Howard J. Wiarda and Harvey F. Kline (Eds.), *Latin American Politics and Development,* 3rd ed. Boulder, Colo.: Westview Press.

Willetts, Peter. 1996a. "Consultative Status for NGOs at the United Nations." In Peter Willetts (Ed.), *'The Conscience of the World': The Influence of Non-Governmental Organisations in the UN System,* pp. 31–62. Washington, D.C.: Brookings Institution.

Willetts, Peter, ed. 1996b. *'The Conscience of the World': The Influence of Non-Governmental Organisations in the UN System.* Washington, D.C.: Brookings Institution.

Williamson, Oliver E. 1985. *The Economic Institutions of Capitalism.* New York: Free Press.

Wolfensohn, James D. and Kathryn S. Fuller. 1998. "Saving Our Trees of Life."*Washington Post,* May 26, p. A17.

Wood, Diane Walton. 1988. "Final Evaluation of Environmental Education Project EDUNAT II." Prepared for Fundación Natura, Quito, Ecuador and USAID/Quito. Quito: U.S. Agency for International Development.

World Bank. 1997. *World Development Report 1997: The State in a Changing World.* New York: Oxford University Press.

World Bank. 1996. *The World Bank Participation Sourcebook.* Washington, D.C.: World Bank.

World Bank, Environment Department. 1996. "Annual Review." *Environment Matters* Fall, pp. 161–84.

World Bank, Operations Evaluation Department. 1988. *Rural Development: World Bank Experience, 1965–86* Washington, D.C.: World Bank.

World Resources Institute. 1994. *World Resources 1994–95: A Guide to the Global Environment.* New York: Oxford University Press.

World Resources Institute. 1992. *World Resources 1992–93: A Guide to the Global Environment.* New York: Oxford University Press.

World Wildlife Fund. 1988. "World Wildlife Fund Letter," No. 1. Washington, D.C.: World Wildlife Fund.

Wurgaft, José. 1992. "Social Investment Funds and Economic Restructuring in Latin America." *International Labour Review* 131, pp. 35–44.

Young, Dennis R. 1986. "Entrepreneurship and the Behavior of Non-profit Organizations: Elements of a Theory." In Susan Rose-Ackerman (Ed.), *The Economics of Nonprofit Institutions*, pp. 161–84. New York: Oxford University Press.

Index

ABOUT THE AUTHOR

Carrie A. Meyer is Associate Professor of Economics at George Mason University. Her interest in Latin America's nongovernmental organizations began when she served as a Peace Corps volunteer in the Dominican Republic and increased during her tenure as an associate at the World Resources Institute. She has also worked as a consultant to the World Bank and the U.S. Agency for International Development.

ISBN 0-275-96621-6

90000>

9 780275 966218

HARDCOVER BAR CODE